# Beyond *Uncle Tom's Cabin*

# Beyond *Uncle Tom's Cabin*

## Essays on the Writing of Harriet Beecher Stowe

Edited by Sylvia Mayer and Monika Mueller

*Fairleigh Dickinson*

FAIRLEIGH DICKINSON UNIVERSITY PRESS
*Madison • Teaneck*

Published by Fairleigh Dickinson University Press
Co-published with The Rowman & Littlefield Publishing Group, Inc.
4501 Forbes Boulevard, Suite 200, Lanham, Maryland 20706
www.rowmanlittlefield.com

Estover Road, Plymouth PL6 7PY, United Kingdom

British Library Cataloguing in Publication Information Available

**Library of Congress Cataloging-in-Publication Data**

Beyond Uncle Tom's cabin : essays on the writing of Harriet Beecher Stowe /
edited by Sylvia Mayer and Monika Mueller.
   p. cm.
 ISBN 978-1-61147-004-8 (cloth : alk. paper) — ISBN 978-1-61147-005-5
(electronic)
 1. Stowe, Harriet Beecher, 1811–1896—Criticism and interpretation.  I. Mayer,
Sylvia. II. Mueller, Monika, 1960–
 PS2957.B49 2011
 813'.3—dc22                                                    2011013872

♾™ The paper used in this publication meets the minimum requirements of
American National Standard for Information Sciences—Permanence of Paper
for Printed Library Materials, ANSI/NISO Z39.48-1992.

Printed in the United States of America

# Contents

# Beyond *Uncle Tom's Cabin*

# Introduction

*Sylvia Mayer and Monika Mueller*

Ever since feminist scholarship began to reintroduce Harriet Beecher Stowe's writings to the American literary canon in the 1970s, critical interest in her work has steadily increased. Rediscovery and ultimate canonization, however, have concentrated to a large extent on her major novelistic achievement, *Uncle Tom's Cabin* (1852). Only in recent years have critics begun to focus more seriously and more comprehensively on the wide variety of her work and started to create knowledge that broadens our understanding of both the writer and the social reformer. During her long writing and publishing career, Stowe was a highly prolific writer who targeted diverse audiences, dealt with drastically changing economic, commercial, and cultural contexts, and wrote in a diversity of genres, among them not only novels and short narrative fiction—variously categorized as reform, social protest, or regionalist, sentimental, domestic, or satirical fiction—but also a geography textbook, books and articles on household management, religious writings, and travel writing. Reflecting a recent trend to move Stowe's "other" texts to the fore,[1] the essays collected in this volume go beyond the critical focus on *Uncle Tom's Cabin* and thus deliberately exclude Stowe's most important novel.

Stowe's writing career spanned more than five decades; as Stowe's biographers and critics have shown, Stowe had already honed her talent as a writer in the decades preceding her major phase.[2] Along with developing the literary themes that have come to be known as "typical Stowe themes" (race, slavery, religion, and domesticity), she also devised trademark literary strategies, such as her deliberate use of sentimentalism in the fight against racial and social injustice.

Many of Stowe's customary themes can be traced back to her childhood and youth in New England, as well as her young adulthood in Cincinnati. After graduating from her sister Catharine Beecher's Hartford Female Seminary, Stowe experienced the problem of having to find a meaningful occupation at a time when females were still barred from going to college. She elegantly solved the problem for herself by combining her interest in perfecting the art of writing with the breadwinning job of teaching composition at her sister's school; several decades later, she thematized the predicament of female education in reference to her protagonist Tina in *Oldtown Folks* in the chapter "What Shall We Do with Tina."

During her tenure as a member of the Cincinnati literary society "Semi-Colon Club," in her phase of contributing primarily to "parlor literature," which was not meant to be published, Stowe authored a *Primary Geography for Children* (1833) (initially published under her sister Catherine's name because she was too shy to admit authorship) and also wrote her famous sketch "Uncle Lot," which would appear in 1843 in her first collection of stories, *The Mayflower; or, Sketches of Scenes and Characters among the Descendants of the Pilgrims*. Both Hedrick and Robbins point out that the sketch "Uncle Lot" reflects the Beecher family agenda of presenting New England ways as a remedy for the "Wild West" that the Beecher family had come to reform (Hedrick 1994, 170; Robbins 2007, 29). As the contributions to this present volume also demonstrate, Stowe would later expand this approach to present New England customs and life as a paradigm for an ideal U.S. society.

In her young womanhood, Stowe, as the daughter of the Calvinist Bible scholar Lyman Beecher, also had to position herself in reference to her father's post-Puritan religious convictions; her mature writing (especially her New England novels and *Agnes of Sorrento*) shows that she succeeded in emancipating herself from both his strict Calvinism and his staunch anti-Catholicism.

As a young wife and mother she closely encountered the domestic issues that she would write about for the remainder of her career. With the help of many examples from Stowe's correspondence, Hedrick powerfully demonstrates that Stowe herself sorely lacked the valued "faculty" in the realm of housekeeping that she attributed to so many of her New England matrons (1994, 127; see also Robbins 2007, 29). Thus, her vision of perfect housekeeping remained to some extent as indebted to her utopian longings and projections as did a perfect society based on a New England model or an unbloody end to slavery.

Literary critics have remarked upon the fact that the city of Cincinnati, where Stowe spent eighteen years of her life, appears to be absent from her body of work (Hedrick 1994, 172) and thus appears to have left no impact. However, as both Hedrick and Robbins show, Stowe's tenure in Cincinnati is indelibly imprinted upon her antislavery novels, *Uncle Tom's Cabin* and *Dred*, since it was in Cincinnati that Stowe first encountered a fierce anti-abolitionist mob in the mid-1830s and since *Uncle Tom's Cabin* is based upon a sketch published in 1845 about a Cincinnati runaway slave named Sam (Hedrick 1994, 172). Moreover, Little Eva's redemptive death is a fictional rendering of the death of Stowe's son Samuel Charles from cholera in Cincinnati in 1849.

But even more importantly, above and beyond making reference to Stowe's formative period in the city of Cincinnati, Stowe's antislavery novels furthered her project of contributing to a unique American literature based on an identifiable American idiom. With the focus on slavery, Stowe participated in inaugurating a truly national American literature featuring a uniquely American subject. In addition to that, Stowe provided a gendered perspective on America and its literature by placing possible redemption in the hands of females; in *Uncle Tom's Cabin* (before masculinizing her antislavery vision in *Dred*) Stowe presents "Christian mothers" as the only propagators of an America that can be free from the sin of slavery.

Despite the focus on Stowe's writings "beyond" *Uncle Tom's Cabin* in this volume, the novel undoubtedly deserves the critical attention it has received. Due to its immediate national and international fame, its contribution to American and transatlantic discourses on race, slavery, and gender, its impact in the realm of popular culture in the United States and internationally, and, finally, its pivotal role in the development of American literary and cultural history, literary and cultural studies critics have rightly acknowledged the novel's immense significance. "*Uncle Tom's Cabin*," as Elizabeth Ammons put it in her introduction to a more recent collection of essays on the novel, "has always stirred debate" (2007, 3). Many of the issues at stake in this debate—most prominently, yet by no means exclusively, the issue of race—are, however, also highly relevant for the field of Stowe criticism at large. Several key themes, narrative and rhetorical strategies, and the multifaceted literary and cultural impact of *Uncle Tom's Cabin* have been and continue to be of significance for the exploration of "other" Stowe texts as well. The thematic issues of race, slavery, religion, and domesticity, for instance, are not only central to *Uncle Tom's Cabin* but to Stowe's oeuvre as a whole, as are such literary modes as sentimentalism, sensationalism, melodrama, and typological writing. In terms of the cultural work Stowe's writings performed during her lifetime, they can all be regarded as pre- and post–Civil War contributions to a discourse of national moral regeneration through their invention of models of family and community that function as core units of region and nation. Ultimately, as Amy Kaplan has first pointed out, they must even be regarded as reaching beyond the national realm in that the "manifest domesticity" that emerges in many of her texts served an emerging American imperialism.[3]

Several of the essays collected in this volume, for instance, further clarify in their analyses of "other" Stowe writings why critical response to *Uncle Tom's Cabin* has been so controversial when it comes to its representation of racial differences.[4] The racialized quality of some of Stowe's portrayals of black characters and the ambiguity of her messages about the status of African Americans in the United States has been pointed out by critics ever since the contemporary responses of black abolitionists such as Frederick Douglass, George T. Downing, and Martin Delaney (Ammons 2007, 4) and has resulted in our current understanding of the novel and its cultural impact as deeply paradoxical: on the one hand *Uncle Tom's Cabin* undoubtedly served as a powerful propagandistic contribution to the abolitionist cause; on the other hand it perpetuated contemporary racialist notions. The essays by Maria Diedrich, William P. Mullaney, and Monika Mueller in this collection show that this problematic issue resurfaces in her New England novels and in *Dred*. They illustrate that, beyond the need to employ specific types of characters for strategic—i.e., abolitionist—purposes, Stowe was deeply entangled in contemporary racial essentialism and kept and promulgated in her writings a belief in Anglo-Saxon racial superiority.

In her introduction to *The Cambridge Companion to Harriet Beecher Stowe*, Cindy Weinstein proposes to address "a heterogeneous and intellectually rich Stowe whose manifold literary productions are best read through as broad a set of contexts as possible" (2004, 6), and the essays collected in *The Cambridge Companion* exemplify this development toward a more comprehensive approach to Stowe's literary and nonliterary textual production. One direction Stowe criticism has taken more recently is to pursue a transnational, or, more precisely, an Atlantic studies approach that puts emphasis on the fact that the United States has always been a crossroads of cultures and that American cultural production has creatively reflected, been fueled by, and strongly contributed to this dynamic. Scholars have begun to more seriously take into consideration that Stowe was not simply an internationally renowned author but a cosmopolitan intellectual whose extensive travel experiences strongly informed her writing. Therefore Stowe's involvement in transatlantic cultural dialog is the focus of the essays in another more recent collection of essays, in *Transatlantic Stowe: Harriet Beecher Stowe and European Culture* (Kohn, Meer, and Todd 2006).[5] As the editors of the collection point out, while nineteenth-century transatlantic male literary relationships have long been of critical interest, Stowe's participation in and impact on European and transatlantic cultures had received rather short shrift before the publication of their volume (12). Neglecting this essential aspect of Stowe's personal development and of her career as a writer had to obstruct the view on various salient issues that are now being investigated: Stowe's literary friendships with George Eliot, Elizabeth Gaskell, and John Ruskin and their impact on her writing; the attraction-repulsion scheme that characterizes her representations of European societies and cultures—a scheme that might be made further productive by linking it to her controversial treatment of African Americans and that puts into relief her ultimate conviction of the superiority of her native New England; and, finally, her extensive explorations—in various texts, set either in the United States or in Europe—of religious differences between Europe and the United States. Several essays in the present collection also address "transatlantic" issues and shed further light on them. The tension between a Protestant United States that functions as moral beacon and a (Catholic) "immoral" Europe is not only addressed in Joseph Helminski's essay that deals with Stowe's American approach to Italian and French Catholicism, but also in Monika Mueller's essay on two New England novels that probe the potentially pernicious influence of Shakespearean "magic" on sober New England life, and in Jennifer Cognard-Black's essay on Stowe's "American" reaction to Lord Byron's licentious lifestyle and the supposedly unjustified vilification of his wife.

Another, fairly new, direction that Stowe criticism can profitably engage in is suggested by the objectives of the still relatively young field of ecologically oriented literary and cultural studies, or, more briefly, ecocriticism. Stowe's post–Civil War writing coincided with the institutionalization of the first American environmentalist movement, and her conscious decision to choose the New England region for a set of novels in which she tries to develop model communities for the nation does not only signal an insistence on the continuing historical and cultural significance of the region, but also a decision to focus on a region that pioneered environmentalist efforts since the late eighteenth century.[6] What needs to be addressed more comprehensively is how her texts responded to the issues at stake in the various organizations that began to form nineteenth-century American environmentalism: the conservation movement, the preservation movement, the animal rights movement, and the home economics movement, all emerging in the second half of the nineteenth century. Critical emphasis on the ethical dimension of her texts can thus be extended from a preoccupation with race and gender to include the realm of nonhuman nature and the quality of the human-nature relationship. As early as 1969 Alice Crozier argued that in Stowe's New England novels "[t]he setting is more than just a backdrop for the action; it is itself the subject of the novels" (89). This claim points toward the first of four criteria that Lawrence Buell has offered for the purpose of defining an "environmental text." An environmental text, he argues, regards the nonhuman environment "not merely as a framing device but as a presence that begins to suggest that human history is implicated in natural history." Furthermore, it understands the human interest not as "the only legitimate interest," and reveals that "[h]uman accountability to the environment is part of the text's ethical orientation"

(Buell 1995, 7). Finally, an environmental text presents "[s]ome sense of the environment as a process rather than as a constant or a given" (Buell 1995, 8). All four criteria can be productively applied to many of Stowe's texts. As Sylvia Mayer's essay on the environmental ethical dimension of the four New England novels demonstrates, studies of Stowe's writings from an environmentally informed perspective—in this case with a focus on human accountability to the environment—can add knowledge about the environmental ethical quality of her New England novels and tales (2004). Another type of text that should yield important insights from an environmentally informed perspective would be her essays on household management in which, for instance, the natural world plays a crucial role as a resource for human use and consumption. Reading Stowe from an environmentally informed perspective will, moreover, strengthen efforts by cultural historians to make visible women's contributions to the history of American environmentalism, which must still be regarded, as Carolyn Merchant has claimed, "an untold story of immense energy, achievement, and dedication by thousands of women" (1996, 110).[7]

Mayer's essay, moreover, is one of several in the collection that try to provide further insight into the role that the region of New England played in Stowe's writing and thinking. The number of studies on Stowe's regionalism—her rich corpus of New England novels and sketches that started with the publication of the story "Uncle Lot" in the *Western Monthly Magazine* in 1834 and her first collection of stories in *The Mayflower* (1843) and ended with the publication of the last of her four New England novels, *Poganuc People*, in 1878—has gradually increased since the publication of major early studies such as Charles H. Foster's *The Rungless Ladder* (1954), but especially since inclusion in Lawrence Buell's *New England Literary Culture* (1986) and since the advent of feminist revisionist studies on regionalist writing in the 1970s. Over the decades the critical focus on her novels and stories has moved from relegating them to the category of "local color"—a genre of supposedly "minor" literary value that was assumed to merely serve the purposes of antimodernist, middle-class nostalgia—toward positioning them squarely within the contemporary cultural processes of national identity formation.[8] Especially the texts' in-depth engagement with New England Puritanism and their creation of a domestic, largely women-centered, culture is today understood as a conscious and in many ways effective contribution to widespread efforts to "invent traditions" that define the American nation in the post–Civil War period.[9] Renewed attention to the fundamental role that processes of ethnic and racial exclusion play in the invention of the regional—and by implication national—community is drawn in the essays of Monika Mueller and Maria Diedrich, both essays making use of methods and insights of American ethnic and postcolonial studies. A fresh look at the creation of a female New England community whose moral vision overcomes received Calvinist notions is taken by Christiane E. Farnan by drawing attention to Stowe's choice of a specific kind of communal narrative voice in *The Minister's Wooing* (1859).

In addition to the three directions of Stowe criticism outlined so far, a fourth field of study has been rekindled by a focus on Stowe's "other" writings, namely the study of her rhetoric, her narrative techniques and stylistic choices. Stowe's interest in questions of composition reached back to her early youth, to her years at Litchfield Female Academy (Hedrick, 27–28), and remained a significant issue in her theoretical writings as well as in her correspondence. In fact, her transatlantic correspondence on matters of composition with writers such as George Eliot and Elizabeth Gaskell again puts emphasis on a transnational approach to her writing. Of particular interest for critics that go beyond the focus on *Uncle Tom's Cabin*, however, is Stowe's response to the transition from popular sentimentalism to literary realism after the Civil War and to the emergence of a concept of "high" culture that was closely tied to a gendered concept of professional authorship. The complexity, and in many ways the ambiguity, of her response was first suggested by Sarah Robbins and Jennifer Cognard-Black, whose essays we regard as seminal in this context and have thus decided to reprint in this collection. However, as several essays in this collection show, the focus on composition yields further results if it is extended beyond Stowe's role as editor-writer who gave advice to aspiring female writers (the issue at stake in Robbins's essay) and her careful crafting of the justification of her politically debatable stance in the controversy surrounding Lady Byron (the issue at stake in Cognard-Black's essay). Farnan's essay on Stowe's choice of a communal narrative voice in *The Minster's Wooing* can be read as shedding further light on the author's struggle with the demands of literary realism. The three essays by Faye Halpern, Martin T. Buinicki, and Astrid Recker on the New York novels *Pink and White Tyranny* (1871), *My Wife and I* (1871), and *We and Our Neighbors* (1875) extend the reach of such a critical focus by linking Stowe's language use to a reassessment of her contribution to contemporary feminism (Halpern), to her anxieties of authorship (Buinicki), and to her response to contemporary developments in the economic realm at large (Recker).

\* \* \*

The essays in this collection are grouped into two sections. The first section brings together those essays that focus on Stowe's language use, on her rhetoric and choices of narrative technique and style. The second section of the collection concentrates on thematic issues, on the representation of race and ethnicity, the role of religion, her participation in the emerging environmentalist movement, and Stowe's response to major economic shifts after the Civil War.

In their focus on rhetoric, narrative technique, and style, the essays in the first section target Stowe's attempts to achieve specific thematic effects and the strategies she developed to create narrative authority. Moreover, they pay close attention to the contemporary cultural discourses out of which her texts emerged, i.e., to the discourses that influenced her narrative choices. As pointed out above, the transition from popular sentimentalism to literary realism and its concomitant relegation of (popular) female writers to the realm of the culturally inferior mark central points of reference as well. Faye Halpern and Martin Buinicki provide such readings of *Pink and White Tyranny*. Focusing on an analysis of the protagonist Lillie Ellis, Halpern goes beyond earlier scholarship that has argued that the novel must either be regarded as a conservative, antifeminist attack on the hotly debated social issue of divorce or as a feminist attack on cultural values and institutional circumstances that shape—and, most importantly, limit—middle-class women's lives. Halpern evaluates the sentimental rhetoric of the novel in the context of the emerging antisentimental rhetoric of postbellum American feminism and sheds light on the difficulties feminist readers may have with the novel's political thrust to this day. Martin Buinicki also transcends earlier scholarship when he focuses on the question of how *Pink and White Tyranny* reflects on Stowe's profound ambivalence about her profession as an author and as authority on the forms of sentimental literature at a time of shifting cultural values. Like Halpern, Buinicki also concentrates on the protagonist Lillie Ellis. He regards her as an "authorial character" whose strategies of manipulation rely heavily on the use—and abuse—of sentimental concepts and rhetorical means. Drawing on the analogy to the sentimental writer, Buinicki closely delineates how the novel can be understood as targeting both the issue of female professional authorship and the issue of "women's work" in general. Ultimately he demonstrates in detail how the novel expresses Stowe's "profound ambivalence about her profession and her own position as an authority on the forms of sentimental literature." Jennifer Cognard-Black's essay investigates Stowe's choice of narrative technique in two texts that placed her at the center of a heated transatlantic public debate on the moral status of the poet Lord Byron, "The True Story of Lady Byron's Life" (1869) and *Lady Byron Vindicated* (1870). Cognard-Black focuses on the impact that the emerging paradigm of post–Civil War professionalism in general, and professional realist authorship in particular, had on Stowe's response to her many critics after the publication of the article in an issue of the *Atlantic Monthly*. Paying close attention to narrative strategy, technique, and style in both texts, she shows that Stowe was able to strategically embrace the realist mode in *Lady Byron Vindicated* while still maintaining an affinity with the sentimental mode. This, Cognard-Black argues, on the one hand demonstrates Stowe's comprehensive artistic abilities and her participation in the emerging literary culture of professional realism; on the other hand, however, it also shows her participation in a development that solidified the gender stigmas that accompanied the rise of professional realism. In her essay that analyzes a series of articles in which Stowe gave advice to aspiring female writers, Sarah Robbins makes a similar point. The four articles, which Stowe published in *Hearth and Home* in January 1869 while coediting the magazine, provide an insight into her attempts to come to terms with women's—and thus her own—professional writing under market conditions that began to relegate sentimental and domestic writers to the increasingly devalued realm of "the popular." Robbins shows that Stowe's articles ultimately send a contradictory message. On the one hand they provide advice and encouragement by, for instance, offering the stages of her own career as a model, thereby putting emphasis on the cultural relevance of sentiment and domesticity; on the other hand, they discourage their female readers by ultimately privileging the emerging male-dominated realms of high culture and professional authorship—realms in which Stowe makes sure to position herself. Christiane E. Farnan's essay, finally, draws attention to the ongoing critical debate about the presumed absence of narrative authority in *The Minister's Wooing*. Drawing on Susan Sniader Lanser's concept of "communal voice," she focuses on how Stowe achieved narrative authority in the novel. "Community," she shows, is not only thematically a key issue, but it is also an issue of narrative technique and strategy that involves narratorial authorization by a variety of (female, often marginalized) characters and a high degree of reader participation.

The essays by Maria I. Diedrich, Monika Mueller, and William P. Mullaney on the representation of race and ethnicity in the light of Stowe's concepts of family and community introduce the second group of essays that focus on single thematic issues. Maria I. Diedrich explores Stowe's racialized negotiations of nationhood in her New England novels by paying special attention to *Oldtown Folks* (1869). The essay investigates Stowe's attempt to develop model communities that—despite their antebellum settings—were to serve the project of redefining American nationhood after the Civil War. Drawing close attention to the factor of race in the construction of these communities, Diedrich exposes the fundamental flaws of texts that at first glance seem to argue in favor of an egalitarian ethos, but at closer inspection are thoroughly influenced by concepts of racial segregation and exclusion. *Oldtown Folks* in particular exemplifies how the three pillars of the nation—the church, the schoolhouse, and the kitchen—emerge as both "loci of national harmony, consensus, and wholeness" and as loci of social and racial division. In her essay on Stowe's appropriation of Shakespeare's *The Tempest* in *The Minister's Wooing* and *The Pearl of Orr's Island* (1862), Monika Mueller shows that Stowe relocates Shakespeare's themes into an "organic," relatively closed, New England (post-)Puritan society. In the two novels, Mueller argues, Stowe explores how unsettling social and spiritual phenomena presented in Shakespeare's play, as, for example, racial alterity and "magic," can be addressed within the context of this strictly religious environment. After showing how strategies of resistance to hegemonic power offered by *The Tempest* are adapted by Stowe for her own presentation of "socially acceptable" black resistance in *The Minister's Wooing*, Mueller analyzes Stowe's adaptation of *The Tempest's* marriage plot in *The Pearl of Orr's Island*. From her discussion of Stowe's presentation of characters, practices, and behaviors that do not fit the New England mold, Mueller concludes that in her attempt to invent a model society for the United States in her New England novels Stowe developed very effective strategies of containment of (ethnic) alterity. William P. Mullaney in his essay uses the figure of the mystic and Stowe's understanding of contemporary mysticism and spiritualism to shed new light on *Dred: A Tale of the Great Dismal Swamp* (1856) as one of the few literary attempts of the time to explore the notion of black masculinity. Mullaney shows how strongly the presentation of the title character—and with it the novel's ambivalence about the future of slavery and the potential of the black race—is informed by feminized concepts of mysticism and hysteria that marked the contemporary spiritualist movement. The role of religion is also central to the essay by Joseph Helminski. He probes deeply into Stowe's participation in nineteenth-century American literary anti-Catholicism whose major function was, as more recent scholarship has shown, to confirm the notions and values of a hegemonic Protestant society. Helminski's essay on *The Minister's Wooing* and *Agnes of Sorrento* (1862) demonstrates that Stowe's revisionist use of anti-Catholic genres and tropes, such as the anticonvent tale and the figures of the morally corrupt priest and the escaped nun, targets the constraints of contemporary patriarchal concepts of femininity and of the discourse of domesticity. By drawing selectively on manifestations of Catholic spirituality—most importantly in the two novels, by endowing her protagonists Mary Scudder and Agnes with Marian qualities—Stowe's novels not only develop a more complex picture of Catholicism and its history than the plethora of anti-Catholic writings of the time, but, even more significantly, destabilize dominant notions of true womanhood and challenge the confines of the domestic realm. Both essays demonstrate the complexity and richness of Stowe's literary involvement with (anti-)Catholicism. The last two essays examine how issues of environment on the one hand and economy on the other figure in some of Stowe's novels. Sylvia Mayer (2004) draws attention to Stowe's contribution to a reform movement largely overlooked by Stowe critics up to this point. She shows how her four New England novels participated in the emergence of the American environmentalist movement in the second half of the nineteenth century.

By applying a taxonomy of value arguments first to the different groups forming contemporary American environmentalism and then to the novels, she charts the complex layer of anthropocentric and physiocentric environmental ethical notions that inform the novels and that position them in a tradition of New England environmentalism that goes back to the late eighteenth century. The essay illustrates how in Stowe's four novels sentimentalism, domesticity, and the concept of a feminized Christianity combine to develop a multilayered environmental ethical dimension. The inclusion at least of parts of nonhuman nature into the moral universe of her texts thus ultimately becomes a part of Stowe's moral project of personal as well as national identity formation after the Civil War. Finally, in her reading of *My Wife and I* and *We and Our Neighbors*, Astrid Recker raises the issue of how the two novels respond to the fundamental shift in the American post–Civil War economy from a house or family economy to a capitalist, consumerist economy in which white middle-class women's role changed from that of producer to that of consumer—a process that Ann Douglas referred to as "feminine disestablishment." Recker shows how the two novels critically assess this economic shift and its effects on the social roles of both women and men. What emerges is a complex picture: first, the novels expose how "female disestablishment" increases women's dependence on men and ultimately commodifies both women and men. Second, especially in *We and Our Neighbors*, Stowe creates a countermodel of consumption, "pious consumption," that returns agency to those women who renounce self-centered, conspicuous consumption in favor of a consumption within the household from which family and community can benefit.

## NOTES

1. More recently Sarah Robbins has pointed out this trend in her review of Stowe criticism. She delineates how critical interest has slowly, but steadily, moved beyond the almost exclusive preoccupation with *Uncle Tom's Cabin* to include Stowe's "other" writings (2007, 99–123).

2. For a discussion of Stowe's career before *Uncle Tom's Cabin*, see Hedrick (1994, 3–217) and Robbins (2007, 1–6, 9–10, 13–31).

3. In "Manifest Domesticity" (1998) Amy Kaplan briefly discusses *Uncle Tom's Cabin* as one of the central mid-nineteenth-century texts that develop an "expansionist logic of domesticity" (602) that creates "notions of the foreign against which the nation can be imagined as home" (582); see also Elizabeth Ammons's "*Uncle Tom's Cabin*, Empire, and Africa" (2000 [2007]).

4. A comprehensive account of the controversial reception of *Uncle Tom's Cabin* since its publication is provided by the essays collected in Ellen E. Westbrook, Mason I. Lowance, and R. C. De Prospo's *The Stowe Debate: Rhetorical Strategies in "Uncle Tom's Cabin"* (1992). In her introduction, Ammons succinctly summarizes:

"*Uncle Tom's Cabin* from the beginning posed problems, especially on the subjects of race, gradualism as a strategy for ending slavery, colonization in Liberia by free blacks, and the whole issue of whites speaking for African Americans" (2007, 4).

5. For a discussion of Stowe as a transatlantic writer, see also Monika Mueller's *George Eliot U.S.: Transatlantic Literary and Cultural Perspectives* (2005).

6. Environmental historian Robert Dorman, for instance, calls New England "the birthplace of American environmentalism" (1998, 9). For further information about and bibliographical references to the history of New England environmentalism, see the essay by Sylvia Mayer in this volume.

7. A first attempt to approach Stowe's writing from an environmentally informed perspective can be seen in Mark Hoyer's essay on *The Minister's Wooing* (2001) and contemporary botanical discourse.

8. Feminist scholarship since the 1970s has been instrumental in overcoming the reductive and aesthetically dismissive notion of "local color" and has demonstrated the multiple cultural functions the genre has performed. For New England, see Donovan (1983); for Stowe's regionalist writing, see in particular Pryse (2004).

9. The phrase "invent tradition" refers to the essays in Hobsbawm and Ranger (1983) that deal with the semiotic construction processes of national identities.

## WORKS CITED

Ammons, Elizabeth. 2000 [2007]. "*Uncle Tom's Cabin*, Empire, and Africa." In Ammons 2007, 227–46.

———. 2007. Introduction to *Harriet Beecher Stowe's "Uncle Tom's Cabin": A Casebook*, ed. Elizabeth Ammons, 3–14. Oxford: Oxford University Press.

Buell, Lawrence. 1995. *The Environmental Imagination: Thoreau, Nature Writing, and the Formation of American Culture*. Cambridge, MA: Belknap Press of Harvard University Press.

———. 1986. *New England Literary Culture: From Revolution to Renaissance*. Cambridge: Cambridge University Press.

Crozier, Alice. 1969. *The Novels of Harriet Beecher Stowe*. New York: Oxford University Press.

Donovan, Josephine. 1983. *New England Local Color Literature: A Women's Tradition*. New York: Ungar.

Dorman, Robert. 1998. *A Word for Nature: Four Pioneering Environmental Advocates, 1845–1913*. Chapel Hill: University of North Carolina Press.

Foster, Charles H. 1954. *The Rungless Ladder: Harriet Beecher Stowe and New England Puritanism*. Durham, NC: Duke University Press.

Hedrick, Joan. 1994. *Harriet Beecher Stowe: A Life*. New York: Oxford University Press.

Hobsbawm, Eric, and Terence Ranger, eds. 1983. *The Invention of Tradition*. New York: Cambridge University Press.

Hoyer, Mark T. 2001. "Cultivating Desire, Tending Piety: Botanical Discourse in Harriet Beecher Stowe's *The Minister's Wooing*." In *Beyond Nature Writing: Expanding the Boundaries of Ecocriticism*, ed. Karla Armbruster and Kathleen R. Wallace, 111–25. Charlottesville: University Press of Virginia.

Kaplan, Amy. 1998. "Manifest Domesticity." *American Literature* 70 (3): 581–606.

Kohn, Denise, Sarah Meer, and Emily B. Todd, eds. 2006. *Transatlantic Stowe: Harriet Beecher Stowe and European Culture.* Iowa City: University of Iowa Press.

Mayer, Sylvia. 2004. *Naturethik und Neuengland-Regionalliteratur: Harriet Beecher Stowe, Rose Terry Cooke, Sarah Orne Jewett, Mary E. Wilkins Freeman.* Heidelberg: Universitätsverlag Winter.

Merchant, Carolyn. 1996. *Earthcare: Women and the Environment.* New York: Routledge.

Mueller, Monika. 2005. *George Eliot U.S.: Transatlantic Literary and Cultural Perspectives.* Madison, NJ: Fairleigh Dickinson University Press.

Pryse, Marjorie. 2004. "Stowe and Regionalism." In Weinstein 2004, 131–53.

Robbins, Sarah. 2007. *The Cambridge Introduction to Harriet Beecher Stowe.* Cambridge: Cambridge University Press.

Weinstein, Cindy, ed. 2004. *The Cambridge Companion to Harriet Beecher Stowe.* Cambridge: Cambridge University Press.

Westbrook, Ellen, Mason I. Lowance, and R. C. De Prospo, eds. 1992. *The Stowe Debate: Rhetorical Strategies in "Uncle Tom's Cabin."* Amherst: University of Massachusetts Press.

# The American Woman Movement Meets the Disingenuous Orator

## Harriet Beecher Stowe's
## *Pink and White Tyranny*

*Faye Halpern*

> What is now called the nature of women is an eminently artificial thing—
> the result of forced repression in some directions, unnatural stimulation
> in others. . . . [I]n the case of women, a hot-house and stove cultivation
> has always been carried on of some of the capabilities of their nature, for
> the benefit and pleasure of their masters.
>
> —John Stuart Mill, "The Subjection of Women," 1869

> He withered all her poor little trumpery array of hothouse flowers of
> sentiment, by treating them as so much garbage, as all men know they
> are. He set before her the gravity and dignity of marriage, and her duties
> to her husband.
>
> —Harriet Beecher Stowe, *Pink and White Tyranny*, 1871

What Harriet Beecher Stowe puts in the mind of the hero of *Pink and
White Tyranny* to characterize his wife's sentimental predilections could
easily describe her own efforts. That is, at first glance Harriet Beecher
Stowe's own sentimental novel appears to be "garbage," and "garbage"
of a particularly antifeminist kind.[1] At second glance, it appears the same
way. Is it possible to rescue this novel according to feminist criteria, a
strategy that literary critics have deployed since the initial rescue of nineteenth-century "woman's fiction" in the 1970s, one that seems especially
suited to rescue one of Stowe's "minor" novels?[2] In the first part of this
article, I examine the difficulty—but not impossibility—of doing so. In
the second part, I step back and examine what it means to measure the
significance of a novel like *Pink and White Tyranny* according to how well

17

it can provide a feminist analysis of culture. What does such a rescue do to this novel? What does it prevent us from seeing?

To see the novel through a feminist lens is not to simplify the novel in any obvious way: it does not mean restricting its significance to topical issues of the time, like whether women should be able to get divorced, the question with which this novel is overtly concerned. A feminist lens can also allow us, among other things, to consider the political ramifications of its sentimental rhetoric. Yet the more a feminist lens produces rich (and varied) readings of the novel, the more we accept the integrity of the lens. We can apply feminist critique to *Pink and White Tyranny*, but we can also apply *Pink and White Tyranny* to feminist critique. Stowe's novel can bring out an aspect of feminist criticism that threatens to remain invisible: the way it goes about persuading others of its points, what we might call its "rhetoricity."[3] It is very easy to drain this novel of its power of metacritique, easy to miss its power to evaluate certain modes of persuasion, especially the one chosen by the women reformers of Stowe's time whom Stowe disagreed with. *Pink and White Tyranny* is not just a disquisition on certain issues that concern postbellum women reformers but an interrogation of how these postbellum reformers went (and most feminist critics still go) about being persuasive and the cost that this particular unsentimental model exacts.

## "RESCUING" *PINK AND WHITE TYRANNY*

Let me begin, however, by showing how, despite first (and even second) appearances, *Pink and White Tyranny* can indeed be rescued—and not just discounted as "antifeminist garbage." *Pink and White Tyranny*, first serialized in Stowe's nephew Edward Everett Hale's journal, *Old and New*, in 1871, recounts the disastrous marriage of John Seymour and Lillie Ellis, she whose "fair, sweet, infantine face" (Stowe [1871] 1988, 2) disguises her ability to manipulate the people around her. Systematically drawing John away from all he (and the author) hold dear—his family ties, his philanthropy toward his workers, the domestic relics of his mother—Lillie, in turn, draws away from him. She escapes to New York society and there narrowly escapes a scandal with an old beau. After this near ruin, she returns to be with John, only slightly chastened. Not even motherhood can end Lillie's "reign of selfishness" (297). What motherhood ends instead is Lillie's health; she slowly sinks into death, supported by her now more discriminating husband: "My wife . . . ! she is worse than nothing" (314). He nonetheless has decided it is his duty to stay by her side.

The ostensible moral of the story, which Stowe helpfully draws our attention to both in the preface and in the course of the novel, is that "once marriage is made and consummated, it should be as fixed a fact as the laws of nature" (320). Thus Stowe rejects the right of women to correct a bad marriage choice through divorce. Stowe considers this argument and responds thus:

> If the woman who finds that she has made a mistake, and married a man unkind or uncongenial, may, on the discovery of it, leave him and seek her fortune with another, so also may a man. . . . [A]re women-reformers going to clamor for having every woman turned out helpless, when the man who has married her, and made her a mother, discovers that she has not the power to interest him, and to help his higher spiritual development? (319–20)

Why is this argument so off-putting? For it seems that Stowe agrees with the highest aim of women reformers: to protect women. It is the method to do so with which she disagrees. We should keep in mind, as well, that Stowe was not alone in her view: many women reformers, including her much more radically feminist sister, Isabella Beecher Hooker, also disagreed with the prodivorce arguments advanced by reformers like Susan B. Anthony and Elizabeth Cady Stanton.[4]

Yet Stowe's antidivorce message is still a hard pill to swallow, as much for the way it is proffered as for its bitter content. This novel is not so much a novel as a pedagogical corrective aimed at certain women reformers of the age (and those readers who might be sympathetic to them), women like George Sand and the native-grown Victoria Woodhull, and those less radical reformers who insisted on defending them. Stowe seems terrified that her message will be lost, so she explicitly tells it to us. Yet if in a novel like *Uncle Tom's Cabin* the didacticism emerges as much through the plight of her characters as through her direct addresses to the readers, *Pink and White Tyranny* has the curious effect of having its characterizations undermine its explicit message.

Reviewing this novel upon the close of its serialization, William Dean Howells suggests the way the novel thwarts its own intention, how it has "[m]uch weightier lessons than this [its antidivorce moral]" ([1872] 1980, 208).[5] The modern reader also feels the pull of "weightier lessons"—though ones different from what Howells imagined them to be. The problem is that the obvious candidate for this weightier lesson can seem as antifeminist as the ostensible one. Modern readers might plausibly see a "weightier lesson" in Stowe's attack not on divorce, but on women. The reason that Stowe's ostensible antidivorce moral seems like a bait and switch is that it depends on our feeling sympathy for Lillie, on not wanting her to be cast out of the Seymour home. Unfortunately, the novel has done too much to make her into an unsympathetic character. Lillie is first presented to us as "a belle by profession" ([1871] 1988, 8); her arts prevent what seems to be her honest misery at her fate of living the life of a self-abnegating wife to a particularly abstemious and upright husband from striking a chord in her readers. Readers can catch a glimpse of Lillie's artfulness upon being asked by John to help him host a party for his workers, whom John is dedicated to "raising up":

> "Oh, well, John! If you say so, I must, I suppose," said Lillie, with a sigh. "I can have the carpets and furniture all covered, I suppose; it'll be no end of trouble, but I'll try. But I must say, I think all this kind of petting of the working-classes does no sort of good; it only makes them uppish and exacting: you never get any gratitude for it." (140)

Now there are many things at work in this passage conspiring to make Lillie unlikable: most saliently, her own unsympathetic attitude toward the "working-classes."[6] There is also the offhand way in which she reveals her materialism and her selfish motive for helping others. Yet the content of what Lillie says is only half the story. It can blind us to what is in fact her deeper sin, which is the way that her words are calculated to produce an effect on her husband: to come across as a martyr, as Stowe spells out toward the end of this episode.

Lillie's habitual disingenuousness leads the reader to long for her unmasking. Since the only person who does not seem aware of the artfulness of her speech is her besotted husband, it is a delectable moment when the shades finally lift from John's eyes after he is told by Lillie that he should sacrifice his good name in order to save his fortune:

> [John] had received this morning his *check-mate.* All illusion was at an end. The woman that he had loved and idolized and caressed and petted and indulged, in whom he had been daily and hourly disappointed since he was married, but of whom he still hoped and hoped, he now felt was of a nature not only unlike, but opposed to his own. (311)

What a disappointment it is to learn that John will not act on his newly acquired knowledge; instead, as I mentioned above, he decides to continue his indulgence. The only thing that does change is John's already high opinion of himself: his loyalty to Lillie allows him to become aware of his own manliness: "Because he is strong, and she is weak, he feels that it would be unmanly to desert her" (322). Because the novel has primed the reader to hope that Lillie gets her just deserts, Stowe's transformation of this novel into an antidivorce argument seems more than a detour. It seems an unkind thwarting of the reader's pressing, if slightly shameful, desire for Lillie to get her comeuppance.

When readers inevitably dismiss Stowe's antifeminist, antidivorce lesson, they are left, instead, with an intense dislike and thwarted sense of revenge for the woman, whom Stowe, making them feel even worse about what she herself engineered, insists on defending. Lillie is a product of patriarchal education, as John's sister and Stowe's spokesperson, Grace, informs her brother:

> Consider how much your sex always do to weaken the moral sense of women, by liking and admiring them for being weak and foolish and inconsequent, so long as it is pretty and does not come in your way. I do not mean you in particular, John; but I mean that the general course of society releases pretty women from any sense of obligation to be constant in duty, or brave in meeting emergencies. (316–17)

Yet Stowe has habitually drained Lillie of sympathy by devoting so much attention to—by making deliciously infuriating, in fact—Lillie's manipulations of those around her. Lillie is a hothouse flower, highly cultivated (though not in the sense of being educated) and artificial, and Stowe gives us example upon example of it. It is a self-undermining strategy. John Stuart Mill and the crafters of the "Declaration of Sentiments," the germinal women's rights document that arose out of the 1848 Seneca Convention,[7] also make the hothouse flower argument, but they choose, to good effect, not to dwell on how these women-flowers act. To do so would deny them the sympathy that the hothouse flower argument initially induces. Stowe's incipient analysis of the patriarchy's deformations of women is subsumed by her portrait of one particular product of these deformations. This is a novel rife with contradictions, one where Stowe's political message is consistently undermined by her characterization of Lillie.

Yet it is a final contradiction having to do with Lillie's characterization that allows us, finally, to rescue this novel on feminist grounds. Lillie does possess a certain canniness, as Stowe periodically points out:

> [Lillie] saw through all the illusions of fancy and feeling, right to the tough material core of things. However soft and tender and sentimental her habits of speech and action were in her professional capacity of a charming woman, still the fair Lillie . . . knew on which side her bread was buttered. (52)

For Stowe, women ought to know about bread and butter only as it relates to culinary endeavors. Lillie's clear-eyed insights into her own material advancement are meant to show what a terrible example of true womanhood she is. For Stowe and her sister Catherine Beecher, women are supposed to gain influence not through offering clear-eyed assessments of the material conditions of men and women but through their ability to dispense a "great moral power," as Beecher and Stowe call it in their introduction to *The American Woman's Home* ([1869] 2002, 21), which depends less on words than on essence. Rachel Halliday, from *Uncle Tom's Cabin*, whom critics like

Jane Tompkins have identified as Stowe's womanly ideal (1985, 141–142), is the prime exemplar of this powerful womanly essence:

> [A]ll moved obediently to Rachel's gentle "Thee had better," or more gentle "Hadn't thee better?" in the work of getting breakfast. . . . Rachel moved gently and quietly about, making biscuits, cutting up chicken, diffusing a sort of sunny radiance over the whole proceeding generally. ([1852] 1994, 121)

Rachel manages to exert her influence less through her words, which are commonplace (and not eloquent at all), than through that intangible "sunny radiance."[8]

In *Pink and White Tyranny*, Grace Seymour is as close as readers get to Stowe's womanly ideal, "a highly cultivated, intelligent, and refined woman" ([1871] 1988, 30). Such high cultivation could have been a danger (Lillie, as I mentioned above, is highly cultivated, too) if Stowe did not show how Grace has been trained to squelch her every insight; again and again, she bites back her tongue upon hearing another example of John's idiocy. There is something eminently unsatisfying about this stifling of Grace: she actually sees clearly into the problem, and the problem is as much about patriarchal manipulations of women's nature as it is about Lillie's particularly disagreeable one. She is the one, remember, who identifies the way that Lillie has been deformed by her male admirers, a version of the hothouse flower analysis that was such a breakthrough for the cause of women.

So both Lillie and Grace see, if not deeply, at least some ways into the institutional circumstances governing women's lives. These insights are what Stowe castigates (although in Grace's case, it seems acceptable that she has these insights as long as she does not make them public). Yet despite Stowe's best intentions, the novel does go some way to offering a feminist analysis of patriarchal conditions. And, actually, it is exactly in these instances of clear-eyed self-awareness that some sympathy for Lillie might flicker into life: "But, you see, I am one of those to whom the luxuries are essential. I never could rub and scrub and work; in fact, I had rather not live at all than live poor" (15). To understand why this statement of Lillie's, which seems to reveal nothing so much as her shallowness, makes her a little bit sympathetic, one must have the experience of reading this novel (and other sentimental novels) in mind. Characters, almost without exception, do not introspect in a sentimental novel. And if they are heroes and heroines, they never do. As one reader of *Uncle Tom's Cabin* memorably, but slightly inaptly, wrote, Eva is "about as complex as a slinky" (Friedman 1996, 84). And even such a celebrator of *Uncle Tom's Cabin* as Jane Tompkins concedes that its characters are two-dimensional (1985, 126).

What gives literary characters complexity? Steven Knapp has noted that the more a character possesses self-consciousness, "the harder it becomes to see the character as exemplifying a general *type* of character (and thus as representing a general *type* of person)" (1993, 63). Along with Augustine St. Clare, Lillie stands as one of Stowe's rare characters who has at least the first inklings of an internal life.[9] This internal life grants Lillie a reality that very few of the other characters in the dimensionless horizon of this sentimental novel or others come close to attaining.

Lillie's moments of self-awareness-linked-to-institutional-awareness bring to mind a later Lily, Edith Wharton's Lily Bart, from *The House of Mirth* (1905). "You know I am horribly poor—and very expensive" ([1905] 1984, 8), Lily tells us early in the novel as a response to her friend and would-be suitor Lawrence Selden as to why she has not found anyone to marry yet. The slight self-mockery—contained in the artfulness of her parallelism—might seem to place her above Lillie, but she is actually quite similar. Though without the lacing of irony, Lillie, in an above quotation, reveals she too requires material comforts; this, in turn, suggests she knows what purpose she has been fitted to fulfill. In recognizing their shared ability to see into the way they have been molded (or deformed, as Lily seems to suggest), one can begin to make a case for a rescue of Stowe since it is exactly this capacity for institutional analysis that feminist critics, who tend to praise Wharton's work, focus on. As Frances Restuccia notes in "The Name of the Lily: Edith Wharton's Feminism(s)," "The story may be read as a social fable that indicts fashionable, fin-de-siècle New York society for producing human feminine ornaments that it has no qualms about crushing" (1987, 223).[10] Though it indicts a population much less sharply drawn (Stowe would probably name it "American men"), *Pink and White Tyranny* works in a similar way.

## WHAT SUCH A "RESCUE" PREVENTS US FROM SEEING

This way of rescuing Stowe requires reading her work completely against the grain. It requires us to ignore what she finds—and wants us to find—most salubrious and to embrace those artful characteristics of modern bellehood that Stowe warns us against. This might seem just fine: a great deal of interesting literary criticism begins in just such against-the-grain reading (especially when the authors under scrutiny have a reputation of being less than artful, like the sentimentalists). Wharton would seem to endorse this kind of reading as well, for she herself undermines the most clearly sentimental character in her novel, Gerty Farrish, who is pathetic exactly to the extent that she takes things to be what they appear.[11] Lily Bart herself seems to put paid to sentimentality and its teary propensities: "But no—I'm not of the tearful order. I discovered early that crying makes my nose red, and the knowledge has helped me through several painful episodes" ([1905]

1984, 215). Here it is Lily's irony—the self-mocking, dry tone of "painful episodes"—that rejects sentimentality as much as the overt rejection of weeping. Weeping, of course, is Stowe's own favorite mode of expression.

Stowe's sentimentality seems like something we must reject because it seems to lead Stowe to embrace positions that are unpalatable to modern feminist readers, like an embrace of heteronormative marriage (let alone a rejection of divorce). Going even further, one could argue that Stowe's sentimentality prevents the kind of institutional analysis that is crucial for feminism. And in fact, Lauren Berlant has argued this: "[W]hen sentimentality meets politics, it uses personal stories to tell of structural effects, but in so doing risks thwarting its very attempt to perform rhetorically a scene of pain that must be soothed politically" (1998, 641). Sentimentality replaces hard-headed institutional analysis with weepy tales of individuals. It not only occludes our clear-eyed vision of what it is that keeps women in their place but offers a false solution, one that we are tricked into thinking is real. It seems that only if we reject Stowe's sentimental values can we find anything of value in her novel.

So this against-the-grain reading of Stowe that I have offered rescues the novel at the same time as it repudiates Stowe's sentimentality—a strange kind of rescue. But I would argue that there might be something of value in her sentimentality. It is not just a valorization of "true womanhood" or a dangerous focus on the traumatized individual. *Pink and White Tyranny* launches an implicit but powerful argument to make us take its sentimentality seriously, both because of the kind of world it promises to bring into being and because of the way it allows us to see as rhetorical things that modern feminists want to be taken as foundational.

The novel does lay bare institutional oppression despite itself, but it also—and it means to do this—offers an analysis of how such clear-eyed, dry-eyed estimations of women's institutional plight might exact a significant cost in terms of persuasiveness. That is, the moments of Lillie's and Lily's institutional analyses go hand in hand with an awareness of themselves as infinitely malleable agents, willing to become what they must in order to triumph in a patriarchal system. We might start estimating the cost of this plasticity by returning to *The House of Mirth*. Unlike Stowe with her Lillie, Wharton seems to celebrate her Lily's ability to seem and be different things and to recognize this doubleness in herself. It is just such a depth of character that, as Wharton knows, makes Lily an interesting character. This depth allows Lily to be self-deprecating (as in her comment about how she avoids weeping), and it also leads to her perspicacity about others. The knowing artfulness of Lily seems to be what allows her to see so clearly the difference between surface and depth of those around her, as in this early scene that allows us to see the wealthy, polished hosts of a dinner party through Lily's eyes:

> She looked down the long table, studying its occupants one by one, from Gus Trenor, with his heavy carnivorous head sunk between his shoulders, as he preyed on a jellied plover, to his wife, at the opposite end of the long back of orchids, suggestive, with her glaring good-looks, of a jeweller's window lit by electricity. ([1905] 1984, 52)

The polish of Lily's rich hosts gets rubbed away under Lily's perceptive gaze, leaving her with a sense of their essential characteristics: Gus's rapaciousness and his wife's vulgar artificiality.

Yet the tragedy of the novel grows out of the mismatch in Lily's world between appearance and reality, which is exactly what allows Lily's circumstances to close like a vise around her. Lily's aunt cuts Lily out of her will because Lily seems to be a girl of a profligate nature (she is not). In perhaps the most painful misapprehension of all, Lawrence Selden, Lily's most suitable suitor, takes Lily's appearance outside of Gus Trenor's house to be proof of her bad character. Why care that Selden makes such a mistake? Readers might censor themselves from admitting to feeling bad about Selden's rejection of Lily because they might not want to admit that they wanted Lily and Selden to be together, either because it might signal their capitulation to impoverished ideas like "true love" or because they might have actually come to loathe Selden, as many critics seem to have done.

But if they look a little deeper into why they might want Lily and Selden to get together they might realize that it is not because they believe in "true love" and that Selden is not as loathsome as he first appears. In fact, what Selden and Lily offer the readers are occasions in which the characters' depths rise to their surfaces. Their coming together offers a respite from the artfulness that eventually ruins Lily's life, after it has already ruined her loveliness. During Lily and Selden's second meeting alone, Wharton describes a deeper communication that occurs between them than their words provide, "an indwelling voice in each called to the other across unsounded depths of feeling" (68). Critics tend to hate Selden, to fixate on his hell-bent desire to fix Lily; Selden, a lawyer, represents the law and its inability to tolerate ambiguity or indeterminacy.[12] Yet at least in the early scene of the indwelling voice, Lily and Selden reveal to each other the depth of their feeling, feeling that registers on the surface of Lily's body, in her tears and in the play of emotions across her face, which Wharton highlights in this scene. This does seem an ideal, one readers are meant to regret when it is removed as a possibility. Wharton or at least Wharton's narrator comments on the lack of loveliness that results once any possibility of depth registering on the surface of Lily's body is foreclosed:

> Scarcely three months had elapsed since [Selden] had parted from her . . . but a subtle change had passed over the quality of her beauty. Then it had had a transparency through which the fluctuations of the spirit were sometimes tragically

visible; now its impenetrable surface suggested a process of crystallization which had fused her whole being into one hard brilliant substance. (182)

Lily has literally begun to turn into a thing, the precious commodity that her suitors (other than Selden) want her to be. Wharton means for her readers to regret this transformation and long for the time in which Lily's feelings could register on the surface of her body. In fact, this observation seems a direct echo, in its inversion, of the earlier scene of the indwelling voice.

The radical elements of this novel—the way it lays bare the double standard and the lack of options for women—require us to reject duplicity: men should not be allowed to be respected as good husbands at the same time as their philandering is permitted; women should not have to make themselves endlessly agreeable or harden themselves so that they not only wear gems but become them. In other words, the clear-eyed analysis this novel offers about institutional conditions surrounding women leads us to reject the duplicity that sponsors these conditions. Ironically, the institutional analysis offered by *The House of Mirth* leads us to long for that sentimental insistence that a world could exist where surface and depth match. Lily's imagined marriage to Selden represents not just a sentimental plot development but a kind of authenticity, a place where Lily could act as she truly feels. In the absence of this world, readers want Lily to get rich. Wealth, in this novel, is not just an avenue of power (or of oppression); its allure derives from the way it could protect Lily from the danger that her world, a world of polished surfaces and lacerating depths, presents. In the absence of wealth, the novel makes us yearn for a place in which we could trust our impressions.

This is the world that sentimental rhetoric would create. The world in which Stowe would like to dwell—the one she tries to achieve with her sentimental rhetoric—is precisely one in which all is always, if sometimes belatedly, revealed. We can see this in the character of Rose Ferguson, a neighbor of the Seymours. Here is the effect she has on her future husband, Harry, who had been hatching a plan to ruin Lillie:

Unperceived by himself, the character of Rose was exerting a powerful influence over him; and, when he met that look of pain and astonishment which he had seen in her large blue eyes the night before, it seemed to awaken many things within him. It is astonishing how blindly people sometimes go on as to the character of their own conduct, till suddenly, like a torch in a dark place, the light of another person's opinion is thrown in upon them, and they begin to judge themselves under the quickening influence of another person's moral magnetism. ([1871] 1988, 269)

Sentimental novels are characterized by conversion scenes, which are often seen by critics in a religious context: conversions to God or at least to walking on a godly path. But we might also see the conversions as conversions into transparency. Harry used to contain hidden depths, embodied not simply in the way that his flirtation with Lillie hid his hatred of her but in the way that he could think of himself as a good person when in fact he was not. What makes him bad is not just the content of his duplicity but the fact that he is duplicitous at all, that his inside does not match his outside. Rose—once again through "essence" (or "moral magnetism") rather than words—allows him to become intelligible to himself. And of course, the moment he does is the moment he quits his duplicity. From now on, readers are led to believe, his appearance will reveal what is inside of him.

We might, of course, also call this a conversion to flatness. Harry henceforth will be a typical, two-dimensional sentimental character. I will not hesitate to say that sentimental rhetoric exerts a cost. But it also allows us, as I have tried to show, a respite from the world in which Lily Bart dwells, one in which surfaces have no necessary relationship to what they cover up. This characteristic is what defines Lily's world of late nineteenth-century wealth, but it also defines "disingenuous eloquence," what an unethical orator could pass off as the truth. According to Janet Gabler-Hover, the fear of "disingenuous eloquence" weighed heavily on nineteenth-century Americans, who suffered under "the suspicion that rhetoric was the study of how best to deceive people" (1990, 39–40). And disingenuous eloquence is what radical women reformers, so quick to condemn Stowe's novel, have no way of guarding against.

## STOWE AND THE "PROBLEM OF CULTIVATION"

What makes the rhetoric of postbellum women reformers unsentimental? Sentimentality, as I have tried to show, is characterized by a particular set of plot conventions (weepy conversion scenes, terminal marriages), but these plot conventions grow out of sentimentality's commitment to a particular model of persuasion, one that relies on the "essence" of the orator far more than on the orator's particular words. Sentimental rhetoric depends upon this "essence" being expressed with no mediation. This is why, I think, that the favored sentimental characters are so often at their most persuasive when they themselves are under duress. Thomas Sheridan, the eighteenth-century Irish actor and elocutionist, provides an insight into why this might be so:

[W]henever the force of these passions is extreme, words give place to inarticulate sounds: sighs, murmurings, in love; sobs, groans, and cries in grief; half choked sounds in rage; and shrieks in terrour are then the only language heard. And the experience of mankind may be appealed to, whether these have not more power in exciting sympathy, than any thing that can be done by mere words. ([1762] 1968, 102)

Words always have the capacity to be duplicitous, but people in pain do not use them; the sounds they make express what they are actually feeling. The ideal sentimental rhetoric is actually a wordless rhetoric, one where "essence" comes to the fore, where there is no possibility of mistaking what is in the sentimental heroine's throbbing heart.

The radical women reformers in Stowe's age explicitly rejected sentimental rhetoric, as in the influential work, "The Enfranchisement of Women" (1851), by John Stuart Mill's wife, Harriet Taylor, which was later turned into a pamphlet and widely disseminated in the States (where it heavily influenced Stowe's sister Isabella). Remarking on the speeches offered at the Worcester Convention of 1850, Taylor writes:

> What is wanted for women is equal rights, equal admission to all social privileges; not a position apart,—a sort of sentimental priesthood. . . . The strength of the cause lies in the support of those who are influenced by reason and principle; and to attempt to recommend it by sentimentalities, absurd in reason, and inconsistent with the principle on which the movement is founded, is to place a good cause on a level with a bad one. (Taylor [1851] 1854, 28)

The opposition structuring this utterance is one between rationality and irrationality. Taylor associates irrationality with "sentimentalities," and these sentimentalities seem to be associated with feeling. Feeling is, not coincidentally, what women of the nineteenth century were associated with, what men and many women believed to be women's natural mode of expression. Taylor envisions a world in which women could find an equal footing with men by severing women's speech (and being) from feeling.

What is disavowed in Taylor's speech, however, is not just what people perceived to be women's true nature but what the nineteenth century believed turned a speech from mere words into action. Nineteenth-century rhetorical theory (heir to the Scottish rhetorical revolution of the eighteenth century) claimed that appealing to the understanding was not enough; an orator had also to inspire the emotions.[13] The Scottish rhetorician George Campbell believed that "[k]nowledge, the object of the intellect, furnisheth materials for the fancy; the fancy culls, compounds, and, by her mimic art, disposes these materials so as to affect the passions; the passions are the natural spurs to volition or action, and so need only to be right directed" ([1776] 1968, 146). The orator needs to make the audience feel in order to inspire them to action. What Stowe adds to the equation is the idea that emotion is best inspired in the audience by the manifestation of the orator's essence. What is assured in a sentimental transaction is veracity. Words could deceive, but an orator could not hide his true character, and this true character is what would lend his words the capacity to affect his audience. Feeling is necessary not just for action but for protection against "disingenuous eloquence."

The women reformers who were anxious to uncouple their rhetoric from feeling were also, not surprisingly, anxious to uncouple it from women's essence. We can see this if we realize that there is an ambiguity at the heart of the "hothouse flower" argument. It could mean that women do have a "true nature" that has been artificially cultivated. That is, women have been artificially cultivated by men to become what men want. Lillie seems the living embodiment of such a cultivation:

> Pretty girls, unless they have wise mothers, are more educated by the opposite sex than by their own . . . and the burden of masculine teaching is generally about the same, and might be stereotyped as follows: "You don't need to be or do any thing. Your business in life is to look pretty, and amuse us." (Stowe [1871] 1988, 47)

Lillie has been made by men into something she is not; her true nature has been warped. Implicit in this understanding is the idea that women have a true nature, though what that comprises is open to debate. What is woman's true essence for Stowe and her sister Catherine? For them it lies in their identity as "moral priestesses" (although they would no doubt prefer the term "ministers"), precisely what Harriet Taylor disavows. But the hothouse flower argument is susceptible to another interpretation.

This hothouse flower argument might claim, instead, that the fact of the matter about woman's true nature is that there is no fact of the matter. Woman is infinitely plastic, capable of anything her circumstances would allow her. She is without essence (even if what defines her is the capacity to reason, this is not so much an identity as a means by which to choose between possibilities). This anti-essentialism, which inspires contemporary feminist theory, might look like liberation, but it brings with it the problem of the gap between seeming and being. If women have no essence, no essential character, then what is left for them is artfulness. They must create themselves from scratch, perform their own femininity. Both Lily Bart and Lillie Ellis show us the lure of artfulness: the way it bestows on the artful person a perspicacity about the duplicitous, patriarchal world around them. But it is exactly this duplicity that caused the problems their own artfulness was necessary to uncover in the first place—the ways in which people's surfaces hide their depths, in which appearance should never be taken for reality. Harriet Beecher Stowe's insistence on the importance of a person's "essence" is thus not only a way of insisting that women feel more than men, that they can form a kind of sentimental priesthood; it is also a way of protecting the public (including women themselves) from disingenuousness. Stowe clearly has objectionable ideas about what woman's essence is, but the idea of essence, a reality that would then reveal itself to onlookers, is not without its attractions, even today. Stowe wants to protect us from exactly the kind of error that John Seymour falls into: mistaking a highly cultivated manipulator for an innocent.

Let me close with a description that embodies the difficult but necessary accounting that the sentimental rhetoric of *Pink and White Tyranny* leads us into:

> Rose Ferguson has one source of attraction which is as great a natural gift as beauty, and which, when it is found with beauty, makes it perfectly irresistible; to wit, perfect unconsciousness of self. This is a wholly different trait from unselfishness: it is not a moral virtue, attained by voluntary effort, but a constitutional gift, and a very great one. (209)

Thus Stowe celebrates Rose for her constitutional incapacity for an inner life. Yet Stowe claims this lack of self-consciousness leads to her magnetism. This might seem baffling in light of what we know about the powers of three-dimensional characters to draw us in. Yet readers should also remember their yearning for Lily to achieve a vantage in the world from which she could finally know where she stands and where people could judge her accurately. It is not that Stowe's argument for sentimental rhetoric comes without its own heavy cost (lack of interesting literary characters, an embrace of some form of essentialism) but that it can also point out problems in modes of rhetoric that reject it completely. These kinds of rhetoric embrace artfulness—in this case, the idea of the "essence-less" woman[14]—without always being aware of the costs. *The House of Mirth* constructs a depressing world of thoroughgoing artfulness, and Stowe's *Pink and White Tyranny* allows us to glimpse its rhetorical foundation.

## NOTES

1.  Dorothy Berkson, for example, one of the only contemporary critics to devote significant attention to Stowe's society novels (*Pink and White Tyranny, My Wife and I,* and *We and Our Neighbors*), reads *Pink and White Tyranny* as evidence of Stowe's unfortunate reaction to the radical feminism of her time: "Nothing could better demonstrate the virulence of Stowe's reaction to radical feminism than this ill-conceived attack on divorce (i.e., *Pink and White Tyranny*)" (1980, 253). Berkson thinks that radical feminism caused Stowe to turn away from the radical millenial politics one can see in her New England novels, like *Poganuc People* and *The Pearl of Orr's Island,* and become a conservative, someone interested only in offering "a defense of traditional feminine domestic virtue" (252). Similarly, Joan Hedrick, a recent biographer of Stowe, notes that Stowe began the novel before her reading of Mill's *The Subjection of Women* and the Lady Byron debacle. She characterizes the novel as evincing a "more characteristic conservatism": "She used *Pink and White*

*Tyranny* to have her say about woman's true role and took swipes at free love and French novels" (1994, 374).

2. See Judith Fetterley's "Commentary: Nineteenth-Century American Women Writers and the Politics of Recovery" for a defense of the rescuing techniques that went on twenty years previously (1954). She issues a call not to abandon them. Fetterley takes to task critics like Richard Brodhead and Shirley Samuels for their attacks on the sentimental novel, fearing that this kind of approach will lead to their reabandonment.

3. I do not mean to suggest that "feminist criticism" is a monolithic entity or that its different strands go about persuading in the same way. Yet many postbellum women reformers and almost all contemporary feminist critics do resemble each other in this way: they insist on women's lack of essence. In our post–Judith Butler critical landscape, it can seem like a novice move to point this out about contemporary feminist criticism, but I would argue that what is powerful about *Pink and White Tyranny* is its ability to bring to our attention something that we might otherwise not even notice since it has become the grounds for our thinking rather than our thinking itself.

4. These tensions were brought to a head in the summer of 1870, when Stowe attacked George Sand in response to an article praising her in the *Revolution*, the print arm of the National Woman Suffrage Association (led by Elizabeth Cady Stanton and Susan B. Anthony). As recounted by Barbara White, the *Revolution* article quoted Sand as calling marriage a "barbarous institution"; Stowe responded in a rival journal by writing that Sand represented the "animalism & atheism" (quoted in White 2003, 160) of the century. Stowe's attack then inspired retaliation by Stanton: "George Sand has done a grander work for women . . . than any woman of her day and generation; while Mrs. Stowe has been vacillating over every demand for her sex, timidly watching the weathercock of public sentiment and ridiculing the advance guard" (quoted in White 2003, 160). Stowe uses *Pink and White Tyranny* as another weapon in this war: there is a flagrant strain of anti-French sentiment that runs throughout it.

5. For Howells, the lesson that this novel teaches is that old New England families like the Seymours should continue to live "simply and sanely in the tradition of their ancestry" ([1872] 1980, 208).

6. Yet this comment about the working class's lack of gratitude has an undermining effect on Stowe's own philanthropic ideas. Stowe has trained us to read this passage (and almost everything Lillie says) by negating it: Lillie has exactly the opposite values and ideas that she should have. Yet if we negate what Lillie says—the working class *is* grateful—the way Stowe seems to lead us to do, we see something unsavory about Stowe's own ideas about philanthropy: that the unfortunate do show gratitude (as in fact the unfortunates who populate Stowe's novels—like the converted Topsy—are sure to do) and, implicitly, this is how it should be.

7. The declaration does not make an explicit mention of hothouse flowers, but it does assume that men have warped women: "He has endeavored, in every way that he could, to destroy her confidence in her own powers, to lessen her self-respect, and to make her willing to lead a dependent and abject life" (Stanton et al. [1848] 1881, 71).

8. Similarly, another womanly ideal in another novel operates more through essence than speech. Here is a description of how Mary Scudder, the protagonist of

*The Minister's Wooing*, converts her friend: "The greatest moral effects are like those of music,—not wrought out by sharp-sided intellectual propositions, but melted in by a divine fusion, by words that have mysterious, indefinite fulness [sic] of meaning, made living by sweet voices, which seem to be the out-throbbings of angelic hearts" ([1859] 1978, 396). Once again, you can see how Stowe disregards words in favor of an inarticulate, yet highly effective, "essence."

9. Like Augustine St. Clare, she can expose other people's foibles. Here Lillie comments on Grace's (her sister-in-law) renunciation of wine: "'Well, really!' said Lillie, in a dry, cool tone, 'I suppose it was very good of you, perfectly saintlike and all that; but it does seem a great pity'" (Stowe [1871] 1988, 155). This reader at least pauses to second Lillie's nailing of Grace's sanctimoniousness.

10. Restuccia goes on to show that to read *House of Mirth* as merely this kind of social fable is reductive; instead, she argues that the novel also works on what she calls a "literary feminist" level (not just a "social feminist" level). Restuccia claims that through Lily, Wharton demonstrates the indeterminacy of the feminine, its immunity to categorization within fixed or "social" categories. Yet since this kind of feminism also serves to expose and critique the law, which it and Restuccia envisions as patriarchal, my summary still, I believe, stands: feminist critics of this novel focus on the way it can perform an institutional critique of the patriarchy.

11. Gerty's finest hour comes when she suddenly stops mistaking appearance for reality, when she realizes that Selden's affection towards her masks his deeper feeling for Lily: "The words [Selden's entreaties to treat Lily kindly] beat on Gerty's brain like the sound of a language which has seemed familiar at a distance, but on approaching is found to be unintelligible. He had come to talk to her of Lily—that was all!" (Wharton [1905] 1984, 150–51). This is the moment when Gerty realizes that the world around her is actually a much more complicated place than she had imagined. To the extent that she had never questioned its appearances, she is a fool; this moment of disillusionment awards her dignity.

12. See, for example, William Moddelmog's assessment in "Disowning 'Personality': Privacy and Subjectivity in *The House of Mirth*," for a discussion of how Selden is unable to find a category to fit Lily into when she returns to his apartment for the second (and final) time. Yet these assessments of Selden scant the way that Selden at first does seem to offer Lily the opportunity to reveal her true self. Moddelmog would no doubt disagree, and that is because he would dispute the idea that Lily ultimately has an essence; he claims she is ultimately unknowable.

13. For a wide-ranging discussion of nineteenth-century rhetorical beliefs see Barnet Baskerville's (1952) "Principle Themes of Nineteenth-Century Critics of Oratory."

14. The form this takes in much contemporary feminist criticism is in the celebration of indeterminacy. Both of the articles on *The House of Mirth* that I quoted above, for example, celebrate this aspect of Lily's, her ability to remain unfixed (and both not surprisingly hate Selden as the "great fixer").

# WORKS CITED

Beecher, Catharine, and Harriet Beecher Stowe. [1869] 2002. *The American Woman's Home*. New Brunswick, NJ: Rutgers University Press.

Baskerville, Barnet. 1952. "Principal Themes of Nineteenth-Century Critics of Oratory." *Speech Monographs* 20:11–26.

Berkson, Dorothy. 1980. "Millenial Politics and the Feminine Fiction of Harriet Beecher Stowe." In *Critical Essays on Harriet Beecher Stowe*, ed. Elizabeth Ammons, 244–58. Boston: Hall.

Berlant, Lauren. 1998. "Poor Eliza." *American Literature* 70 (4): 638–68.

Campbell, George. [1776] 1968. "The Philosophy of Rhetoric." In *The Rhetoric of Blair, Campbell, and Whately*, ed. James L. Golden and Edward P. J. Corbett, 139–271. New York: Holt, Rinehart, and Winston.

Fetterley, Judith. 1954. "Commentary: Nineteenth-Century Women Writers and the Politics of Recovery." *American Literary History* 6 (3): 600–11.

Friedman, George S. 1996. Letter to the Editor. *Harper's Magazine*, March, 84.

Gabler-Hover, Janet. 1990. *Truth in American Fiction: The Legacy of Rhetorical Idealism*. Athens: University of Georgia Press.

Hedrick, Joan. 1994. *Harriet Beecher Stowe: A Life*. New York: Oxford University Press.

Howells, William Dean. [1872] 1980. "Reviews of *Pink and White Tyranny, My Wife and I*, and *Oldtown Fireside Stories*, by Harriet Beecher Stowe." In *Critical Essays on Harriet Beecher Stowe*, ed. Elizabeth Ammons, 207–9. Reprint, Boston: Hall.

Knapp, Steven. 1993. *Literary Interest: The Limits of Anti-Formalism*. Cambridge: Harvard University Press.

Moddelmog, William. 1998. "Disowning 'Personality': Privacy and Subjectivity in *The House of Mirth*." *American Literature* 70 (2): 337–63.

Restuccia, Frances L. 1987. "The Name of the Lily: Edith Wharton's Feminism(s)." *Contemporary Literature* 28 (2): 223–38.

Sheridan, Thomas. [1762] 1968. *A Course of Lectures on Elocution*, ed. R. C. Alston. Menston, UK: Scholar.

Stanton, Elizabeth Cady, et al. [1848] 1881. Vol. 1 of *History of Woman Suffrage*, ed. Elizabeth Cady Stanton et al. New York: Arno.

Stowe, Harriet Beecher. [1852] 1994. *Uncle Tom's Cabin*. New York: Norton.

———. [1859] 1978. *The Minister's Wooing*. Hartford, CT: Stowe-Day Foundation.

———. [1871] 1988. *Pink and White Tyranny: A Society Novel*. Boston: Roberts Bros.

Taylor, Harriet. [1851] 1854. "The Enfranchisement of Women." In *Woman's Rights Tracts, No. 3*, ed. Wendell Holmes et al., 1–28. Boston: Wallcut.

Tompkins, Jane. 1985. *Sensational Designs: The Cultural Work of American Fiction, 1790–1860*. New York: Oxford University Press.

Wharton, Edith. [1905] 1984. *The House of Mirth*. New York: Bantam.

White, Barbara A. 2003. *The Beecher Sisters*. New Haven, CT: Yale University Press.

# Pink and White Tyranny and Harriet Beecher Stowe's Ambivalent Views on Authorship

*Martin T. Buinicki*

"This story is not to be a novel, as the world understands the word," Harriet Beecher Stowe writes in the preface to her novel *Pink and White Tyranny* ([1871] 1988, v), and modern critics have largely accepted this assertion, giving the text scarcely a passing glance. Those who have paused to consider the book at all have described it as little more than a tract espousing Stowe's views on domestic life and her critique of aspects of the feminist movement. In her important biography of the author, Joan D. Hedrick provides one of the more sustained discussions of the novel, spending approximately a page of her volume on the work. Like other novels Stowe wrote during the early 1870s, Hedrick argues, the book represents "a kind of journalistic fiction, half editorial, half story. Loosely plotted and often carelessly constructed, these 'society novels' still sparkle with Stowe's satirical asides and seemingly effortless metaphors" (1994, 378). While Hedrick gives one example of such a metaphor, she does not concentrate on either the style or content. Primarily she sees Stowe using the text "to have her say about woman's true role and [to take] swipes at free love and French novels" (374).

It is perhaps the vision of "woman's true role" that Stowe presents in the text that accounts for at least a degree of the critical silence that surrounds it. The novel tells the story of John Seymour, a well-meaning, philanthropic bachelor who is "hooked" by Lillie Ellis, an aging belle whose prospects are fading ([1871] 1988, 9). Full of romantic inspiration and stunningly poor insight, he marries Lillie, much to the dismay of his more clear-eyed sister Grace who recognizes an opportunist when she sees one. After the marriage, Lillie becomes the tyrant alluded to in the title, uprooting the comfortable life of her husband and draining his resources and his patience

35

until finally he faces financial and emotional collapse. Although she is
eventually forced by necessity and parenthood to live under straitened circumstances, and John learns to make the best of a bad situation, it is only
on Lillie's deathbed that she truly comes to see the errors in her ways. In a
striking act of exchange, she leaves behind a daughter, her namesake, who
takes her place at her husband's side: she is now "the tender confidant, the
trusted friend of her father. . . . The Lillie who guides his household, and is
so motherly to the younger children; who shares every thought of his heart;
who enters into every feeling and sympathy,—she is the pure reward of his
faithfulness and constancy" (330–31). Stowe's stated moral in telling the
story is to counter calls from women's rights activists for making it easier
for couples to pursue divorces by demonstrating how such a change could
leave women like Lillie without support (319–20).

Stowe is dealing with more than the proper conduct of married women
and the obligations of matrimony, however. The text is also an exploration of women's occupations; indeed, a great deal of her writing addressing women's issues during the years that preceded the publication
of the book in 1871 is concerned with the issue of work. For Stowe, a
professional author accustomed to receiving queries from hopeful (and
hopeless) writers, her own trade was never far from her mind when she
considered the subject. Yet, unlike many of her literary contemporaries,
Stowe does not highlight a female novelist in her fiction. In her portrayal
of Lillie Ellis, however, she comes closest to presenting an "authorial"
character, a woman who is skilled both in recognizing the expectations
of others and producing language and imagery designed to fulfill those
expectations. By presenting such a character as a "tyrant," Stowe reveals
a profound ambivalence about her profession and her own position as
an authority on the forms of sentimental literature. Correspondence with
an aspiring author in 1865 further demonstrates Stowe's view of reading
and writing as a courtship, an exchange in which the most accomplished
belle/writer can win the affection of the suitor/reader. Read in this light,
*Pink and White Tyranny* offers unique insight into Stowe's perspective regarding her profession and the power of the literary style and symbolism
that she helped to create and to popularize.[1]

In *The Limits of Sisterhood*, an analysis of the Beecher sisters and the
women's movement, the omission of Stowe's novel from discussion of the
author's works is most evident in the following passage discussing a letter
she wrote pitching *Pink and White Tyranny* to one of her editors:

> In a letter written to Edward Everett Hale, the editor of *Old and New*, Harriet
> Beecher Stowe offered an illuminating portrait of herself. Telling Hale in April
> 1869 that she was beginning a novel dealing with contemporary issues, she
> informed him that she was "to some extent a woman's rights woman, as I am

to some extent something of almost everything that goes." Indeed she was. However, the extent to which Stowe supported the postbellum movement's leaders and their demands was determined by her conception of womanhood. (Boydston, Kelley, and Margolis 1988, 258)

The lack of even a mention of the work's title in this context is telling. While the authors are correct to point out that Stowe's views regarding women's rights were tied to her more conservative feelings regarding domesticity, she was explicit in her letter to Hale regarding the "contemporary issues" she wished to discuss: the oppression of men by their wives. She wrote of the planned book, "It will be in a quiet way an offset to a class of writings which I am sorry to see which represent men in most cases as oppressors and women as sufferers in domestic life" (Stowe quoted in Martin 1988, vi). Stowe completely reverses her feminist contemporaries' portrayals of gender hierarchies, and her position on this issue would appear to be vexingly at odds with any argument that Stowe was "[d]etermined to establish female hegemony in the private sphere" (Boydston, Kelley, and Margolis 1988, 259), for why endanger such a hegemony with an apparently unflattering portrayal of female power?

Stowe's contemporaries saw the potentially reactionary quality of the novel. In publicizing the work, Stowe's Canadian publisher remarks,

Mrs. Stowe does justice to that sex which is not enough remembered in the discussion of the wrongs of woman. For she describes, as no one else can describe, the tyranny under which a loyal and chivalrous gentleman suffers. This, the latest work of one through whose efforts the black slavery of centuries was broken, will render a service not less considerable, if it so awakens the conscience of men and women that Pink and White Tyranny of women over men shall be impossible. (quoted in Martin 1988, vi–vii)

As Judith Martin wryly notes of this advertisement, "Ah, yes. Uncle Tom's mother speaks out on domestic injustice—to condemn her own sex" (vii). Martin goes to great lengths in her introduction to the only modern edition of the novel to complicate this assessment, pointing out that Stowe places much of the blame for the tyrant's behavior on the male-dominated society in which she was raised: "In her fairness, the author has delineated the pastel tyrant's own social grievances . . . going beyond her stated intention of sympathizing with men who have pretty wives to explore the social forces that made them what they were" (ix). While this is true, the causes of Lillie's behavior are not the primary concern of the novel, and there is no denying that the text troubles our understanding of the author's views on "the woman question." As the advertisement makes clear, Stowe's reputation as a spokesperson for social justice gave her writing a particular weight in the debate over gender equality, and it is difficult not to interpret her actions in this regard as working counter to the goals of the women's movement.

The timing is particularly problematic. Events like the scandal over her article on Lady Byron and the accusations of adultery that Victoria Wood-hull lodged against her brother Henry Ward Beecher have been offered as explanations for some of the more conservative ideas Stowe expresses in her work in the 1870s (Hedrick 1994, 374). For example, Hedrick theorizes that Stowe became disillusioned by these personal crises and pulled away from the more progressive factions of the women's movement. While her explanation is convincing, particularly in her discussion of *My Wife and I* (1871), there is no clear catalyst to account for the stridency of *Pink and White Tyranny*, which, as Hedrick notes, Stowe pitched to her editor prior to these incidents (374).

Rather than a reaction to any particular personal event, the novel and its domestic dictator Lillie Ellis appear to be the dramatization and elaboration of views that Stowe began espousing in her 1865 *House and Home Papers* and reiterated in her series of articles for the *Atlantic* in 1868, *The Chimney-corner*, both also published and sold as bound volumes. In one such essay from *House and Home Papers*, "Home-Keeping vs. House-Keeping," Stowe's male narrator, Christopher Crowfield, tells the story of Bill Carberry, an early prototype for the oppressed husband of *Pink and White Tyranny*. Bill watches in dismay as his dreams of a restful home life entertaining friends with his new wife are shattered by his bride's family's obsession with fashion and order. His hope for "social freedom," a life marked by relaxed visits with close friends, is "crushed under a weight of upholstery" (1865a [2003], 34):

> Poor Bill found very soon that his house and furniture were to be kept at such an ideal point of perfection that he needed another house to live in,—for, poor fellow, he found the difference between having a house and a home. . . . Bill would often drop in upon us, wistfully lingering in the cosey arm-chair between my writing-table and my wife's sofa, and saying with a sigh how confoundedly pleasant things looked there, so pleasant to have a bright, open fire, and geraniums and roses and birds, and all that sort of thing, and to dare to stretch out one's legs and move without thinking what one was going to hit. (36)

Bill suffers from his in-laws' dual obsessions with fashion and with order, and he is forced to flee his own residence.

Stowe returned to this well of male domestic discontent in describing the living situation of Lillie's male vassal, John Seymour:

> He never felt like lolling at ease on any of those elegant sofas, as of old he used to cast himself into the motherly arms of the great chintz one that filled the

recess. . . . There was not, in fact, in all the reorganized house, a place where he felt *himself* to be at all the proper thing; nowhere where he could lounge, and read his newspaper, without a feeling of impropriety. . . . [H]e took long rests every day while he went to [his sister] Grace's, on Elm Street, and stretched himself on the old sofa, and sat in his mother's old arm-chair, and told Grace how elegant their house was . . . and how much Lillie was delighted with it. ([1871] 1988, 139)

Like Bill, John must leave the impersonal and uncomfortable surroundings of his "house" in order to feel at "home," a sensation that seems to derive from the ability to "stretch out" and "linger." Home is a refuge, a place where a man can feel at ease, and in both of these passages, though written several years apart, husbands are forced from their sanctuary by the coldly aesthetic desires of their wives. The accommodating man in these episodes is rendered powerless by his marriage vows, the standards of gentlemanly conduct, and, in John's case, the emotional manipulation of his spouse.

There are some differences in the two portrayals, however. Stowe goes to great lengths in her 1865 essay to describe Bill's wife Sophie as a victim of her family's preoccupation with fashion as much as her husband is:

Sophie was solemnly warned and instructed by all the mothers and aunts,— she was warned of moths, warned of cockroaches, warned of flies, warned of dust; . . . and bundles of receipts and of rites and ceremonies necessary for the preservation and purification and care of all these articles [of furniture] were stuffed into the poor girl's head, before guiltless of cares as the feathers that floated above it. ([1865a] 2003, 35–36)

While Bill may have been a prototype for the suffering husband, Sophie seems a far cry from the scheming Lillie Ellis, who convinces John that the house must be made over in order to revive her flagging spirits: "[O]ur rooms are lovely; but they are n't modern and cheerful, like those I've been accustomed to. They make me feel pensive and sad all the time" ([1871] 1988, 105). Sophie cries over her cares; Lillie cries in order to gain her husband's assent to her demands. She is not concerned with upkeep of the house; she simply expects John to hire the appropriate servants to manage it:

Lillie cried, and said she had never had any trouble before about "getting her things done." She was sure mamma or Trixie or somebody did them, or got them done,—she never knew how or when. . . . John kissed and embraced, and wiped away her tears . . . and declared she should have everything just as she desired it. (70–71)

Lillie may not be able to handle a household, but Stowe demonstrates time and again that she can rally her emotions and her beauty to manage her husband.

In her 1868 *Chimney-corner* essay "Woman's Sphere," Stowe posits that women such as Lillie are a product of either a lack of employment or a lack of appropriate employment. The first, which Stowe describes as producing "girls and women who *can or will do no earthly thing well*," seems to have much in common with Lillie (43). A girl who belongs to this category is well-versed in the latest styles and manages to use her knowledge to meet her monetary and social goals:

> [She] finds means, by begging, borrowing, living out, to keep herself extremely trim and airy for a certain length of time, till . . . the lace hat and parasol, and the glib tongue, have done their work in making a fool of some honest young mechanic who earns three dollars a day. She marries him with no higher object than to have somebody to earn money for her to spend. And what comes of such marriages? (46)

In *Pink and White Tyranny*, Stowe informs the reader that Lillie marries John with this objective in mind: "A husband, she knew very well, was the man who undertook to be responsible for his wife's bills: he was the giver, bringer, and maintainer of all sorts of solid and appreciable comforts" ([1871] 1988, 52). While her chosen target is certainly more than a mechanic, the union in the novel seems to represent Stowe's lengthy response to her earlier hypothetical question, "what comes of such marriages?"

As dangerous as not having gainful employment can be for the moral education of a woman, Stowe argues, the specter of having the wrong sort of employment can be even worse. Christopher Crowfield's wife expounds on the grim fate that awaits the young girls who have gone to work in the factories. These jobs have put them into unwholesome environments with inadequate oversight and insufficient training in the domestic arts. The result, Stowe writes, is a woman who seems destined to do little more than prey on her unsuspecting husband:

> Many times it has been my lot to try, in my family service, girls who have left factories; and I have found them wholly useless for any of the things which a woman ought to be good for. They knew nothing of a house, or what ought to be done in it; they had imbibed a thorough contempt for household labor, and looked upon it as a *dernier resort*; and it was only the very lightest of its tasks that they could even begin to think of. . . . They were pretty, and their destiny was to marry and lie a dead weight on the hands of some honest man, and to increase, in their children, the number of incapables. ([1868] 2003, 52–54)

Both of these descriptions seem equally apt for Lillie, though one deals with a woman who does not work, and the other with a woman who does the wrong sort of work. In each instance, the women Stowe describes are inordinately concerned with fashionable trends, associate freely with men, and are too uninterested in the ways of "home-keeping."

As these parallels between the novel and Stowe's earlier writings on domestic affairs suggest, there is no denying the prominent role gender issues play in the novel. The book seems to represent a lengthy discourse on questions that the author had begun exploring several years earlier. What these parallels also suggest, however, is that for Stowe any discussion of the proper domestic behavior of a wife must also address women's proper employment, and this is true in the case of *Pink and White Tyranny*. Lillie is not a factory girl, yet it would be a mistake to include her in the class of women who do nothing or do nothing well. Stowe's female tyrant is, in a sense, an expert in the very trade that the author herself practices. She is skilled in reproducing the rhetoric of romance and sentimentality. As the author depicts the ways in which Lillie first ensnares and then manipulates her husband, time and again she emphasizes the professional way that she approaches her pursuits and her use of language and romantic symbolism: "However soft and tender and sentimental her habits of speech and action were in her professional capacity of a charming woman, still the fair Lillie, had she been a man, would have been respected in the business world, as one that had cut her eye-teeth, and knew on which side her bread was buttered" ([1871] 1988, 52). She approaches her courtships in a business-like fashion, her "habits of speech and action" little more than tools of her trade. Like Stowe herself, Lillie manipulates the tropes of sentimentality to fulfill her ambitions. Indeed, there is a striking similarity between the character and her accomplished creator, for, while Stowe constructs Lillie as a woman defined by "poetical similes" (2), Lillie herself is an expert who knows how to employ the tropes popularized by Stowe to her own advantage.

It is not surprising then that Stowe demonstrates a persistent concern with language and representation in the text, exploring her own literary authority as a sentimental novelist and the uses and abuses of symbolic power. The title itself both signifies and displaces the "tyrannical" woman who is the apparent subject of the text, presenting instead the tyranny of the "pink and white" metaphor; it is symbolic language itself that seems to be the agent of excessive power here. In the preface, Stowe highlights her awareness of language and attempts to exercise authorial control over it, as with her assertion that the novel is not a novel "as the world understands the word" (v), arguing that the word no longer signifies what it is expected to signify. She presents herself as an authority of both morals and meaning, setting the terms by which her work will be read and interpreted: "[The text] is, moreover, a story with a moral; and for fear that you shouldn't find out exactly what the moral is, we shall adopt the plan of the painter who wrote under his pictures, 'This is a bear,' and 'This is a turtle-dove'" (vi). Stowe declares herself the arbiter of interpretation, pledging to provide the captions that will illuminate (and restrict) the meaning of her images and convey the proper social lesson.

Both author and character, therefore, attempt to wield symbolic power for their own ends in their "professional capacity." In "Woman's Sphere," Stowe suggests that authorship offers one of many suitable modes of employment available for women. Christopher Crowfield lists it as the first option: "'In the first place,' said I, 'come the professions requiring natural genius,—authorship, painting, sculpture, with the subordinate arts of photographing, coloring, and finishing'" ([1868] 2003, 38). While Stowe does not provide an example of a female author in her novel, her negative portrayal of Lillie indicates some ambivalence regarding the power that she herself employs as a writer.

Mary Kelley argues that this is an ambivalence that Stowe shared with other "literary domestics." In Kelley's view, when Stowe describes herself to her editor Hale as "to some extent something of almost everything that goes," she is expressing the simultaneous pull of domestic life and inherent dissatisfaction with that life: "Stowe spoke more truth than she realized, for the literary domestic, in conflict within herself, did indeed stand on all sides of the 'woman' issue" (1984, 318). Writing offered a way for Stowe and other women of the nineteenth century to extend their sphere of influence outside the home; at the same time, Kelley argues, such employment threatened the familiar notions of womanhood and the female role by revealing their limitations and deprivations:

> Just as the literary domestics felt compelled to look within the circle of domestic concerns for satisfaction, for all joys, and for ultimate purpose, so was it inevitable that they found within themselves the stirrings of discontent, the sum of fears, and the basis for disillusionment. Their eagerness to glorify woman in the name of her mandated ethic of life, selfless service to others, warred with their apprehension that woman's condition was actually demoralizing and debilitating. (251)

Writing could allow for the celebration of traditional home life, but it also had the potential to undermine it. In *Pink and White Tyranny*, Stowe appears to be simply elaborating upon her earlier essays, outlining the proper occupations and behaviors of young women. Her descriptions, however, constantly deal with how Lillie represents herself in the world. She is intimately linked with the writing process, and Stowe herself seems to have linked writing with the flirtatious conduct of a young woman, as indicated in a statement Stowe wrote in a letter to another of her editors, James T. Fields: "[A]t times and seasons a story *comes*—grown like a flower—sometimes will and sometimes won't like a pretty woman" (Stowe quoted in Kelley 1984, 276). *Pink and White Tyranny*, as she describes it in her letter to Hale, will "show the domestic oppression practiced by a gentle pretty pink and white doll on a strong minded generous gentleman who has married her in a fit of poetical romance because she looks pretty" (Stowe quoted in Kelley 1984, 318). "Poetical romance" can mislead and trap even those with the best natures. Stowe's language suggests that her novel is as much an exploration of the power of writing as a seductive and manipulative force as it is an argument for the proper domestic behavior of women.

If a story comes only of its own accord, "like a pretty woman," then it is no surprise that Stowe's "tyrant" first appears to the reader and her ill-fated future husband not so much as a fully drawn character but as a literary symbol, a "light, sylph-like form" ([1871] 1988, 1). Like the mythic figure that Stowe references, Lillie is a graceful, if perhaps empty, female signifier, whose outlines are soon filled in by her male spectators. To the experienced man-about-town, one whose knowledge allows him to "read" her properly, she is "the most adroit 'fisher of men' that has been seen in our days," but to John Seymour, the luckless hero of the text, she is "pretty" (2). This lack of critical discernment should not make us question John's character, however. We are assured that he is "as good and honest a man as there is going in this world of ours. He was a generous, just, manly, religious young fellow" (2). Nothing in his upbringing seems to have prepared him for the idea that there may be a gap between signifier and signified, that the vision may not match the reality.

Representation seems to be all that matters in this encounter, and Lillie is little more than a series of metaphors: "John gazed, and thought of all sorts of poetical similes: of a 'daisy just wet with morning dew;' of a 'violet by a mossy stone;' in short, of all the things that poets have made and provided for the use of young gentlemen in the way of falling in love" (2). To the naive eye of John, who "had deep within himself a little private bit of romance" (3), Lillie is simply a construction of clichés, a form of forms. His friend Ethridge also views her in textual terms, but in a decidedly different fashion: "I know her like a book. I know all her smiles and wiles, advices and devices; and her system of tactics is an old story with me. I shan't interrupt any of her little games" (10). Rather than an innocent poetic simile, Ethridge sees in Lillie a "story" of systematic seduction, a manual of romantic devices designed to ensnare unsuspecting (male) readers. She reads John much more accurately than he reads her, and she says and does exactly the right thing when the two are introduced. Stowe's narrator remarks, "Miss Ellis was a belle by profession, and she understood her business perfectly. In nothing did she show herself master of her craft, more than in the adroitness with which she could soothe the bashful pangs of new votaries" (8).

If Lillie is indeed a "master of her craft," one must ask what exactly makes her so. It is apparent that her skill seems to lie in her ability to manipulate the very tropes and symbolic language that suitors like John ascribe to her. She delivers "unconscious, baby-like smiles" (6), and speaks with a "sweet, unconscious simplicity of manner" (8). As the narrator remarks later in the text, "Lillie had always found her prettiness, her littleness, her helplessness, and her tears so very useful in carrying her points in life that she resorted to them as her lawful stock in trade" (110). Beauty, tears, vulnerability; these are tools employed to achieve specific ends. In addition to these devices, Lillie also includes maternal affection in her repertoire. John writes to his sister, "Lillie remarkably resembles the ivory miniature of our dear sainted mother. She was very much affected when I told her of it. I think naturally Lillie has very much such a character as our mother" (17–18). In order for John's virtue to go unquestioned, and, in order to strengthen his role as a victim of this drama, Stowe highlights the fact that Lillie appears to be very much the ideal spouse. Lillie's performance of affect when she sees the miniature is critical in Lillie's self-construction as the iconic sentimental heroine. She is mother and babe, the childlike, innocent beauty that is at the same time an icon of maternal wisdom, the very hallmark of sentimental fiction, a woman that John sees as a "little fairy . . . leading him into wonderland" (10). This wonderland is not simply the creation of John's fancy; it is the very stuff of novels.

Stowe does not critique her protagonist's interpretive skill, even as she points out that he is utterly mistaken in his view of Lillie:

> John is not in love with the actual Lillie Ellis, but with that ideal personage who looks like his mother's picture, and is the embodiment of all his mother's virtues. The feeling, as it exists in John's mind, is not only a most respectable, but in fact truly divine one, and one that no mortal man ought to be ashamed of. (44–45)

John's motives are pure, and even his oddly unobservant behavior largely escapes censure because Lillie is so adroit in her handling of him. Stowe is more preoccupied with revealing the abuses of symbolism than she is with failures of interpretation. Rather than linger on John's shortcomings in this regard, she emphasizes Lillie's representative nature; before marrying him, Lillie lives in a world where those who know her best are named Mrs. Chit and Mrs. Chat, and Billy This and Harry That (11), and she is attended by seamstresses known as Miss Clippins, Miss Snippens, and Miss Nippens (40). Her social circle, like her nature, is composed of literary devices.

Stowe contrasts Lillie's poetic nature with John's sister, Grace, who has been his companion and housemate for his entire adult life:

> [H]is sister was all plain prose,—good, strong, earnest, respectable prose, it is true, but yet prose. He could read English history with her, talk accounts and business with her, discuss politics with her, and valued her opinions on all these topics as much as that of any man of his acquaintance. (3–4)

As this description indicates, Grace is not a character of sentiment or simile, despite what her name suggests; if Lillie is defined by poetic metaphor, then

Grace seems to be a woman of mathematic precision. Lillie leads John into a wonderland, while his sister is explicitly an inhabitant of the "real" world of politics and business. Stowe contrasts the "respectable prose" of the sister with the sentimental language that is Lillie's stock and trade.

Not that the Seymours have no literary turn of mind. Describing their staid social world in Massachusetts, Stowe writes,

> There is also a literary aroma pervading their circles. Dim suggestions of "The North American Review," of "The Dial," of Cambridge,—a sort of vague "*miel-fleur*" of authorship and poetry,—is supposed to float in the air around them; and it is generally understood that in their homes exist tastes and appreciations denied to less favored regions. (186)

It does not take a close examination to note the literary type of the family. It is determinedly conservative, intellectual rather than emotional. Their reading lies outside the popular trends of the time. Judge Ferguson, the noble patriarch of their community represents those timeless values that stand in opposition to the popular trends Lillie symbolizes:

> [He] was a gentleman of the old school, devoted to past ideas, fond of the English classics, and with small faith in any literature later than Dr. Johnson. He confessed to a toleration for Scott's novels, and had been detected by his children both laughing and crying over the stories of Charles Dickens; for the amiable weaknesses of human nature still remain in the best regulated mind. (188)

The fact that being affected by such popularly and critically regarded authors as Scott and Dickens is evidence of weakness in the novel indicates a surprising distrust of sentimental writing, one that Lillie's behavior bears out in the text.

Prose is the language of reality, poetry the language of fiction, and it is poetry that fails to meet the needs of everyday life: "The plain prose of life must have its turn, after the poetry and honey-moons—stretch them out to their utmost limit—have their terminus" (63). In the world that John and his sister inhabit, symbolism alone is not adequate, and it is in this atmosphere that the husband at last begins to reinterpret his wife: "[S]he wasn't like his mother, he thought with a sigh. The 'je ne sais quoi de saint et de sacre,' which had so captivated his imagination, did not cover the saintly and sacred nature; it was a mere outward purity of complexion and outline" (101). As before, Stowe highlights Lillie's existence as a form to be read, and John discovers that, while Lillie can reproduce the image well, the substance is lacking.

The irony, of course, is that the same symbolic language that defines Lillie's world and "profession" marks Stowe and her profession as well. It is as if Lillie and John have learned how to act in and interpret the world by reading sentimental novels; she has learned how to behave and he what to expect. Nowhere is this more evident than in Lillie's death scene, the event that is supposed to represent Lillie's apotheosis. John first fell in love with her because she so perfectly reproduced the imagery of romance. After being forced to deal with her true nature and to learn to live with her in a kind of uneasy truce, his love for her is renewed when she once again speaks and acts in familiar sentimental fashion. Her farewell is little more than a reiteration of little Eva's death in *Uncle Tom's Cabin* (1852) and Mara's in *The Pearl of Orr's Island* (1862). Rather than representing her entry into the "real," serious world inhabited by the likes of the Seymours, at the moment of her death she once again enters the world of poetic expectation and, once again, John falls for it completely:

> She put out her little wasted hand; "John dear," she said, "sit down; I have something that I want to say to you. . . .
>
> I was never the woman to have made you happy; and it was not fair in me to marry you. I have lived a dreadfully worldly, selfish life. . . . You dear good man, your trials with me are almost over; but I want you to know that you really have succeeded. John, I do love you now with all my heart, though I did not love you when I married you. And, John, I do feel that God will take pity on me, poor and good for nothing as I am, just because I see how patient and kind you have always been to me when I have been so very provoking. You see it has made me think how good God must be,—because, dear, we know that he is better than the best of us."
>
> "O Lillie, Lillie!" said John, leaning over her, and taking her in his arms, "do live, I want you to live. Don't leave me now, now that you really love me!" (328–29)

While throughout the course of the novel Stowe has shown us time and again that Lillie can manipulate tropes to her own ends, now we are meant to believe that Lillie "really means it" and that John's sudden outpouring of affection is both genuine and deserved. The problem is that rather than demonstrate Lillie's transcendence of the world of literary forms and tropes to a more authentic spiritual realm, this scene simply replicates once more the "poetic" language that seduced John in the first place. Lillie and Stowe are once again producing the language that both he and the reader most expect. Rather than representing her renunciation of the forms that she deploys so well, Lillie's death is a last instance of her absolute mastery of them.

Stowe's condemnation of Lillie, who excels in the same art that she does, appears to embody an ambivalence the author felt about her profession and her own symbolic power. Such ambivalence seems at odds both with the author's stature at this point in her career and with other writings in which Stowe seems to represent herself as comfortable in her role as purveyor and arbiter of popular fiction. In her analysis of a series of articles Stowe wrote for *Hearth and Home* in 1869 giving advice to female writers, Sarah Robbins points out how the author confirms her own status and seems reluctant to encourage others to follow in her footsteps:

> An outline of Stowe's entire "How Shall I Learn to Write?" sketch highlights her tendency to shift back and forth between empowering and constraining her women readers who wished to become writers. She observes that "the best writing is done by men," then attributes American women's general authorial shortcomings to their deficient educations. . . . In short, Stowe's position on the possibility that (other) women might become successful professional writers—much less highly regarded ones—is unclear even in an essay where she purportedly seeks to help female readers achieve just such a goal. (2001, 56–57)

Robbins ultimately concludes that Stowe finally identifies herself as "the writer-editor . . . on the side of high culture, espousing an increasingly elitist, male-dominated vision of what professional authorship in the United States should be" (61). She argues that Stowe has, in effect, reached a safe perch as an author and is now aiding the masculine literary establishment in pulling up the ladder behind her. Stowe's comments might also suggest a discomfort with that form of "women's fiction" that she herself practices, the kind that Lillie embodies so well.

Stowe's views on authorship coincide with a larger critical movement that, as Nancy Glazener demonstrates, elevated literary realism over popular literary sentiment and conflated realism with professionalism. Authors that appealed too strongly to readers' emotions were most likely amateurs and, even more telling for the present discussion, manipulative: "The production of tears in readers also highlighted the problem of authors' motives, exactly the issue that professionalism was designed to address" (1997, 125). Truly professional authors might evoke emotions from their readers, critics argued, but it was done deliberately and not for the sake of feeling alone. Jennifer Cognard-Black, writing of Stowe's entanglement in these controversies as a result of her article on Lady Byron, describes the dilemma in which women sentimental writers found themselves in vivid terms: "[S]ince the instantaneous delight of sentimental reading must be continually renewed through buying and selling repeated pleasures, such practice could be construed as a kind of prostitution. Inevitably, then, professional male realists could adopt positions of cultural management, labeling women writers who participated in the sentimental or the sensational as authorial amateurs or literary whores" (2004, 97). Stowe's portrayal of Lillie as a woman whose performances repeatedly make her attractive to male suitors, even after her marriage, certainly seems to reinforce this critique of sentimentality: "With a ravishing morning-dress, and with a killing little cap of about three inches in extent on her head, she enacted the young matron, and gave full permission to Tom, Dick, and Harry to make themselves at home in her room, and smoke their cigars there in peace" (1871, 114). Lillie's sentimental powers lead men to view her as a "fast one" (123).

Stowe's efforts to exclude herself from the ranks of the "amateur" sentimentalists predate her portrayal of Lillie: they are also evident in an article she wrote in 1868 for *The Chimney-corner*. The paternalistic tone of the title, "What Will You Do with Her? Or, the Woman Question," is heightened by the presence of her male narrator, Christopher Crowfield. The essay begins with a description of the arrival of an aspiring author. Stowe writes,

> [S]he is poor, and she has looking to her for support those that are poorer and more helpless than herself: she has tried sewing, but can make little at it; tried teaching, but cannot now get a school,—all places being filled, and more than filled; at last has tried literature, and written some little things, of which she sends you a modest specimen, and wants your opinion whether she can gain her living by writing. You run over the articles, and perceive at a glance that there is no kind of hope or use in her trying to do anything at literature; and then you ask yourself, mentally, "What is to be done with her? What can she do?" (1868 [2003], 2)

One cannot help but notice that Stowe here is both reiterating and debunking the story of Fanny Fern and her famous literary protagonist Ruth Hall, both of whom turned to writing as a last means of support. While many young women might seek to emulate these literary personages, few will succeed, and Stowe is now in a position to make judgments regarding their chances. Here the author is the voice of pragmatic reality, seeking to answer the question of "what to do with" the literary supplicant with some career more prosaic than authorship.

Stowe can be seen exercising the same kind of literary authority described above in a letter she wrote to a woman named Josephine Ruggles who contacted her in 1865 in much the same manner she describes in her article. In her reply to the woman's entreaty and manuscript, the author shows both compassion and expertise, sympathizing with the woman's plight while making very specific suggestions regarding both style and subject matter. Stowe emerges as an arbiter of popularly accepted literary tastes and values, even as she repeatedly appears to defer to the judgments of her husband Calvin Stowe, who has also read parts of the work. The letter begins by referring to opinions that Calvin has already shared with the writer, but, Stowe writes, as she fears Calvin's handwriting may be illegible, she offers her own views as well. While initially presenting herself as doing little more than agreeing with her husband, Stowe quickly and decisively positions herself as a mentor for Ruggles: "I judge there is in you power enough and passion thought & experience enough to make an effective writer but you write at present as one paints who has only painted from his own brain without the help of models & masters" (1865b, 3). After praising her imagination and generally critiquing her art of expression, Stowe offers her services: "If you will come up here & spend a day with me sometime I can put you on a track that I think will improve you—I think you are worth improving" (4). Stowe is thus both judge and instructor, determining the writer worthy and then proceeding with her lessons.

When she speaks of style in this instance, however, Stowe defers to an earlier male authority figure when presenting her advice. After pointing out a couple of basic rules that Ruggles breaks, she writes, "The rules in Blair's rhetoric under the head of structure of sentences are worth a careful & thoughtful study I was drilled in them as a child & have never ceased to be grateful to my excellent teacher Mr Brace for his drilling" (4). Her expertise is a result of Brace's "drilling" more than her own skill. In speaking of the content of the work, however, it is clear that Stowe's opinions emerge directly from her own moral values and conceptions of what is appropriate for sentimental fiction: "I would omit from the character of Mr [illegible] the account of his systematic drinking bouts—they will excite prejudice & disgust—I would also leave out the prolonged reflection on his swearing" (8). While she is clearly concerned with the effect that the apparently realistic description of a male character will have on readers, Stowe is even more adamant regarding the conduct of the tale's heroine. After once again invoking her husband's opinion, Stowe offers her own view:

> In regard to the night scene Mr Stowes suggestions express my mind. A young girl of seventeen found in an open cabin on the sea shore dressed in white embroidered muslin with a scarlet shawl going at midnight on board a yacht with two strange men—is a tough incident to present to a readers credulity & needs a great deal of skillful & delicate treatment to make it at all go down. As it stands I would venture to say that a reader who has been really charmed with the first chapters will throw down the story & say—"Oh its all going off into a crasy [sic] headed [illegible] story"—. . . . (8–9)

While Stowe seconds Calvin's judgment regarding how readers will react to the late-night rendezvous, what is most important to her is the consideration of how an author can handle such an episode in the course of a story. She is not reluctant elsewhere to tell Ruggles to omit inappropriate material, but here she suggests that it is essential that an author know how to present such incidents with tact, without driving the reader away. It appears that a reader must be kept "charmed" by a story, and any incident that might risk breaking that spell requires careful handling.

This "courting" of the reader, always keeping in mind his or her expectations, parallels nicely Lillie's careful handling of John in *Pink and White Tyranny*. When she faces a challenge requiring "skillful & delicate treatment"—

John's discovery that she is twenty-seven years old and not twenty—she knows just how to handle her husband's anger and disappointment:

> Lillie sobbed, and seemed in danger of falling into convulsions; and John's heart gave out. He gathered her into his arms. "I can't help loving you; and I can't live without you," he said, "be you what you may!" Lillie's little heart beat with triumph under all her sobs; she had got him, and should hold him yet. . . .
>
> John may of course be excused for feeling that his flattering little penitent was more to him than ever; and as to Lillie, she gave a sigh of relief. *That* was over, "anyway;" and she had him not only safe, but more completely hers than ever. ([1871] 1988, 99–100)

Lillie, like the skilled author, need not fear driving her husband/reader away, provided she can couch questionable actions in the reassuring attitudes of sincerity and sentimentality. Once again John escapes the narrator's censure for his failure to see through the act; he has simply been taken in by Lillie's bravura performance. Stowe makes this same lesson clear to Ruggles: "[Y]our girl loses the sympathy of the reader at the outset and appears coarse bold and indelicate—freely jesting with a perfectly strange man at midnight—going on board a strange ship—&c" (1865b, 10). To counter this, Ruggles must make it clear that the heroine maintains her "mature womanly delicacy" (11) in order "to win for your girl the favor of the reader" (12). Reading and writing are acts of courtship for Stowe, demanding that the author present unpleasant events in a manner designed to elicit sympathy. Seen in this light, Lillie Ellis emerges as the consummate professional author. She comports herself in such a way as to completely meet John's romantic expectations, and, at her death, confirms one last time her abilities to manipulate sentimental tropes.

In spite of Stowe's coaching, Ruggles apparently failed in her efforts to become a successful author, although Stowe did meet with the woman at least once, spoke to editors on her behalf, and corresponded with her on at least one other occasion (1865c). Her experience with Ruggles may have led her to produce the simultaneously instructive yet discouraging articles on writing for *Home and Hearth* in 1869. The experience certainly appears to have informed her *Chimney-corner* article on "what to do with" aspiring female artists. If a story is like a pretty woman, as she suggested to Fields, perhaps she came to believe that the skill needed to produce a story could not be successfully taught. One had to be born with it, just as Lillie had been endowed with great beauty. Regardless of how one became an author, Stowe's condemnation of her heroine in *Pink and White Tyranny* suggests that perhaps she had come to question the profession itself, at least in the form that had led to her popular success. The portrayal of Lillie, a woman blessed with gifts that allow her to negotiate the romantic tropes that are the common tools of her trade, indicates a deep ambivalence regarding

Stowe's own expertise and perhaps a suspicion of the power of the sentimental language that she had helped to popularize. The novel, largely dismissed by modern critics, offers a revealing portrait of her opinions regarding her craft and suggests an anxiety that, in achieving literary fame, Stowe had also assumed a potentially tyrannical authority.

## NOTE

1. While this study emphasizes a close reading of Stowe's use of metaphors and sentimental tropes in her novel, these elements are best understood when read in the context of what Gerard Genette (1997) has termed the "paratext," those elements outside of the text itself that inform our interpretation of a work. In the present study, these include Stowe's magazine publications, literary reviews of *Pink and White Tyranny*, and correspondence with her editors and with an aspiring female author. While Joan Hedrick's 1994 biography is crucial in providing a clearer picture of the background from which Stowe's works emerged, and, while the Internet has allowed for greater access to Stowe's numerous publications, many of the primary documents that might further inform a reassessment of the author's lesser-known texts are not yet widely available. *Pink and White Tyranny* shares many traits of the sentimental novel, particularly in its "deathbed" conclusion, yet the paratextual elements reveal the preoccupation with her profession that underlies Stowe's apparent attack on female authority in the text. I am grateful to the curators of the Harriet Beecher Stowe Center in Hartford, Connecticut, for their aid in my research and for granting permission to quote from Stowe's remarkable 1865 letter to Josephine Ruggles.

## WORKS CITED

Boydston, Jeanne, Mary Kelley, and Anne Margolis. 1988. *The Limits of Sisterhood.* Chapel Hill: University of North Carolina Press.

Cognard-Black, Jennifer. 2004. "The Wild and Distracted Call for Proof: Harriet Beecher Stowe's *Lady Byron Vindicated* and the Rise of Professional Realism." *American Literary Realism* 36 (2): 93–119.

Genette, Gerard. 1997. *Paratexts: Thresholds of Interpretation*, trans. Jane E. Lewin. New York: Cambridge University Press.

Glazener, Nancy. 1997. *Reading for Realism.* Durham, NC: Duke University Press.

Hedrick, Joan D. 1994. *Harriet Beecher Stowe: A Life.* New York: Oxford University Press.

Kelley, Mary. 1984. *Private Woman, Public Stage.* New York: Oxford University Press.

Martin, Judith. 1988. Introduction to *Pink and White Tyranny*, by Harriet Beecher Stowe, vii–xiv. New York: Plume.

Robbins, Sarah. 2001. "Gendering Gilded Age Periodical Professionalism: Reading Harriet Beecher Stowe's *Hearth and Home* Prescriptions for Women's Writing." In *"The Only Efficient Instrument": American Women Writers and the Periodical,*

*1837–1916,* ed. Aleta Feinsod Cane and Susan Alves, 45–65. Iowa City: University of Iowa Press.

Stowe, Harriet Beecher. [1865a] 2003. *House and Home Papers.* Boston: Ticknor and Fields. http://www.letrs.indiana.edu/web/w/wright2/.

———. 1865b. Letter to Josephine Ruggles [Baker]. March 1865. Katherine S. Day Collection. Stowe Center, Hartford, CT.

———. 1865c. Letter to Josephine Ruggles [Baker]. September 1865. Katherine S. Day Collection. Stowe Center, Hartford, CT.

———. [1868] 2003. *The Chimney-corner.* Boston: Ticknor and Fields. http://www .letrs.indiana.edu/web/w/wright2/.

———. [1871] 1988. *Pink and White Tyranny.* New York: Plume.

# The Wild and Distracted Call for Proof

## Harriet Beecher Stowe's *Lady Byron Vindicated* and the Rise of Professional Realism

*Jennifer Cognard-Black*

In an 1869 cartoon from the October *Merryman's Monthly*, Harriet Beecher Stowe wields an immense quill and conjures Lord Byron in the shape of a satyr. Byron rises on a dark cloud from a great black inkwell, a snake at Stowe's feet is marked "scandal," a horned toad sits on copies of *Uncle Tom's Cabin* and *Dred*, and, in the background, a human skull as well as a jarred fetus rest on a shelf. The caption reads: "Mrs. H—— B—— S——'s Great Incantation. Who have we here?—The great poet Byron or the D——l?"

The cartoon's surface critique is obvious: Stowe's writing is witchcraft. More subtly, however, the parody targets three specific attributes that had comprised Stowe's rhetorical ethos ever since the publication of *Uncle Tom's Cabin*: her tripartite position as woman, Christian, and abolitionist.[1] The Christian critique is the most apparent. An emissary of the "D——l" (manifested in the serpent that names her writing practice "scandal"), Stowe's art transforms Byron from a great poet into a satanic incarnation, insinuating that Stowe's own writing is not great—it can only defile and debase the great. In turn, the elements of witchcraft, especially the pickled fetus, suggest that Stowe's womanhood has gone awry. Rather than nurture and protect the republic's children, her writing or sorcery pollutes the domestic space. And, indeed, the entire portrait is not just magic but *black* magic: the stuff of Stowe's art, her ink, drips thick and black, and Stowe's two slavery novels, *Uncle Tom's Cabin* and *Dred*, are the representative productions of this art. By implication, the sketch racializes all of Stowe's writing, suggesting her treatment of Byron is inflected by a different kind of "blackness."

This cartoon is but one response of many to Stowe's article "The True Story of Lady Byron's Life." Published simultaneously in the September 1869 issues of the *Atlantic Monthly* in America and *MacMillan's* in

53

England, this piece initiated a transatlantic media attack so virulent and widespread that Oliver Wendell Holmes called it the "Byron whirlwind" (Morse 1896, 183).[2] In short, the article accused Lord Byron of committing incest both before and during his marriage. Even though this gossip had been around for over sixty years, such a blatant and public accusation against the revered male poet by a female pen explains, in part, the caustic nature of the critics' response. However, the professional and realist assumptions motivating the precise quality of these condemnations are less transparent, and Stowe's response to these censures reveals her participation in an emerging literary culture of professional realism—a realism both historic and deeply paradoxical.[3]

Indeed, the criticisms aimed at Stowe's "True Story" spurred her to approach narrative in a new, more "factual" way. In less than six months after the appearance of the "True Story," Stowe rewrote her tale into a very different kind of text, *Lady Byron Vindicated*, a book-length work that embraces certain precepts of professional realism, including a self-conscious use of professional style and an emphasis on fact-as-value. At the same time, *Vindicated* maintains an affinity with the kinds of sentimental appeals Stowe had employed ever since the publication of *Uncle Tom's Cabin*. As a result, even though the text is in part a historical commentary, *Vindicated* operates as a kind of realist fiction, thereby highlighting the slippage between cultural categories of fact and fiction that actually engendered the professional realist project. As such, *Vindicated* both exposes and helps to solidify the gender and commercial stigmas that were necessary to the rise of professional realism in late nineteenth-century America.


## PROFESSIONAL REALISM AND FEMININE READING

Stowe's original essay and its sequel adapt the same story as their centerpiece. On a trip to England in 1856, Lady Byron granted Stowe a tête-à-tête, one in which Stowe learned the secret reason behind Lady Byron's marital estrangement: that Lord Byron had fathered a child with his half-sister Augusta Leigh and maintained an incestuous relationship even after his marriage—all the while blaming Lady Byron's frigidity as the source of his dissipation. Thirteen years following this confidence, and after Lady Byron's death, Stowe happened upon a memoir by Byron's last mistress, the Countess Guiccioli. This work perpetuated the oft-repeated portrayal of Lady Byron as a "narrow-minded, cold-hearted precisian" (Stowe 1869c, 295) who stifled Byron's art and drove him to seek solace in other women.[4] Then Stowe alleged to have come across an article in England's *Blackwood's* praising Guiccioli's memoir and offering it as a true representation of Byron's wedded woes.[5] Angered at what she felt to be a one-sided attack on Lady Byron's character and frustrated that no English writer would come to her defense, Stowe argues in the "True Story" that since "Lady Byron has an American name and an American existence, and reverence for pure womanhood is, we think, a national characteristic of the American" (295), she deserves a conclusive "refutation of the slanders" (313) from an American author.

At one level, then, Stowe's "True Story" works as a national corrective, not merely one woman speaking in defense of another's honor but as America tutoring England on how to treat its pure women—not unlike how *Uncle Tom's Cabin* sought to teach Southerners how to "feel right" on the issue of slavery. But Stowe's piece on Lady Byron troubles the very gender position she claims as a credential, her appeal as a symbol and defender of pure womanhood. Indeed, Stowe's detractors accuse her of behaving in an unwomanly manner by spreading sexual scandal and breaking confidence. The editor of London's *Illustrated Times* jibes in "The Lounger," "[Stowe's] rash and utterly unjustifiable [*sic*] conduct only illustrates once more the melancholy truth that man's inhumanity to man is as nothing compared with woman's uncharitableness to woman" (1869, 231). In turn, a letter to the editor of the *Pall Mall Gazette* claims that "women, especially when jealous, are not very scrupulous in their assertions, and, moreover, after a certain time actually believe in the truth of their assumptions. They will in fact, to use a common expression, stick at nothing" (1869, 3). And another critic quoted in *Public Opinion* exclaims, "[Stowe] is false to the instincts of her own sex; it is theirs to draw the curtain over the faults of the living, and to cherish sympathy for those whom genius endows with her noblest gifts" (1869, 381).

Two impulses are at work in these censures: first is an equation between sentimentalism and hasty, feminized emotion. The assumption that Stowe's article is founded on feminine-based susceptibility to feeling is a direct result of her former reputation as a sentimental author. Thus, to the *Illustrated Times* editor, Stowe's revelation is "rash," the result of impulse rather than a measured process of judgment. The *Times* calls Stowe's conduct "uncharitable," which echoes *Public Opinion*'s charge that Stowe has gone against the "instincts of her sex." Not only, then, is Stowe weakly sentimental: she is unladylike, failing to exercise her forgiving nature and exposing "faults" that she is supposed to "veil," especially if such faults reside in "genius." By implication, the second and related impulse here is in keeping with one of the critiques raised by the *Merryman's* cartoon: a sentimental writer is the instrument of (feminine) sympathy, not (masculine) genius.

But in addition to charging Stowe with debasing pure womanhood, her detractors construed her article as a text made up of lies. The *Pall Mall Gazette* engages bandwagonism to suggest that *all* women, including Stowe, "stick at nothing," while the London *Standard* refuses to quote from the

"True Story" because doing so would "allow the authoress . . . to employ over again in these pages the well-known dexterity of the romance writer when fiction has to be made to look like fact" (quoted in *The Stowe-Byron Controversy* 1869, 56). Importantly, the *Standard* confounds the accuracy of Stowe's article by suggesting that an acknowledged romance writer would dupe readers through her fictional "dexterity," a substitution of fancy for fact. In this manner, the *Standard* codes narrative unreality as feminine, aligning a number of nineteenth-century genres—including sentimental and sensational texts—with stereotypes of female equivocation.

Such indictments of Stowe's feminine corruption and falsehood reveal one set of stigmas necessary to the ideology of professional literary realism that was, by 1869, gathering high-culture cachet. As Nancy Glazener has detailed, certain precepts of the emerging professionalism in disciplines such as medicine and law provided the means by which a new coterie of male realist writers could shift "the intertwined effects of commercialism and consumerism onto women's culture" (1997, 95).[6] Professionalism allowed for this dislocation by its basic contradiction between expertise and entrepreneurship: male authors could both participate in the perhaps distasteful economics of the literary marketplace while maintaining intellectual transcendence as public arbiters of high-cultural taste. Of course the relationship between a sentimental woman writer and her female reader traded on emotional sensitivity, not intellectual or spiritual elevation, and such sensitivity was dangerously addictive, inspiring immediate gratifications rather than the timeless ones offered by the professional male realist. Further, since the instantaneous delight of sentimental reading must be continually renewed through buying and selling repeated pleasures, such practice could be construed as a kind of prostitution. Inevitably, then, professional male realists could adopt positions of cultural management, labeling women writers who participated in the sentimental or the sensational as authorial amateurs or literary whores. The *Merryman's Monthly* cartoon is a case in point: Stowe's hair and dress are in dishabille, and she lifts her skirts to display her ankles—clear signs of sexual permissiveness.

But it is not just Stowe's virtue or veracity that are at stake. The *Merryman's* caricature also implies that Stowe's writing is fantastic—not just dishonest but beyond the realm of the "real." The cartoon's humor trades in a conflation of pagan and Christian mythologies: in satyrs and witches and the Devil in his proverbial serpent's skin. Such imagery suggests that Stowe's claim of Byron's incestuous infidelities is merely a fable, thereby playing into indictments of the "True Story" that, like the *Standard*'s, insisted that all of Stowe's "romances" were "fiction . . . made to look like fact" (quoted in *The Stowe-Byron Controversy* 1869, 56).

This particular strain of criticism against the "True Story" epitomizes a larger cultural unease over what Michael Robertson has termed the pervasive "fact-fiction discourse" in America at the end of the nineteenth century. Akin to the fact-fiction slippage in the 1700s that had brought about the modern form of the Anglo-American novel,[7] between 1865 and the turn of the century, many fictions read like relations of fact, whereas newspapers "indiscriminately mixed news, fiction, and feature articles that had an indeterminate truth status" (Robertson 1997, 6). The job of a professional realist writer, then, was to counter the fictionally induced unreality of quotidian life by producing a fiction more real than reality—a narrative more factual than fact.

Though seemingly contradictory, this belief that a high-art, realist, masculine text could provide a culturally redeeming narrative more factual than fact is in keeping with nineteenth-century professional ideologies that repeatedly privileged scientific objectivity and fact-as-value. Thus, an American realist writer appropriated a grammar of fact—dates, names, figures, events—and simultaneously withheld his personality from the text in order to distance himself from an authorial position coded as feminine. One need only think of Hawthorne's infamous complaint about scribbling women, or Poe's insistent adoption of personas, or Melville's Ishmael, or Whitman's expansion of "self" beyond all possibility of an identity defined by domestic relationships to see how a withholding of personality performed "the real." And Stowe's detractors repeatedly argued that the "True Story" revealed itself as an unrealistic product of sentimental hokum.

Indeed, review after review called on Stowe to produce "facts," hard proof of Byron's crime. In 1851, Southern critics had denounced the veracity of Stowe's fiction, prompting her to write A Key to Uncle Tom's Cabin, a compendium of real-life stories that allegedly served as the basis of controversial scenes Stowe had incorporated into her novel.[8] Twenty years later, however, a much more comprehensive body of readers, including educated Northerners, were denouncing the veracity of her nonfiction. "The wild and distracted calling on me for proof," Stowe protested, "utterly ignoring the only kind of proof that I have to give, shows that the public is yet not in a proper state to weigh anything" (1869a). In the largely sentimental reading culture of the 1850s, "proof" had been a matter of effecting a convincing narrative to arouse Christian sympathy—the very kind of proof Stowe had to give. Now, with the advent of professional realism as a high-culture benchmark, Stowe's emotionally based ethos no longer granted her automatic authority, especially on a historical topic dealing with real people and lacking verifiable data.

Taken together, the deluge of criticism against the "True Story" reveals a complex of ideas privileging an authorial ethos and a kind of narrative that were at odds with Stowe: an ethos simultaneously masculine, secular, and cosmopolitan that produced either fact-based texts or texts that rendered a mimetic reality. As such, it is little wonder that within half a year of the publication of her "True Story," Stowe rewrote her article into a book-length study, one that emphasized fact-as-value and reframed her rhetorical position from woman-Christian-citizen to that of professional realist writer.

## SENTIMENTAL VERSUS PROFESSIONAL REALIST FORMS

The *Independent*, a newspaper that had printed many of Stowe's articles, carried a prototypal indictment of the "True Story" from its editor, Theodore Tilton. In his review, Tilton admonishes, "Startling in accusation, barren in proof, inaccurate in dates, infelicitous in style, and altogether ill-advised in publication, [Stowe's] strange article will travel round the whole literary world and everywhere evoke against its author the spontaneous disapprobation of her life-long friends" (1869, 1). Tilton's specific condemnations are telling. Stowe's piece is "startling"—which meant shocking or disturbing rather than merely surprising—and the reader's sensibilities are "startled" by a text that cannot, according to Tilton, justify the consequence of such disturbance: the story contains no proof; it is inaccurate; it is stylistically gauche and generally "strange." Thus, the article fails because it does not adhere to Tilton's unspoken prejudice for exact evidence and a straightforward writing style. If a reader is "startled," Tilton suggests, then there had better be objective proof to mitigate a reader's exposure to an offensive idea: i.e., the form of the text must assuage the text's function.

Indeed, Tilton was accurate that the form of the "True Story" was not one that suggested "truth": the article is clearly a product of 1850s sentimentality, employing heuristic and didactic techniques upon which Stowe had founded her career as a sentimental novelist. For instance, the article confuses dates, misquoting how many years the Byrons were married. Lord Byron's poems are cited as unalloyed autobiography—passages from *Don Juan* demonstrate Byron's mistreatment of Lady Byron and excerpts from *Cain* and *Manfred* show how he "justified himself in incest" (1869c, 304). In keeping with the style of historical romance, the text refers to the narrator as "the writer," never providing Stowe's name.[9] The syntax is the opposite of economy, a maze of sinuous constructions, and the piece relies on pathos-based allusions, including the requisite tears: "Lord Byron's 'Fare thee well . . .,' was set to music and sung with tears by young school-girls, even in this distant America" (1869c, 296). The plot structure resembles a moral tale. The "True Story" first establishes the traditionally caustic portrayal of Lady Byron as a crime perpetuated on innocent readers. The narrative then retells the same story through new eyes, including all the damnable actions on Byron's part—the "secret adulterous intrigue with a blood relation" and the fact that he asked Lady Byron to allow a "continental latitude" in their marriage, "in which complaisant couples mutually agreed to form the cloak for each other's infidelities" (306). Finally, the article's symbolism follows the pattern of *Uncle Tom's Cabin*, embodying the redemptive love of Christ in a Little Eva exemplar—"Lying so near the confines of the spiritual world, [Lady Byron] seemed already to see into it" (310–11)—and making a prophetic analogy between Byron and a fallen angel whose evil doings had influenced gullible readers. In short, the article is a romance.

But in response to rebukes such as Tilton's, Stowe produced a very different sort of text: *Lady Byron Vindicated*, an archive of dates, manuscripts, and named sources—a self-consciously professional document. As Stowe sought to meet the rhetorical demands of a public calling for "proof," like her realist contemporaries, she appropriated words from the burgeoning professions, especially law and psychiatry. "As it is too late to have the securities of a legal trial," Stowe explains, "certainly the rules of historical evidence should be strictly observed. All important documents should be presented in an entire state, with a plain and open account of their history" (1870, 322). Here, Stowe attempts to cast herself in the role of the impartial, investigative lawyer, the one who will provide the "plain and open account" of all documents and will put Byron on a kind of literary trial. Later in the text, she simulates the voice of the psychiatrist, the one who will establish Byron's moral illness and its infection of the entire British nation. The consequence of miming such professional postures, however, is the tension Stowe creates against her own sentimental ethos—a tension against her own established artistry.

The professional form and tone of much of *Vindicated* are designed to teach Stowe's readers the proper state in which to read both her text's proof and her own position as a credible narrator. Unlike the "True Story," Stowe autographs the book, referring to herself in the preface and elsewhere as "I" and "me" instead of as "the writer."[10] Punctilious in naming names and quoting sources, Stowe devotes an entire chapter to the notorious interview, providing the who, what, where, when, and how hitherto absent. Stowe numbers, footnotes, and dates; *Vindicated* moves in a rough chronological fashion, inserting an entire chapter abstracting the most salient events. The text justifies the error previously made over the marriage dates by precisely citing a source, thereby impugning someone else's faulty research. For the most part, *Vindicated* turns away from Byron's poems as biographical material to analyze his personal correspondence.[11] Overall, the substance of *Vindicated*'s approach changes from what Stowe herself characterizes as the "most general terms" (261) of her original article to "just where I would stand were I giving evidence under oath before a legal tribunal" (258).

With this evocation of a courtroom, Stowe appropriates the language of an expert witness as well as the voice of a defense lawyer. For the chapters requiring data to demonstrate the "criminal" aspects of her case, pertinent documents are quoted at length, often in their entirety, and are structured like a legal brief. Here is one example of many:

> IV. Aug. 9, 1817.—Gives to M. G. Lewis a paper for circulation among friends in England, stating that what he most wants is public investigation, which has always been denied him; and daring Lady Byron and her counsel to come out publicly. Found in M. G. Lewis's portfolio after his death; never heard of before, except among the "initiated". (79)

By placing the date first, this passage makes it appear as one in a series—a reassurance that the following information is linked to a specific day in a specific year. Sentence fragments form the body of the paragraph as if the investigator merely jotted down the most striking facts. All of the information comes from a named document. Indeed, this excerpt provides the reader with the "plain and open account" Stowe herself had said was imperative, the knowledge of who had the documents, where they were found, and how preserved. And in reference to Byron's actions, the passage chooses two words that connote culpability: "daring" and "initiated." Byron dares his wife like an overgrown child picking a fight—he does not request, demand, or expect her to make a public accusation. And clearly Byron is a member of some mysterious band called the "initiated"; the quotation marks highlighting this term imply that the word is Byron's own, further implicating him in some covert activity.

Read against the following paragraph from the original "True Story," *Vindicated*'s appropriation of legalistic discourse is all the more evident:

> Madame de Staël commenced the first effort at evangelization immediately after [Byron] left England, and found her catechumen in a most edifying state of humility. He was metaphorically on his knees in penitence, and confessed himself a miserable sinner in the loveliest manner possible. Such sweetness and humility took all hearts. His conversations with Madame de Staël were printed and circulated all over the world, making it to appear that only the inflexibility of Lady Byron stood in the way of his entire conversion. (1869c, 297)

The syntax here is literary, consisting entirely of independent clauses rather than sentence fragments. In addition, the text applies a number of literary devices: strings of value-laden descriptors highlight Byron's artifice (e.g., "edifying," "miserable," "loveliest"); metaphor portrays Byron's affect on others (e.g., "[his] sweetness and humility took all hearts"); and the diction suggests a belletristic narrator (e.g., "evangelization," "catechumen," "penitence"). There are no dates nor documents. Distilled to its informational content, this excerpt has very little in the way of hard fact: the reader knows Madame de Staël got involved in some way to persuade the public that Lady Byron was at fault for the separation, although de Staël's manner of involvement is not specified, and the reader learns that Byron engaged in confession, but the transcript of this confession is absent.

But unlike the "True Story," *Vindicated* moves fluidly from one professional accent to another. Taking on the voice of the psychiatrist, Stowe devotes an entire chapter to what is called a "Physiological Argument"—a chapter intended to convince the reader that Byron was an alcoholic as well as a hysteric. When needing the opinion of an expert, especially a medical man, *Vindicated* quotes long passages from Dr. Forbes Winslow and his article "Obscure Diseases of the Brain and Nerves" (1870, 387). Yet the text goes beyond mere citation to ventriloquize medical discourse itself:

> Modern physiological developments would lead any person versed in the study of the reciprocal influence of physical and moral laws to anticipate the most serious danger to such an organization as Lord Byron's, from a precocious development of the passions. Alcoholic and narcotic stimulants, in the case of such a person, would be regarded as little less than suicidal, and an early course of combined drinking and licentiousness as tending directly to establish those unsound conditions which lead toward moral insanity. (374)

Here, the diction insinuates scientific jargon with such turns of phrase as "reciprocal influence," "precocious development," and "unsound conditions." By forgoing the use of "I" in favor of a third-person, passive voice, this excerpt suggests a universal, objective point of view, and the writing hints that the narrator herself is one of those people versed in this esoteric study without actually having to claim that she is or is not. In essence, this example mimes classic textbook prose, adopting the inflection of a distanced, intelligent narrator whose opinion is axiom.

## THE NECESSARY SENTIMENTAL

Such legalistic and pseudoscientific concessions to a public calling for proof throw into relief points where *Vindicated* returns to the sentimental, revealing something about the narrative that necessitates an intimate, emotional stance. *Vindicated* adopts just such an approach for the most sensational chapter, "Lady Byron's Story as Told Me"—the one relating the all-important moment of Lady Byron's confession. It was this piece of evidence (or, rather, the lack thereof) that produced the most skepticism against Stowe's "True Story." Thus, for this most contestable chapter—a chapter containing no documents to bolster its claims, no spectators to reinforce its merit—Stowe adopts the form of fiction: scene, setting, dialogue, and character.[12] Even this chapter's title is telling: "Lady Byron's Story as Told Me." For while Stowe takes a certain authorial responsibility for *Vindicated* by signing the book and writing a preface, she also obscures her role as the story's mediator in order to insert a distanced, profession-alized ethos in place of material proof. As a result, all preceding chapters from part 1 of *Vindicated* offer no sense of a narrative "I" or "me" in the text, and all subsequent chapters lose this first-person perspective. (The chapter just prior to the infamous one is the only other to adopt the first-person, "Lady Byron as I Knew Her"—a point discussed below.) Taken together, then, these titles suggest that *Vindicated's* summaries, arguments, and résumés are not "authored"; rather, they represent a compendium of publicly owned evidence. Moreover, these chapters add thick layers of documental evidence on either side of the confession, bookending a moment meant to be taken on faith by the reading public; as such, these chapters create an illusion of inner substance as well as a further mystifi-cation of the terrible secret.

The narrator's difficulty with "Lady Byron's Story as Told Me" rests with a professional's dependence on print—clear, precise words that function as the binding vehicles between writer and reader. A carefully chosen word connotes authenticity, objectivity, and timelessness (the masculine Public), while the spoken implies hearsay, personal opinion, and the immediate (the feminine Private). Stowe's audience could scrutinize a letter, an affida-vit, a catalogue of dates, and by wrapping her volatile chapter in so much information, *Vindicated* responds to typographic prejudice in like form, admitting that straightforward prose more closely approximates truth. However, by feeding this prejudice, the book also reveals its dependence on intimate, private exchange and oral testimony, thus subverting its own logic. As such, Stowe had to try to remake orality into fact, and, further, herself into a kind of objective, professional witness.

For this reason, before relating the crucial interview, *Vindicated* includes a chapter on "Lady Byron as I Knew Her." The narrator explains, "Lady By-ron's communications were made to me in language clear, precise, terrible; and many of her phrases and sentences I could repeat to this day, word for word" (202). Here Stowe's confessional idiom deliberately imitates the language of the professions. In *The Culture of Professionalism*, Burton Bled-stein explains that with the rise of professionalism in America, "A man was his 'word' or the words others used about him. . . . To place an opinion in writing was to make it final, commit the writer to its veracity, document a position and submit that position to the impartial reading of a third party" (1976, 73, 75). Bledstein stipulates that the professional's words had to be clear, plain, and direct, and these are precisely the quality of words that emit from Lady Byron's mouth: "clear, precise, terrible" (Stowe 1870, 202). In this manner, Stowe suggests that the words she remembers and records are real, true, irrefutable.

In turn, Stowe represents her own memory as lexic. It is not, Stowe in-sists, that she cannot remember Lady Byron's testimony; rather, if she had reproduced Lady Byron's precise language in her "True Story" word for word, "the public horror and incredulity would have been doubled" (202). Thus *Vindicated*'s narrator takes on the role of a realist writer choosing words that will convey brutal, irrevocable truth. This move further serves to maintain Stowe's pure womanhood, for feminine modesty as much as professional restraint are at work.

Once Stowe insists that the most significant statement can be produced verbatim or "scripted," her next step is to credentialize her source:

> I am now about to complete the account of my conversation with Lady Byron; but as the credibility of a history depends greatly on the character of its narrator, and as especial pains have been taken to destroy the belief in this story by representing it to be the wanderings of a broken-down mind . . ., I shall preface the narrative with some account of Lady Byron. . . . (204)

While the narrator obviously means to rescue Lady Byron's integrity, she also alludes to those critics who accused Stowe herself of having misunderstood or lied about Lady Byron's confession. As a result, Stowe's brief history of her subject's virtue is a displaced reparation of her own damaged reputation, and the qualities this chapter chooses to elucidate—purity, exceptionalism, and intelligence—stand as testimony to Stowe's own role as a professional witness.

Having now "proven" their mutual qualifications as accurate sources, the narrator is ready to relay the "most painful interview which has been the cause of all this controversy" (232). And here the text's ethos dramatically shifts: it delivers its climactic conversation in dialogue, thereby gaining a sense of the dramatic as well as the feeling that the interview is happening before the reader's eyes; and with the insertion of a specific "me" in the text, Stowe risks compromising her carefully calculated position as a distanced, professional expert. Although other chapters certainly include statements in the first person,[13] this chapter is unique in that it requires Stowe take the dual part of critic and subject.

Thus, at one level, this scene's writing style returns to the kinds of descriptions, details, and images abundant in Stowe's sentimental writing. As previously mentioned, in the "True Story," Lady Byron is characterized as a class of Little Eva who compels her reader with suffering and forgiveness. In *Vindicated*, Lady Byron is less an artless, puerile embodiment of Christ and more a rational Christian, one who approaches religion from a position of maturity and consideration, while still representing a stock figure of pure womanhood:

> She answered quickly, and with great decision, that . . . she felt sure [Byron] had finally repented; and added with great earnestness, "I do not believe that any child of the heavenly Father is ever left to eternal sin."

> I said that such a hope was most delightful . . ., but that I had always re-
> garded the indulgence of it as a dangerous one.
>     . . . She looked at me so sadly, so firmly, and said,—
>     "Danger, Mrs. Stowe! What danger can come from indulging that hope, like
> the danger that comes from not having it?"
>     "The danger of losing all faith in God, . . . all hope for others, all strength to
> try and save them" (247).

It would be easy here to discuss other aspects of sentimental convention
and Christian tautology Stowe employs at the crux of *Vindicated*, even
though these narrative techniques are not as exaggerated as in the "True
Story." In a Tompkins vein, it would be obvious to argue that with conversations like the one above, Stowe drew on her audience's rich literacy as
sentimental readers, their recognition of certain archetypal characters and
scenes and the sympathy she expected to realize from their use.[14] After all,
Stowe had written to Oliver Wendell Holmes that "[t]he interview [with
Lady Byron] had almost the solemnity of a death-bed confession" (quoted
in Charles Stowe 1889, 453)—clearly a familiar theater.[15]

However, it is not accurate to separate sentimental from professional
realist attributes. Rather, what makes *Vindicated* so compelling within its
historical moment is its demonstration of how necessary the sentimental
was to realistic writing. *Vindicated* is indicative of professionalized discourse
throughout the 1860s and 1870s that crossed fact and fiction and that
functioned in a similar manner, and with a similar cultural purpose, as
emerging literary realism. Nineteenth-century professionals (social scientists, lawyers, academics, and the like) writing about human behavior provided particular interpretations evidenced with examples—character case
studies or generalizations about certain groups of people. Unlike empirical
scientists whose subjects of study had no interiority of their own (a leaf, an
asteroid, a liver), interpretations made by such "social" professionals could
not be tested for their falsity but would be accepted or rejected on the basis
of the detail and depth of their explanations as well as the credibility of
their narrative positions. And all such professionals had didactic intents:
the psychiatrist wanted to curb sexual deviance; the lawyer wished to argue
that women should be allowed limited rights of property in marriage. Milieu, métier, and personal bias delimited all such writings.

In this professional culture, the technical supplanted the moral; or,
rather, the technical *was* the moral. Even though professional text abjured
subjectivity and held up data and method as the things that "spoke," the
new professionals and realist writers alike provided images of and for their
culture that were meant to excite an appropriate sympathy, a morality with
qualities more culturally sustaining than what William Dean Howells—
that metonymn for American realism—once disparaged as the "artfully-
wrought sensations" of the newspaper or the sentimental novel ([1895]

1911, 178).[16] In terms of *Vindicated*'s troublesome chapter, then, what emerges is an emphasis on disciplined emotion over emotion for its own sake—i.e., species of literary realism. The text's moment of true confession, sans documentary evidence, induces *Vindicated* to cross sentimental writing with professional technique and realigns narrative discourse into mimetic representation. In other words, because Stowe's story must rely on realistic fictionality in order to present itself as true, *Vindicated* fits Howells's own description of literary realism: "the very highest fiction is that which treats itself as fact" ([1895] 1911, 76).

As such, Stowe's chapter "Lady Byron's Story as Told Me" opens with backstory, key characters, and setting. "My sister and myself were going from London to Eversley," begins the narrator. "On our way, we stopped, by Lady Byron's invitation, to lunch with her at her summer residence on Ham Common, near Richmond . . . as she said she had a subject of importance on which she wished to converse with me alone" (1870, 232). So might a Henry James novel start, with the evocation of a class-bound *donnée* and the slightest hint of social intrigue. From here, the narrator sets the stage for a tête-à-tête: "After lunch, I retired with Lady Byron; and my sister remained with her friends" (233). Now the text constructs and arranges the two principal characters: the credible interviewee—calm, dignified, quiet, lucid—and the professional witness. Stowe even goes so far as to admit the possibility of error in order to accent the words she will insist are exact. "In recalling the conversation at this distance of time, I cannot remember all the language used," Stowe confesses. Yet "[s]ome particular words and forms of expression I do remember, and those I give" (234–35). Now the terrible accusation is furnished, "word for word":

> There was something awful to me in the intensity of repressed emotion which she showed as she proceeded. The great fact upon which all turned was stated in words that were unmistakable:—
> "Mrs. Stowe, he was guilty of incest with his sister!"
> She here became so deathly pale, that I feared she would faint. (235)

Here, then, is the true center of *Vindicated*: the "great fact" stated in words "unmistakable," including what the narrator later refers to as "that one word": incest. To accurately observe this moment, the narrator is required to speak plain, exacting, harsh language. To make up for the deficiency of documents to prove her claims, the book is equally required to textualize the moment via verisimilitude in setting, dialogue, and the portrayal of convincing character. And to guard against the kinds of criticisms Stowe had already received, she is required, finally, to articulate the charge of incest but professionalize its articulation.

But just as *Vindicated* evokes professional realism, the text's very technique indicates the emotionality, the sentimentality, of the story. The narrator experiences an "awful" emotion—the awe-inspiring, intense empathy of an ecstatic witness—while her subject of study enacts a "deathly pale" aspect, reminiscent of Christ's death as well as a paleness and propensity to faint that connote female virtue.

Further, in addition to employing these soteriologic transformations, the narrator reveals the fictionality of her facts. By reasoning that she could not "remember all the language used," yet would provide "[s]ome particular words and forms of expression" she could recall, Stowe puts into question what parts of the chapter are literatim, what parts "the substance of what was said." For example, one passage reads:

> I inquired in one of the pauses of the conversation whether Mrs. Leigh was a peculiarly beautiful or attractive woman.
> "No, my dear: she was plain."
> "Was she, then, distinguished for genius or talent of any kind?"
> "Oh, no! Poor woman! she was weak, relatively, to [Byron], and wholly under his control."
> "And what became of her?" I said.
> "She afterwards repented, and became a truly good woman." (245)

The rhetorical devices for textualizing this moment actually alert the reader to invention: the dialogue tag "I said," quotation marks to bracket speech, a line of indirect dialogue, and a presentation of everyday speech that normalizes the breaks, pauses, and incoherencies inherent in real-life communication into a seamless, polished exchange. A reader could easily suspect the narrator's assertion that these are the exact "forms of expression" used by Lady Byron and Stowe thirteen years earlier. Could Stowe possibly recollect whether Lady Byron had said, "No, my dear," or "My dear, no"? How about the order of "Oh, no!" and "Poor woman!"; might not have Lady Byron exclaimed, "Poor woman! Oh, no!"? And if the reader disputes these superficial phrases, the text cannot insist on the exactitude of the whole.

That Stowe does insist on just that points toward a use of fiction as fact. "Of course," Stowe says, after having recited the whole of the interview, "I did not listen to this story as one who was investigating its worth. I received it as truth. And the purpose for which it was communicated was not to enable me to prove it to the world, but to ask my opinion whether *she* [Lady Byron] should show it to the world before leaving it" (251). Because a confessional moment demands that the narrator present herself as a friend of Lady Byron's, Stowe cannot be the objective investigator she claims. As Stowe herself admits, a friend receives a painful disclosure as truth, not as a statement that must be reviewed, contested, substantiated. Thus Stowe makes her role as a professional witness liable by the very act of claiming full responsibility for the truth of her story.

Here, Stowe's credibility problems have everything to do with gender. As Stowe wrote in a letter to her publisher Osgood, "Nobody has ever called for *proof* from any of the numberless writers who reported their conversations with Lord Byron" (1869a). The inverse is true for the problem of silence: since Lady Byron failed to assert her side of the story in her own lifetime, her reticence worked as "proof" of her culpability, even though silence, in and of itself, proffers no conclusions. Lady Byron's silence was consequently scripted by Byron's poems and letters into slander (i.e., her silence meant she had something to hide), and because Byron was male, his assertion was accepted without proof. "Of course," notes Stowe, "there is no stronger power than a virtuous life; but, for a virtuous life to bear testimony to the world, its details must be *told*, so that the world may know them" (1870, 160). Bearing witness to Lady Byron's story is the precise act that in itself is true. Stowe claims that the instant she takes up the pen, her fiction becomes fact: "When a noble name is accused, any person who possesses truth which might clear it, and withholds that truth, is guilty of a sin against human nature and the inalienable claims of justice. I claim that I have not only a right, but an obligation, to bring in my solemn testimony upon this subject" (196). Thus the vindication Stowe attempts to achieve in her book is three-fold: a vindication of Lady Byron, a vindication of Stowe herself, and a vindication of the crucial role of feminine sentimentalism in all projects of culture making, even in a professional realist climate.

In essence, *Lady Byron Vindicated* reveals the gendered hypocrisies necessary to professional realism. If her critics require more proof than Stowe has to give, by inference, they cannot accept Byron's version of his marriage and divorce. In turn, if they believe Lord Byron in spite of his own lack of proof, they must simultaneously accept Stowe's version. "All this is not proof," Stowe says, referring to the iteration of Lord Byron's allegations. "It is mere assertion, and assertion made to produce prejudice. It is like raising a whirlwind of sand to blind the eyes that are looking for landmarks" (319). What Stowe does not say, however, is "all this is not real." What she's describing is how one writes realist fiction, and, of course, this is the exact method Stowe employs.

## REALIST PROFESSIONALISM AND ADVERTISING

There is a final layer to these series of paradoxes so rife in Stowe's book, one that exposes how commercial stigma both served and worked against professional realism. The repetition of an assertion to such an extent that the concept becomes truth is not only a technique of professional experts but a key component of advertising, although advertising repeats assertions in combination with images until the idea or statement is synonymous to its image. Advertising as a corporate industry in America did not fully emerge until after the Postal Act of 1879, an act that provided cheap mailing privileges to periodicals, but even a decade earlier, Stowe's *Vindicated* provides a powerful venue for Stowe to link her text with potent, conspicuous images.

Like any professional realist writer, Stowe relied on the workings of consumer culture, especially advertising, in order to propagate her moral expertise. In *Vindicated*, the key components were the documents, so much weight in facts, figures, and dates. Before the 482 pages of *Vindicated* went to press (463 pages longer than her original article), Stowe stipulated to Osgood that he "choose a good, clear, plain type for the *documents* so that nobody may skip them as fine print, and then have a larger type for my own words. The documents are the very marrow of the thing, and every care must be taken to make them flash clearly on the eye at a glance" (1869b). Stowe manipulated the same documents she used to inculpate Byron to serve her own claims to truth. The typeface itself was to perform the effect of her words—"good, clear, plain" type would equal Stowe's good, clear, plain purpose. The substance of the Byron documents mattered little; they provided eye-catching support for the "larger type" of Stowe's own text.

Thus, Stowe marketed *Vindicated*'s documents as advertisement—advertisement fashioned to rouse an inevitable sympathy from her readers. Indeed, it was crucial for Stowe to retender these documents as surface, not substance: ironically, as the "marrow," the vital lifeblood of her case, she had to disinfect them from further promulgating Byron's contaminants, the language that was his lie. Otherwise Stowe might breed infection in the sentence, since, after all, she sought to engage in exactly the enterprise she most reviled in Byron: writing slander.

Yet advertising worked against Stowe even more than it worked for her. While Stowe had comprehended the import of speaking out on such a topic and against such a favorite as Byron—especially as a woman and an American—she could not have foreseen the universal wrath she would incur for having uttered "that one word." Stowe was condemned for using propaganda similar to Byron's own and for spreading an even more virulent social disease. "The ruthless hand of the sensational authoress of 'Uncle Tom's Cabin' has invaded our shores," cries one columnist for *Vanity Fair*, "and torn the veil from the figure which might just as well have remained veiled" (1869, 146). Through the periodical press, Stowe metamorphosizes from defender to invader, advocate to assailant, cure to infection. "Mrs. Stowe has been guilty of . . . extremely bad taste," pronounces another writer in the *Saturday Review*. "[S]he has let loose a flood of immoral talk and immoral speculation on loathsome subjects which has deeply defiled, and will long defile, European and American society" (1869, 343). Like Stowe's own treatment of Byron in the "True Story," now Stowe herself is labeled innately wicked—seeking fame and money, or according to one satirist in the *Period*, merely living up to her own evolution.[17] "If we were to dissect her encephalon, we should in all probability find imprinted upon the inmost recesses of her brain the words she has herself placed in the mouth of one of her most popular characters: *'I 'spects I'se awful wicked'*; for only by natural and innate weakness can we account for the mischievous character of her writings" (1869, 2).

Like the depiction of Stowe as a black-magic witch in the *Merryman's Monthly* (1869), many a satirist makes race the central dynamic of his or her insult, a throwback to the media contention surrounding *Uncle Tom's Cabin* but also a typical nineteenth-century elision, collapsing gender with racial degeneracy and, in so doing, threatening Stowe's most powerful claim to social power: her whiteness. If her brain is inscribed with Topsy's famous phrase, Stowe, herself, harbors an essential blackness—a constitutional weakness but also, by association, a lurking animalism. The black woman in Stowe denotes her "wickedness," her sexual knowledge, but especially her knowledge of incest, for, as the logic goes, who would know more about incest than a black slave woman? In a *Will-O'-the-Wisp* cartoon from 25 September 1869, for instance, Uncle Tom crouches behind a horrified-looking Stowe and asks a weeping Little Eva, "How could she paint one of her own brethren so *black*?" From the *Comic Monthly*, another shows Topsy telling Byron, "I'se so glad you'se come. Is'e got company now. Is'e wicked—but Missis saz you goes ahed o' me," while still another pictures Uncle Tom, playing a great harp and pleading, "Go 'way from me, Massa Byron—my Missus saz you're too wicked to 'sociate wid spectable cullud sperrets" (1869). In these caricatures, Stowe is often in the act of self-blackening or striating black streaks across a gleaming statue of Byron or performing "black magic." Alternately, she is a prim-and-proper Alice-in-Wonderland type, besmirched with the very mud she slings (*Comic Monthly* 1869); a hag, scuttling up Byron's noble visage trailing muck from her hands and feet (*Merryman's Monthly* 1869); or a witch, brewing a cauldron of calumny.

As these examples demonstrate, the backlash against Stowe became an enterprise of advertising. The sacred connotations she had hoped to instill with her portrayals of Lady Byron as a noble martyr and herself as a fearless defender were quickly drained of their import through a process of swift trivialization. By distorting Stowe's image, showing her here as a witch, there as a peevish old woman, her representation was exhausted—just another bit of sensational gossip from a ridiculous, sentimental woman.

Even those periodicals who claimed moral indignation against Stowe's "one word" served to proliferate the sensationalism surrounding the tale, for the technologies of mass iconographic distribution that had just started up when Stowe wrote *Uncle Tom's Cabin* were in full swing by 1869.[18] In

1852, readers may have seen Stowe's portrait in the frontispiece to her novel or, perhaps, in a shop window—a pirate copy from an engraver's original. If her face sold anything, it sold her book or, by abstraction, the American abolition movement: serious items and ideas. But the convergence of mass transit, mass media, and mass information deprived Stowe's face of its gravity, using it, instead, to sell trivia and sensation, "entertainment." Thus the meaning of Stowe's critique was not in the content of her analysis but transferred to the act of consumption itself, to whatever the consumer wanted her face or text to mean. Since Stowe had tried to portray Lord Byron as a liar and a cheat, the press retaliated in like kind. English and American critics disliked Stowe's commodity, and so they realigned the terms of the market by revising the look, and thereby the meaning, of what she had tried to produce. And once Stowe and her text no longer stood for righteous action or decorous womanhood, once the symbol was detached from its rational signification, it failed to carry any cultural relevance. "Sold" as the paragon of American abolitionism and pure womanhood with *Uncle Tom's Cabin*, with *Lady Byron Vindicated*, Stowe was now "sold" as an indecorous woman out to make a quick buck.

Stowe's friend and correspondent, George Eliot, wrote about the Byron controversy to her acquaintance Sara Hennell, commenting, "As to the Byron subject . . ., [t]he discussion of the subject in newspapers, periodicals and pamphlets, is simply odious to me, and I think it a pestilence likely to leave very ugly marks. One trembles to think how easily that moral wealth may be lost which it has been the work of ages to produce, in the refinement and differencing of the affectionate relations" (1954–55, 5:56–57). With the advent of advertising as a basis of meaning making, it is no wonder that, as a high-art realist, Eliot would worry that the "refinement and differencing of affectionate relations" she had spent her life's work trying to promote was undergoing rapid-fire annihilation through popular print. But while Eliot condemned the media that had made Stowe's claims into a "pestilence," she also forgave what she believed to be her friend's motive. In a letter to Stowe, Eliot consoles, "[W]ith regard to yourself, dear friend, I have felt sure that in acting on a [unique] basis of impressions, you were impelled by pure, generous feeling" (1954–55, 5:71–72).

And, in fact, Stowe's critique of Byron from within his own providence reveals a tenacious "feeling," one that is "pure" if not necessarily "generous." For Stowe clearly holds up a sphere of aesthetic transcendence that rises above and stands beyond all other social discourse—reified, perfect, and, one might say, pure. To criticize Byron for using his poetry as propaganda is to posit that true literature is not commodifiable or is somehow beyond the designation of mere advertisement: precisely the claim made by professional male realists. Stowe censures Byron for possessing a sentimentalized aesthetic, a bankrupt notion of what literature is and should be. By showing

Byron's art as insufficient—especially lacking in moral ideality—Stowe pays allegiance to the professional realist faith in a perfect, continuous realm of art. At the same time, Stowe intimates that she, like a professional male realist, is a true artist, one through whom timeless moral sentiment makes itself known to the general public. As a result, Stowe's *Vindicated* and Stowe herself serve as emblems of the late nineteenth-century ideology of professional realism that would, ironically, contribute to the ultimate decline of Stowe's own standing in the age of New Criticism.

## NOTES

This article is reprinted from *American Literary Realism* 36 (2004): 93–119.

1. A year after completing *Uncle Tom's Cabin*, on 20 September 1853, Stowe explained to Lord Denman, an English admirer: "I wrote what I did because as a woman, as a mother I was oppressed & broken-hearted, with the sorrows & injustice I saw, because as a Christian I felt the dishonor to Christianity—because as a lover of my country I trembled at the coming day of wrath" (Stowe 1853).

2. "We have had three storms this autumn," Holmes wrote to his friend John Lothrop Motley, "1. The great gale of September 8th, which I recognized while it was blowing as the greatest for fifty-four years. . . . 2d. The Byron whirlwind, which began here and travelled swiftly across the Atlantic; and 3d, the goldstorm, as I christened the terrible financial conflict of the last week. About the Byron article I confess that, great as I expected the excitement to be, it far exceeded anything I had anticipated" (Morse 1896, 183).

3. "Realism" here is not meant simply to concede to the traditional rubric of the late nineteenth-century high-art canon, i.e., Howells or Eliot as social realists, Twain as a regional realist, or James as a psychological realist. Rather, "realism" is meant as an aesthetic term that both presupposes a set of standard "realistic" criteria at the same time that it embodies the appropriation of aspects of other aesthetic movements that, at first glance, seem antithetical to realism's form and function: chiefly appropriations of textual and readerly "sentimentalism" as created in and by sentimental novels.

4. Note that "The True Story of Lady Byron's Life" was published simultaneously in the September issues of the *Atlantic Monthly* in America and *MacMillan's Magazine* in England. For the sake of clarity, in this article all page numbers for "The True Story of Lady Byron's Life" come from the *Atlantic Monthly*.

5. This point has been debated by one of her modern biographers, Forrest Wilson, who writes, "It is remarkable that none discovered the astonishing fact that much of [Stowe's] argument . . . was based on a misrepresentation of fact, and a deliberate one. Not one critic or enemy ever found it, and Harriet died with her guilty secret intact. . . . Critics picked at such flaws as her misspelling of Miss Milbanke's name and her inaccurate statement that the Byrons' married life had lasted two years, but never once saw that in her *Atlantic* paper, which, she cried so passionately in her book, she had written in answer to the review in *Blackwood's*, she did not

mention that review at all. The explanation is, of course, that when she wrote her dreadful gossip for the *Atlantic*, she did not know of the *Blackwood's* review. It had not yet been published" (1941, 549–50).

6. Authors are imperfect professionals. Unlike doctors, lawyers, and academics, authors do not establish nor control set procedures of credentializing that function as gatekeeping mechanisms. While there are, of course, accepted methods for attaining the recognized position of "professional author" (e.g., publication), these methods are not regulated nor, ultimately, required.

7. For a study of how the fact-fiction slippage in the eighteenth century gave rise to the British novel as well as the construction of female authorship, see Catherine Gallagher, *Nobody's Story: The Vanishing Acts of Women Writers in the Marketplace, 1670–1820*.

8. In addition to Southern criticisms of *Uncle Tom's Cabin*, Stowe received censure from English reviewers as well. See Wendy F. Hamand, "'No Voice from England': Mrs. Stowe, Mr. Lincoln, and the British in the Civil War."

9. The editor's preface to the *Macmillan's* issue did, in fact, name the author as "Mrs. Beecher Stowe," although in the article itself, as in the American version, the narrator calls herself "the writer."

10. Though it may seem, at first glance, that a first-person narrator is less authentic than a universalized third-person voice, *Vindicated* is indebted to a long history of readers equating first-hand experience with credibility: examples are Aphra Behn's *Oroonoko*, Benjamin Franklin's *Autobiography*, or Olaudah Equiano's *Interesting Narrative of the Life*. One of the reasons Stowe's text can be seen as, in part, a kind of realist "novel" is that the narrator slips between first person and third person throughout the book; the convergence of fact and fiction that opens a space for the creation of the modern novel brings together the assumed integrity of a first-person perspective with the equally assumed integrity of normalized, third-person objectivity.

11. Stowe also contends that Byron himself reacted to the public criticism of his poetry—especially *Blackwood's* initial condemnation of Byron's representation of Lady Byron as Donna Inez—as if his art were the substance of fact: "March 15, 1820.—Writes, and dedicates to I. Disraeli, Esq., a vindication of himself in reply to the 'Blackwood' on 'Don Juan,' containing an indignant defense of his own conduct in relation to his wife, and maintaining that he never yet has had an opportunity of knowing whereof he has been accused" (1870, 80).

12. After *Lady Byron Vindicated* came out, the *Nation*—a periodical that had roundly abused Stowe's "True Story" and had a history of publishing negative reviews of Stowe's novels—recognized that the "only additional proof" Stowe had added was "more extended and explicit reports of the conversation in which Lady Byron revealed the secret" (1870, 2).

13. For instance, the second paragraph of the book begins, "I have not thought it necessary to disturb my spirit and confuse my sense of right by even an attempt at reading the many abusive articles that both here and in England have followed [my] disclosure" (1870, 1). It should be noted that this assertion is false, insofar as it is clear Stowe read many of her critics because *Vindicated* is a point-by-point refutation of claims made against her argument in the "True Story," going so far as to quote many of her detractors.

14. See Jane Tompkins's chapter on *Uncle Tom's Cabin* in *Sensational Designs*.

15. Stowe iterates this line in her "True Story": "The interview had almost the solemnity of a death-bed avowal" (1869c, 311).

16. Howells admitted that he experienced "impossible stress" from the Sunday paper, "which with its scare-headings, and artfully-wrought sensations, had the effect of fiction, as in fact it largely was" ([1895] 1911, 178).

17. As Susan Wolstenholme points out in "Voice of the Voiceless: Harriet Beecher Stowe and the Byron Controversy," most everyone who has written about the Byron controversy has speculated about Stowe's motives, i.e., whether Stowe's intentions were pure or profane in revealing Lady Byron's secret.

18. A commentator for the *Tomahawk* unwittingly yet aptly assesses the paradox of claiming to abhor libel at the same one writes and rewrites it: "We fearlessly challenge that reckless malignancy which, biting its lips over such a congenial morsel of scandal as this, imputes to all who will not join in its rabid assumption of virtuous indignation, the crimes that it gloats over while it deplores. We are content to be classed by such creatures with the irreclaimable votaries of vice, because we have protested against the beastly curiosity which lays bare the repulsive secrets of the lives of those who were great in spite of their moral blemishes" (1869, 125).

## WORKS CITED

Bledstein, Burton. 1976. *The Culture of Professionalism: The Middle Class and the Development of Higher Education in America*. New York: Norton.

*Comic Monthly*. 1869. Cartoon. October.

Eliot, George. 1954-55. *The George Eliot Letters*, ed. Gordon S. Haight. 7 vols. New Haven, CT: Yale University Press.

*Fun*. 1869. Cartoon. 18 September.

Gallagher, Catherine. 1994. *Nobody's Story: The Vanishing Acts of Women Writers in the Marketplace, 1670–1820*. Berkeley and Los Angeles: University of California Press.

Glazener, Nancy. 1997. *Reading for Realism: The History of a U.S. Literary Institution, 1850–1910*. Durham, NC: Duke University Press.

Hamand, Wendy F. 1988. "'No Voice from England': Mrs. Stowe, Mr. Lincoln, and the British in the Civil War." *New England Quarterly* 61:3–24.

Howells, William Dean. [1895] 1911. *My Literary Passions: Criticism and Fiction*. Reprint, New York: Harper.

———. [1897] 1957. "Preface to English Society by George du Maurier." In *Prefaces to Contemporaries (1882–1920)*, ed. George Arms, William M. Gibson, and Frederic C. Marston Jr., 73–77. Reprint, Gainesville, FL: Scholars' Facsimiles and Reprints.

*Illustrated Times*. 1869. "The Lounger." 9 October, 230–31.

*Merryman's Monthly*. 1869. Cartoon. October.

Morse, John T., ed. 1896. *Life and Letters of Oliver Wendell Holmes*. Cambridge, MA: Riverside.

*Nation*. 1870. Review of *Lady Byron Vindicated*, by Harriet Beecher Stowe. 6 January, 2.

*Pall Mall Gazette*. 1869. Letter to the Editor. 7 September, 3.

*Period*. 1869. "Polychromatic Portraits.—No. 1." 30 October, 2.

*Public Opinion*. 1869. "The Byron Scandal." 25 September, 380–81.

Robertson, Michael. 1997. *Stephen Crane, Journalism, and the Making of Modern American Literature*. New York: Columbia University Press.

*Saturday Review*. 1869. "The Byron Case. 11 September, 343–44.

*The Stowe-Byron Controversy: A Complete Résumé of Public Opinion; with an Impartial Review of the Merits of the Case, by the Editor of "Once a Week."* 1869. London: Cooper.

Stowe, Charles Edward. [1889] 1967. *The Life of Harriet Beecher Stowe Compiled from her Letters and Journals*. Reprint, Detroit, MI: Gale Research.

Stowe, Harriet Beecher. 1853. Letter to Lord Denman. 20 January. Fields Papers. Huntington Library.

———. 1869a. Letter to James R. Osgood. n.d. [August or September] Fields Papers. Huntington Library.

———. 1869b. Letter to James R. Osgood. 16 October. Fields Papers. Huntington Library.

———. 1869c. "The True Story of Lady Byron's Life." *Atlantic Monthly* 24:295–313.

———. 1870. *Lady Byron Vindicated: A History of the Byron Controversy, from Its Beginnings in 1816 to the Present Time*. Boston: Fields, Osgood, and Co.

Tilton, Theodore. 1869. "The Byron Revelations." *Independent*. 26 August, 1.

*Tomahawk*. 1869. "The Byron Scandal." 18 September, 125–26.

Tompkins, Jane. 1985. *Sensational Designs: The Cultural Work of American Fiction, 1790–1860*. New York: Oxford University Press.

*Vanity Fair*. 1869. "The Byron Scandal." 11 September, 146.

*Will-O'-the-Wisp*. 1869. Cartoon. 25 September.

Wilson, Forrest. 1941. *Crusader in Crinoline: The Life of Harriet Beecher Stowe*. Philadelphia: Lippincott.

Wolstenholme, Susan. 1987. "Voice of the Voiceless: Harriet Beecher Stowe and the Byron Controversy." *American Literary Realism* 19 (2): 48–65.

# Gendering Gilded Age Periodical Professionalism

## Reading Harriet Beecher Stowe's *Hearth and Home* Prescriptions for Women's Writing

*Sarah Robbins*

In the top left corner of its front page, the 1860s–70s periodical *Hearth and Home* regularly rendered its own title in image form, reflecting and reinforcing the popular culture's view of white, middle-class American domestic life in the decade after the Civil War. The array of objects in this recurring illustration carried easily recognizable messages about nineteenth-century family literacy practices for the publication's anticipated readers.[1] Perhaps predictably, a hearth with a comfortable fire dominated the midsection of the picture and, though the particular objects on the mantelpiece were obscured by the periodical's nameplate, other visual cues suggested this home was a properly educated and refined one. Beside a stuffed chair facing the fireplace, for instance, stood a reading table and its lamp, and the other side of the illustration included another side table with a carefully draped cloth and a dainty vase of flowers, signaling a close relationship between the homemaker's attention to aesthetically pleasing decor and the family-based development of the mind in a middle-class domestic setting. The centerpiece of the image foregrounded a third small table holding several books, with one thick volume perched on top at an angle that seemed to invite an opening of this text or of the periodical itself.

Anyone who opens the tabloid-size pages of *Hearth and Home* at the dawn of the twenty-first century is probably doing so, as I have been recently, because Harriet Beecher Stowe served as its coeditor during its early life. In the wake of moves to reposition *Uncle Tom's Cabin* in the field of American literary studies, whether as a prime example of an alternative feminine aesthetic or as an embodiment of women's significant cultural work, we are beginning to take a closer look at other writing Stowe produced in her long career as a professional author. Reevaluations of novels

75

like *Dred* and *The Minister's Wooing* have been one result of this scholarly
recovery process. Eager as we are to celebrate Stowe the author, however,
we may be a bit disappointed, at least at first, when we turn to her weekly
columns for *Hearth and Home*. To put the case too bluntly perhaps, Stowe
the 1860s' periodical writer was no Fanny Fern.[2]

Today I find myself scanning a good bit of the writing Stowe did for
*Hearth and Home* with impatience, irritated to see the same writer who
had galvanized the world against the major sociopolitical issue of her day
redirected toward filling column inches with passages like this one about
"beauty as applied to the living-rooms of houses": "And now our friends
having got this far, are requested to select some one tint or color which shall
be the prevailing one in the furniture of the room. Shall it be green? Shall
it be blue? Shall it be crimson? To carry on our illustration, we will choose
green, and we now proceed . . . to create furniture for our room" (1869g,
200). Unlike the satirical stance of Stowe's recently reappreciated *Atlantic*
essays on carpet selection, this column was unstintingly straightforward, offering practical help for women readers eager to create a tastefully decorated
parlor—for example, those who wanted to purchase a "very pretty curtin
muslin" and who needed to know how many yards of fabric to buy for a
typical window. ("Six," Stowe advised.)

Stowe's labor on such prose may seem to be lacking in subtlety and
polish, and thus in aesthetic interest as well. On the one hand, "How to
Treat Babies" may have been genuinely reassuring for readers whose col-
icky infants really could drive them to near distraction: after all, if such
moments made the world-famous author of *Uncle Tom's Cabin* feel "like
crying [her]self" (1869e, 104) what could be expected of anyone else? On
the other hand, even if I try to follow Patricia Okker's advice to appreciate
such social value as Stowe's "sisterly editorial voice" (1995, 23) in these
texts,[3] I still find myself reluctant to see something like "Growing Things"
(1869f) as substantial cultural work. Even if I re-view it within a feminist-
materialist framework, sensitively aware of the complex role gardening
could play in the lives of women of earlier eras,[4] "Growing Things" basically offers little more than quick summaries of two books about garden
techniques that Stowe recommends to her readership. Clear calls to social
action, like "The Woman Question," are relatively scarce in Stowe's *Hearth
and Home* columns. Certainly, in that one piece she righteously exhorts
her audience to read "John Stuart Mill's account of what the legal position of woman is under English common law" and to reflect that, in the
postbellum United States, a married female "can make no contract and
hold no property," that she is essentially in a position "precisely similar to
that of the negro slave" (1869i, 520). But in the rest of that year's worth
of sketches, the politicized author of *Uncle Tom's Cabin* is far harder to
find. So, what are we to make of this seeming shift to conservatism?[5] And

how do we reconcile our continuing moves to position Stowe among the "best" makers of American literature with the notably uneven quality of her writing for *Hearth and Home*?[6]

Answering these questions requires situating Stowe's work for the periodical within the marketplace context for such publications in her own day, as well as distinguishing between the advice she gave others when acting as a work-a-day editor and the artistic aspirations that she seems to have cherished for herself as an American author whose best work could be expected to meet more permanent aesthetic criteria. Beginning to address such questions also involves taking a look at Stowe's life as a practicing professional against a larger backdrop of gendered literature making in the post–Civil War United States. Therefore, it includes situating the particular venue of *Hearth and Home* within a network of publications competing for white, middle-class national readership in that marketplace while trying to recapture a sense of who those readers were and how Stowe imagined herself as meeting their needs in her columns. In addition, it includes cultivating an awareness of how our own reading practices, as well as our beliefs about "literary" value, shape our interpretations of nineteenth-century texts; of the authors' specific processes for writing and circulating them; and of the original readers' interactions with those printed products.

One especially fruitful site for such an analysis is the series of essays Stowe wrote *about* women's professional writing during her year as editor. Originally appearing in January 1869, these sketches now provide a kind of window into the range of forces operating in the periodical marketplace during the late 1860s, and they convey a sense of Stowe's own efforts to negotiate a gendered professional position—for herself and other aspiring women writers—within that shifting set of values and practices.[7] Beginning with "Can I Write?" (1869a) and progressing in order through "How Shall I Learn to Write" (1869b), "Faults of Inexperienced Writers" (1869c), and "How May I Know That I Can Make a Writer?" (1869d), the essays reflect tensions then inherent in the evolving, frequently contested views of what professional American literature making should and could entail. By exploring Stowe's efforts to acknowledge but also to manage these tensions in her series on authorship for *Hearth and Home*, we can better understand both her particular professional writing career and the periodical context in which it continued to develop.

That Stowe chose to write on this topic in this particular periodical may have served to heighten some of the tensions inherent in her own position as a major American literary figure, since the character of the publication matched some aspects of her gendered professionalism but challenged others. *Hearth and Home*, established in 1868 as a weekly publication with Donald G. Mitchell and Stowe as coeditors, entered a national literary scene that had moved since midcentury from a long tradition of genteel amateurism to an expanded print culture selling literature as a commodity necessarily reflecting mass-market values and interests. That its owners and founders were the advertising firm Pettengill, Bates and Company suggests the extent to which this venture was seen from the outset as a business operating within the burgeoning U.S. literary marketplace. According to Frank Mott, the niche the publication sought to fill was not unique: while committed to publishing works of domestic literature, *Hearth and Home* also offered a wide range of nonfiction self-help fare about the hearthside, the garden, and the farm (99). In that vein, although *Hearth and Home* lasted only seven years, its association with other 1860s–70s New York–based periodicals centered in American home life (such as *Wood's Household Magazine, Domestic Monthly*, and *Our Neighborhood*), underscores ways in which literature writing in the United States was increasingly being seen as a money maker. But this same linked construction of imagined readership and periodical content also points to another trend in Gilded Age publishing: the growing divide between an urban, "high culture," masculine model for literature making and an increasingly distanced alternative tradition, grounded in the values and practices of a more rural or domestic, middlebrow—and feminized—space for textual consumption *and* production.

Stowe served as coeditor of *Hearth and Home* for only a year. Yet, although her editorial tenure was relatively brief, her taking on the job in the first place reminds us that, for Stowe at this point in her life, her writing was as much a generator of domestic income as anything else. As Joan Hedrick has pointed out, Calvin Stowe had retired from his professorial position in 1863, leaving his wife as the primary breadwinner for a large and demanding family that included adult children who had proven themselves incapable (or at least unwilling) to support themselves (1994, 310). In the interval between the end of the Civil War and the start-up of *Hearth and Home*, the Stowe family's expenses had been on the rise (given the added expense of their new Hartford home) so that Harriet's efforts to increase the amount of money she made with her pen became even more pointed (as reflected, for instance, in her correspondence with publishers like James Fields). Thus, Stowe's taking on the duty of a weekly publication needs to be seen in part as an example of her growing sense of herself as a professional (read "for pay") author.[8]

This emphasis on earning money through writing helped gender Stowe's work for *Hearth and Home* by connecting it with a network of other women, periodicals, authors, and editors whose labor had already begun to distinguish male from female literary professionalism during the antebellum era. Specifically, Sara Parton (Fanny Fern) had gained as much attention for the amount of money *New York Ledger* editor-publisher Robert Bonner was willing to pay for her columns as for the quality of her prose.[9] Similarly, as Okker has noted in her recent study of Sarah Josepha Hale, that redoubtable "editress" consistently conceived of professionalism in women's writing as writing for pay as opposed to producing "unpublishable, amateur writings" (1995, 99). From Okker's perspective, one result of this stress on becoming financially successful as a mark of professionalism was to distance Hale's view of serious writing from the continued calls for "artistry" over income in the rhetoric (if not in the life practices) of male cultural arbiters like Hawthorne. In other words, whereas Hale herself would have argued that top women writers who earned good salaries were not merely "pander[ing] to their audiences" but instead showing that "they had talent *and* worked hard" (100), another kind of contrast associated men's presumably more elitist authorship with "an eighteenth-century model of the leisured gentleman author" and women's with "scribbling" perceived as less worthy (100). Later in the century and on into the twentieth, such African-American women writer-editors as Josephine Ruffin and Ida B. Wells-Barnett would also devote notable energy to the money-making side of their work as writers, especially since publications like the *Woman's Era* were dependent on such female business acumen to survive and thereby to carry out their race-oriented uplift missions.[10] American women writers, in other words, have often written within a gendered tradition of entrepreneurship. Viewed in this context, Stowe's labor for *Hearth and Home* was part of an ongoing process associating *women's* writing more with money making than with art for art's sake.

Stowe's tenure at *Hearth and Home* should also be set against the pragmatic political background of her growing interest in women's social issues, to the extent that she even flirted with the idea of joining, in some influential capacity, the political movement led by Susan B. Anthony and Elizabeth Cady Stanton (Hedrick 1994, 358). Within this context of Stowe's increasing fascination with women's rights, a consideration of her work at *Hearth and Home* would also take into account Hedrick's observation that Stowe "for the first time [had] a shaping power over columns other than her own, a power she used . . . to promote women writers such as Lucy Larcom" (1994, 361), as well as issues like woman suffrage.[11] Seen in this light, Stowe's occasional forays into women's rights issues in *Hearth and Home* take on more weight. One of those issues, for example, was a question that had held her attention from as early as her coteaching days at the Hartford Seminary in the 1820s—the proper education of young, middle-class ladies, both in school and at home. Scattered through her *Hearth and Home* sketches were recurring complaints about the still-constraining limits of female education, and two columns in June 1869 specifically addressed the topic of what young girls should study at home.[12] Like her assumptions that professional female authorship involved serious work for pay, Stowe's support of women's learning in *Hearth and Home* affiliated her work with a gendered tradition of restrained yet persistent editorial advocacy nurtured by Hale's *Ladies' Magazine* and *Godey's*.[13] Along these lines, we might note, too, that Stowe left the publication after just one year, not because of philosophical or artistic differences but because she was eager to throw her energies into her book-length, protofeminist defense of Lady Byron (366).

Considering that Stowe was evidently preparing to enter into a battle that would lead a number of her contemporaries to classify her writing as distinctly and dangerously unfeminine,[14] Stowe's recommendations to other would-be authors in the series of columns printed during the four weeks of January 1869 may seem surprising. The bulk of her advice urged aspiring women writers to start off modestly, in terms of both content and monetary aspirations, and then move gradually, through study and practice, to a strategically maintained professionalism. One way of interpreting this apparently conservative stance is to see it less as restraining than as mentoring—that is, to note that the trajectory Stowe described for other aspiring writers was something of a record of her own development as an author. The advice Stowe offered to novices in her *Hearth and Home* series came straight out of her own experience during her attendance at Litchfield School, her membership in Cincinnati's Semi-Colon Club, and her earlier magazine writing for women's venues such as *Godey's*. Stowe's essays, in other words, encouraged would-be writers to follow in her footsteps, imitating both the specific stages she had progressed through and her basic acceptance of the gendered expectations for feminized authorship. For example, John Brace, her favorite composition teacher during her own schooling, was the source of one tenet she stresses here: "FIRST THINK OF WHAT YOU WANT TO SAY, AND THEN SAY IT" (1869a, 40). Stowe explained: "It is not enough to have a general desire to write; the author must have a very particular and definite conception of something that she wants to say. We would say to such a person: 'Is there any subject on which you feel so deeply and vividly, that it seems to you that you have something to say on that subject?' If it be so, then try to put that something into the very clearest, plainest, and simplest words that you can" (40). According to a reminiscence by Stowe and a later retelling of that same tale by her sister Isabella Hooker, John Brace had given just such guidance to young Harriet when she was a student in his writing course at Miss Pierce's famous Litchfield School many years earlier, and it remained a cornerstone of Stowe's composing process for the rest of her life. Though Harriet first encountered Brace at Litchfield, they both were also associated later with the Hartford Female Seminary, and Stowe drew upon his teaching strategies when she instructed young ladies while working there with her sister Catherine Beecher.[15] Stressing his ability to build on shared conversations about topics of interest, Stowe often praised Brace's particular talent in "teaching composition" and associated her early development as a writer with his approaches (1993, 28). Specifically, in recalling Brace's model for teaching writing, she described two of her own successful papers, written at ages nine and twelve respectively, as apt examples of *his* pedagogical skill. The first, though devoted to the ambitious topic "The Difference between the Natural and the Moral Sublime," Stowe insisted was not too difficult to write since "the discussions which he held with the class not only made me understand the subject as thoroughly as I do now, but so excited me that I felt sure I had [the] main requirement" for success at writing (28).

By advising would-be authors to write of something they knew and cared about, Stowe may appear to us today to be offering little more than a cliché. But her elaborations on this point in the introductory sketch for the 1869 series clarify that part of her goal was to help her audience of potential *female* writers value the rather limited domestic subjects most available to them. In that vein, the shift from "men and women" writers to "a woman" in a later passage of "Can I Write?" is worth noting:[16]

> Now, a great many men and women, when beginning to write, attempt too much; they take some great general subject, and flood it with platitudes and commonplaces. There is a whole class of ideas and words that go floating around the newspaper world, that belong no more to one person than another, and that by this time one person can say about as well as another. . . .
> But now, to come down to a practical point. If there is a woman who could take this subject, "how to quiet a fretful baby," and write a good, sensible, shrewd article on it, though she were not literary at all, and though there might not be a fine figure in it, yet if there were a good share of practical sense and evident experience, we think her article would make a hit. (1869a, 40)

Stowe went on to catalogue other "specimens of a certain class of topics," all of which she described as "a homely and practical kind," "relating to the whole field of matter covered by the HEARTH AND HOME paper"—that is, "subjects . . . where a person who would follow our rule of thinking what *she* wanted to say, and then saying it, might get opportunity" (emphasis added). These suggested topics included "How to keep boys at home evenings," "How best to unite warmth and ventilation in a house," and "How to make Sundays both pleasant and useful to children" (40).

On first reading, this series of topics may seem to embody just the kind of overdetermined gender-based distinctions that feminists have resisted in our own lives and in portrayals of nineteenth-century "spheres" that oversimplify the separations between male and female cultures in that era. A closer look at Stowe's advice here, however, especially in the context of her ongoing efforts to stake out effective positions for her writing in the years after *Uncle Tom's Cabin*, indicates that at least one aim for this essay was savvy and pragmatic: to help would-be authors for *Hearth and Home* understand and adapt to the increasingly gendered position such periodicals might need to stake out in a marketplace moving unremittingly toward an urban and male-dominated view of "the literary."[17] One positive point that Stowe offered, accordingly, was that, despite the increasing influence of forces like the male-run, highbrow *Atlantic*, there might still be available niches for small-circulation papers devoted to women-oriented audiences, much as today's television broadcasting and cablecasting includes specialty "narrowcasting" slots such as the History Channel and the Home Shopping Network. With this point in mind, her reference to "a certain class of topics" and her listing of specific examples represent a defensive yet potentially useful demarcation of relevant women's work in writing, work that need "not [be] literary at all" in order to be professional; work that, if not likely to be printed in a place like the *Atlantic*, could still find an audience.

In the second series entry on 16 January, Stowe would explain: "Now, the kind of writing for which there is a call in our paper, HEARTH AND HOME, is writing about domestic and rural subjects, and subjects of a practical nature, such as lie more fully within the sphere of woman's knowledge and observation than in that of ordinary men" (1869b, 56). Besides arguing that such writing could find a place in her own particular periodical, Stowe also insisted that it could have a value in its own right. After all, she wrote:

> [I]t is a fact that the experiences of woman in real life, in all that comes to her in her domestic capacity as mistress of a family, sister, daughter, wife, and mother, do furnish a class of subjects wherein a woman, trained to think wisely and justly, may find a great deal to say that is worth saying. She may have subject matter of peculiar weight and importance—subject matter which woman, and only woman, could possibly be able to present. (56)

Valued as something "which woman, and only woman, could possibly be able to present," Stowe's list of topics in the first sketch for the series is elevated beyond the mundane level of the literal ("How to keep boys at home," "How best to unite warmth and ventilation in a house") to a special compact between writer and reader, one bound to the unique experiences of womankind.[18] In this sense, Stowe's recommendation to avoid "some great general subject" (1869a, 40) becomes not an injunction assuming others' inability to take on just the kind of grandiose topic she herself had tackled for John Brace (in "The Difference between the Natural and the Moral Sublime") but rather a celebration of women's own space of experience and communication. That this space deals with the everyday is one of its strengths, not a fault, according to Stowe: "There is a great deal of writing," she asserted, "very charming, very acceptable, and much in demand, which consists simply in painting by means of words the simple and homely scenes of every-day life" (1869b, 56).

Stowe's formula positioned women's writing and the particular periodical she was editing within a gendered tradition of genteel entrepreneurship—one affiliated with venues like Hale's *Ladies' Magazine*, from its inception earlier in the nineteenth century, and also anticipating eventual descendants such as *Better Homes and Gardens* and *Ladies' Home Journal.* By implication, achieving the first two traits she cited—being "charming" and "very acceptable"—could ensure successful attainment of the third—having a product that was "much in demand." Indeed, writing for magazines and newspapers was a way that middle-class women could make money without surrendering their genteelness, since composing a "charming" piece (e.g., depicting decorous and uplifting feminized behavior in parlor, school, or village) with an "acceptable" topic (e.g., temperance, courtship, child rearing) would not violate expectations for female social action.

Within just such a set of expectations, Stowe's early-career pieces for James Hall's *Western Monthly Magazine, Godey's Lady's Book,* the *Evangelist, Christian Keepsake,* and other periodicals had often taken the form of brief descriptive sketches and "charming" short narratives of everyday life. For instance, "Feeling," which was later reprinted in the *Mayflower,* offered detailed descriptions of the students in a country schoolroom, where one seemingly unproductive boy was singled out by the narrator because, although not a great scholar, he exhibited "the very temperament which often makes the noblest virtue"—compassion, or intense feeling (1855, 141).[19] At the end of the sketch, the reader discovers that the young boy eventually became a vibrant orator, beloved friend, and caring citizen-neighbor—precisely because he had "quick perceptions, the tenderness, the gentleness of an angel" (143). Similarly, Stowe's sketches of "Old Father Morris" and the "Alice H." of "Frankness" are not frequently read today, but they at least avoided the errors Stowe critiqued in the "Faults of Inexperienced Writers" column for her *Hearth and Home* series. Both pieces used focused themes and straightforwardly colloquial language instead of the overly "fine writing" or "hifalutin' style" Stowe would decry in her "Faults" essay: they aimed instead for "the simple language of ordinary conversation" and the unpretentious content she would extol in the *Hearth and Home* prescriptions (1869c, 72).

Stowe's advice to aspiring lady authors, then, was that they follow a path she had taken by positioning their professional goals within the circulation venue most readily available for them—the periodical marketplace—even though the price of that access would be accepting gendered constraints on their writing. If Stowe seemed, in 1869, to be urging would-be women writers away from the very path she had chosen with *Uncle Tom's Cabin*—taking on the most crucial social issue of the day and then writing page after page until she had created an impassioned, novel-length work—she would probably point out that her first bestseller was not her first piece of professional writing; that she began it, in fact, planning to produce just a short series of sketches; and that she churned out the original version facing all the exigencies of periodical serialization.[20] And she could also have emphasized that, before expecting to succeed as a well-paid professional, she had herself carried out exactly the kind of patient training program she outlined for her *Hearth and Home* readers. Her original writings for the Semi-Colon Club and for the "little" magazines of the antebellum era perfectly fit the rules for novices she proposed in "Can I Write?": "Young writers must begin by giving away their writing while they are learning to write. In fact, some [like Stowe herself] who were [eventually] reaping large incomes from writing began by sending articles to magazines, with no other expectation of remuneration than the insertion of them" (1869a, 40–41). Overall, even as she asserted the need for patient "practice in writing," for the acceptance of gendered norms, and for a commitment "to give their minds seriously to the work of forming themselves into good writers," Stowe offered her column readers some hope of success, if they followed her advice.

One caveat already present in the series' early stages, however, received more and more emphasis as Stowe's exploration of professional writing continued throughout the month of January. From the outset, if not at first too insistently, Stowe cautioned that she was basing her directions on the assumption that her would-be protégés would be capable of producing "really good writing," which she declared would "always bear its price in the market" (41). Interestingly, as the series on professional writing progressed, Stowe placed more and more stress on this issue of quality. Her later installments exhibited repeated, increasing slippage between celebrations of the special, productive, and relatively open place for women's writing in a burgeoning marketplace and her continued revisitings of an idealized model for serious writing more devoted to aesthetic, "genius"-associated values than to an impressive paycheck. Perhaps such tensions in Stowe's portrayal of authorship were inevitable, given the fluctuating state of literary professionalism in 1860s American culture. But they are fascinating, nevertheless, since they suggest she may have been struggling to define a position for herself in the already emerging pantheon of "great" American writers and to do so in a way that would prevent her being excluded because of her gender. This goal would naturally be at odds with efforts to open up professional writing to any woman willing to work hard and play by the rules. That is, if Stowe wanted to carve out a unique place for herself as a great writer according to the developing framework of the high-culture model for American literature, she could hardly argue at the same time that the profession was fully accessible to anyone willing to learn the craft by way of steady practice.

This dilemma of mixed goals helps explain what would otherwise seem an unfathomable inconsistency in tone and content when Stowe addressed or depicted aspiring women authors in the series on professional writing. In the January 1869 articles on women's writing, she may have occasionally taken on the voice of a lecturing schoolmarm, but she still conveyed a faith in the potential worth of her readers' writings, assuming they were willing to follow the dictates she recommended at the end of her first article. In such passages, Stowe positioned herself as the novice's experienced mentor but also her companion in suffering the restraints of their shared gender. Thus, in "How Shall I Learn to Write" she contrasted the extended opportunities for education enjoyed by men with the constraints suffered by women, and her satirical attack on those limits situated her firmly on the women's side. Similarly, she frequently shifted throughout the series from third-person description of novice writers to the more collegial use of second person. In "Faults of Young Writers," for example, she first imagined "a writer," then slid into the friendly "you": "Now, as a general rule, a writer should take this caution: keep yourself from those authors who impress you too powerfully. If there is a general style that is running loose through all the literature of your country, and is coloring all the magazines and stories, try as much as possible to lift yourself out of it, by choosing for yourself, resolutely, quite another circle of reading" (1869c, 72). In addition, Stowe occasionally addressed her anticipated reader for the series quite affectionately, as in a passage from "How May I Know That I Can Make a Writer?" when she directly called the novice writer "my dear friend" (1869d, 88).

However, for every time she reached out to embrace and encourage aspiring women writers throughout her January series, Stowe also made moves to distance herself from them. One sign of this tendency was her repeated citing of male rather than female writers as positive models. For instance, in "How Shall I Learn to Write?" after inviting her female readers to take on the "subject matter which woman, and only woman, could possibly hope to present" and suggesting that, to do so, her readers need only "*get* the gift of expression" (emphasis added), Stowe went on to explain that such a "gift," though a "fine art," could be "studied" and "practised"—thereby indicating that her readers could work their way to professionalism (1869b, 56). But just a few paragraphs later, when she began offering models for her readers—presumably female—to emulate, all three of those provided were male: Washington Irving, Honoré de Balzac, and Nathaniel Hawthorne, whom Stowe designated "the greatest American writer" (56).[21]

An outline of Stowe's entire "How Shall I Learn to Write?" sketch highlights her tendency to shift back and forth between empowering and constraining her women readers who wished to become writers.[22] She observes that "the best writing is done by men," then attributes American women's general authorial shortcomings to their deficient educations. She moves to proposing that some subjects for writing are the particular property of women, who could learn to depict those topics by practicing carefully; then limits her examples of "the most celebrated and most admired writing" available for imitation to male-written texts. She creates an analogy for such study of models that cast the aspiring writer as another male ("a gymnast [who] becomes graceful by constant use of his muscles"), then offers specific examples of pages in Hawthorne's *American Note-Books* that combine both masculine and feminine experiences (e.g., "digging potatoes" and working as a "little seamstress"). In short, Stowe's position on the possibility that (other) women might become successful professional writers—much less highly regarded ones—is unclear even in an essay where she purportedly seeks to help female readers achieve just such a goal.

Another relevant point should be raised about Stowe's depiction of would-be women authors and her attitude toward them. Many of her less encouraging comments exemplify the perspective of someone already vested with professional authority determining to share it with others only *after* they have earned it—a common stance in other traditionally male professions, such as medicine and the law. Admittedly, such conceptions of professionalism as having carefully regulated membership do not always exclude in the end. In other words, just because Stowe depicts writing as difficult does not mean in itself that she expresses doubt that other women could ever succeed at it. We should surely note, however, that her repeated emphasis on the *degree* of difficulty involved in achieving success is often cast in distancing terms. The opening paragraph of "Can I Write?" is consistent with that kind of monitoring and even with a rather exclusionary perspective toward other would-be women professionals. Invoking an editorial "we" and moving toward a distinction between already-professional authors like herself and mere aspiring ones, Stowe notes that "[w]riting is becoming a source of income to many women in these days, and we get many letters, the general drift and purport of which is to ask the question ["Can I Write?"] we have put at the head of this article." Stowe then confides that she "often" finds these letters "touching, eloquent, interesting—of a kind which make us wish with all our hearts that the authors of them could, as they desire to do, make writing a source of profit" (1869a, 40). Even as she portrays herself as feeling sympathy for these correspondents, however, Stowe declares their submissions to be "not of a kind which would justify our giving encouragement to the writers." Why not? "In short," her editorial voice intones, "the style of a graceful, easy, feminine letter-writer is something so different from what is necessary in newspaper or magazine articles, that one can seldom form a judgment from a lady's letter as to what she could do" (40). By claiming that she finds these letters from women readers to be "touching, eloquent and interesting" but that she also feels herself to be unable to "form a judgment from a lady's letter as to what she could do," Stowe distances herself—the published author-editor and thus the arbiter of professional writing—from the milieu of *unprofessional* literacy, which she casts in feminine terms and for which (mere) letter writing could not suffice to make meaning in a public, professional sphere. Though she eventually moves on within the body of the article to provide numerous helpful suggestions both global and specific, Stowe takes an initial stance toward her female correspondents that still contains them in a culture of letters distinct from her own, especially given that, even in her most supportive passages, she continues to hold back from full affirmation of their wishes or their abilities. The rhetorical devices she calls upon to maintain this distance include repeated invocation of a rather royal editorial "we" (implying her close association with the male community of already professional authors like Hawthorne and Irving), frequent use of subjunctive verb forms and qualifying connectors when describing aspiring women writers' work (e.g., "If it be so . . . "); repetition of negatives in connection with their writing (e.g., "It is not enough," "have not succeeded"), and the choice to frame three of the four titles for the series in very tentative question forms, from the point of view of the would-be writer ("Can I Write?" "How Shall I Learn to Write?", and "How May I Know That I Can Make a Writer?").

If Stowe's attitude toward her female readers-who-would-be-writers seems ambivalent through most of the series, her negative stance toward them is most pronounced in the 30 January installment, where she offers her striking final thoughts on the topic of female literary professionalism. Stowe opens "How May I Know That I Can Make a Writer?" with an attack-like description of an "unfortunate class of persons troublesome [both] to themselves and others from the fact that they suppose themselves to have a call and a talent for doing certain things, when, in fact, these are the very things for which they have neither call nor talent" (1869d, 88). After asserting that spending as many hours as the hard-working Paganini trying to make music would never make a tone-deaf amateur into a true musician, she complains that such "persons forget one thing: it is not merely practice that makes perfect, but *practice resulting from a natural aptitude* in a certain direction . . . " (88). While her reference to the well-known male artist Paganini as an unreachable model is telling in and of itself, perhaps even more notable in the opening salvo against the inept amateur is Stowe's insistent pulling back from her earlier emphasis on hard work as the main ingredient for success as a writer. We should juxtapose this column's dismissive lead paragraphs against the comforting suggestion in "Can I Write?" that aspiring authors might start learning the craft "the way that artists begin to draw," "not . . . [by trying] the cartoon of an historical picture," but with more modest practice activities such as sketching "an eye, a hand, a foot," and then moving on to more challenging pieces (1869a, 40). Similarly striking is the contrast between her insistence in the last installment that having "a restless desire to be a painter or sculptor" would not ensure success even for someone who practiced incessantly and her encouraging earlier suggestion "to our young students" that they study and then work to emulate "some special pages of Hawthorne's *American Note-Books*" (1869b, 56).

By the final installment of her series, Stowe appears to have shifted her position on the qualifications for serious authorship from a flexible (or unstable) view allowing for hard-working lady writers to achieve professional status, at least within some venues and for some audiences, to a more elitist stance affiliating her own work and current status with masculine-gendered standards of excellence. Interestingly, she depicted this firming up of her position not as a shift but rather as a clarification:

> We have endeavored, in our last papers, to induce persons who have a natural talent for writing to cultivate themselves by sedulous and careful practise, and have set before them the example of one of our greatest American artists, whose industry in self-cultivation was equaled only by his genius. But if Hawthorne had not had a natural genius for writing, do you suppose keeping a journal and writing down minutely the particulars of every squirrel and walnut-shrub, and bird and leaf and flower and man and woman he saw, would have enabled him to compose the *Scarlet Letter*?
>
> . . . Our remarks as to culture, then, were directed to those who have confessedly some natural gift—or what is called, for want of a better word, *genius—for writing*; and our object was to show them how this gift or *genius*, supposing it to exist, was good for very little without laborious and careful study and culture. (1869d, 88, emphasis added)

Along with these rather obviously labored moves to portray herself as consistent, another intriguing aspect of Stowe's assertion of elitism was her effort to justify her exclusionary stance by referring to the correspondence that she had been receiving in response to the series' earlier installments: "Since writing these articles, we have received other letters, saying over again what we so often hear—that their authors wish to become writers for the papers, because writing for the paper is an easy way of earning money." Stowe's response to these wishes to use writing for "easy . . . money" was markedly sarcastic:

> So it is, dear lady, if Providence has given you talent for saying things—if you have a natural gift of expression; but some of your letters do not indicate this. They do not show, so far as we can see, either that you have anything to say which you think it might be useful to have said, or that you have any particular facility in the matter of expressing yourself at all, but only that you would like to make money by writing. (88)

In this record of a dialogic encounter with her "dear lady" reader, Stowe most clearly unveils a stronger affiliation with masculine conceptions of "the success of genius" than in her earlier pieces. Here her address to this would-be "lady" author eschews the maternally mentoring tone of her earlier sketches in the series and replaces it with a deprecating lecture, dismissing both the letter writer and her goal, which Stowe *now* judges inadequate—"to make money by writing." In the final piece for this series of essays, Stowe rejects the model of open access to the professional women's authorship that her earlier sketches had affirmed, however tentatively. Furthermore, by indirectly asserting her own position among those possessing "a talent for saying things" or "a natural gift," Stowe erases the social support systems that had nurtured her own writing to link her personal story of professionalization with a model of individual genius, whereby "[a] young man (or woman), unknown, without patronage or means of putting himself forward" draws upon special talents (like those of "Dickens, Thackeray, all the best writers") to excel. At another extreme, she declares, the hapless pretenders who simply wish they could be writers had better give up the goal: "There are a great many persons setting their hopes on writing as a profession to whom a friend could do no greater kindness than to convince them . . . that it would not be worth their while to try. Better plant a peach-orchard, and flood the world with rosy peaches . . . than to write second-rate poems and trashy stories" (88). Such doomed aspirants to the role of professional author, Stowe indicates, should step aside for the few who, even if they started out as a "nameless power," would eventually "burst forth," like the great Hawthorne, to full-fledged success (88).

Stowe returns to a more rousingly populist tone for her essay's last paragraph, predicting that "[i]f the public want to hear you, if they call for you, if what you say begins to pass from hand to hand, and heart to heart, then go at it with courage" (88). However, since this scenario is limited to those who could be true "artists," the end note of the series is still one of clear constraint and elitism, positioning Stowe the writer-editor, at this point in her own career, on the side of high culture, espousing an increasingly elitist, male-dominated vision of what professional authorship in the United States should be. Leaving a part of her own legacy behind, then, in her *Hearth and Home* series, Stowe articulates and promulgates a model of professional literature making that would exclude others trying to follow the road she had originally taken herself. Thus, whatever the aesthetic shortcomings we might identify today in this particular series of essays and in the whole body of her work for the periodical, we can see that some of her labor there helped undermine the very traditions of domestic, popular authorship that had supported her own progress into gendered professionalism.

## NOTES

This article is reprinted from Aleta Feinsod Cane and Susan Alves, eds. 2001. *"The Only Efficient Instrument": American Women Writers and the Periodical, 1873–1916.* Iowa City: The University of Iowa Press, 45–65.

1. See Heininger's *At Home with a Book* (1986) discussions of reading habits and the furnishings associated with them in nineteenth-century culture. I wish to thank Diana Royce, then librarian at the Stowe-Day Library in Hartford, Connecticut, for suggesting

that I review Stowe's writing on authorship in *Hearth and Home* and for finding copies of the periodical for me. Support for my research was provided by the regents of the University System of Georgia, with Stowe's essays being recovered in part for a team-taught course on American women's work during the nineteenth century.

2. Fern (1811–87), whose real name was Sara Payson Willis Eldredge Farrington Parton, is today remembered for her novel *Ruth Hall* (1855) but was best known in her day as a vibrant journalist. She was the first woman in America to write a signed column in a newspaper. Her witty and engaging work for Robert Bonner's *New York Ledger* (which ran from 1856 to 1872) helped increase the newspaper's circulation from 100,000 to 400,000 by 1860.

3. Okker characterizes this stance as one of "relative informality and an assumed equal and personal relationship between editor and readers," making use of such friendly addresses as "old friends" for readers (Okker 1995, 23). Along those lines, in the "How to Treat Babies" sketch cited earlier, Stowe began by declaring that a "friend has sent us an article on a subject suggested by us" (1869e, 104). Similarly, "What Shall the Girls Read?" opens by referencing a letter from "a young friend in the Female Seminary at Steubenville" and then moves to a response, with the salutation "My Dear Rose" (1869h, 408).

4. See Alice Walker's moving essay, "In Search of Our Mother's Gardens" (1983).

5. Certainly Stowe was not an extreme radical. She identified herself as non-abolitionist while living in Cincinnati. Even *Uncle Tom's Cabin* (despite its initial publication site in the *National Era*) drew as carefully on the conservative rhetoric of republican motherhood as it did on the more liberal stance of white women's abolitionist writing. See my "Gendering the History of the Antislavery Narrative." See also Hedrick's "Woman's Rights" chapter, where she says that, despite being drawn to the women's movement, Stowe could not imagine her name "on the masthead of a journal called the *Revolution*" (1994, 361).

6. Of course, many male canonical writers of the nineteenth century produced work judged, in our own time, as uneven or even pedestrian. Melville's *Pierre*, Hawthorne's *Marble Faun*, as well as several of Twain's works, have incurred critical attack at times.

7. Examining Stowe's series of writing thus seems quite consistent with Susan Albertine's recent observations in the introduction to *A Living in Words*. Albertine cautions against setting "a fixed reading of women's participation in print culture," and stresses that "there is no one female response to the print business, any more than there is a set patriarchal reaction to women who venture into traditionally male preserves" (1995, xvi).

8. One helpful context for interpreting Stowe's work for this and other periodicals, as well as her advice to aspiring authors, is offered by Christopher P. Wilson's chapter "'Magazining' for the Masses," where he points out that "[s]ince mid-century, the magazine had occupied a middle landscape between the frenetic world of newspaper work and the status of book writing," and that magazines had an "intermediary position" in publishing, often providing "a vocational springboard" (1985, 41). See also Wilson's discussions of "the commercial motive" driving work by editors and writers for magazines (46).

9. See Warren's treatment of the productive, mutually respectful relationship between Bonner and Fern. Warren includes details about Bonner's announcing in

print that he was paying Fern the until-then-unheard-of sum of one hundred dollars per column and his later bragging in another issue of the *Ledger* that his investment had already been paid back "three times over" due to increased circulation (56).

10. See Streitmatter's essay on Josephine St. Pierre Ruffin in *A Living in Words*. As Streitmatter points out, "Ruffin devoted most of her energies to the business side of publishing," including trying out a number of strategies for increasing circulation of her newspaper, the *Woman's Era*: "She did not intend to make a financial profit from her newspaper, but she expected it to pay for itself" (1995, 53, 54–58).

11. John R. Adams described Stowe's duties at *Hearth and Home* as "slighter than her title of associate editor suggested," that is, "limited to supplying a weekly column, with [coeditor] Mitchell shouldering the main labors" (1989, 80). Both Hedrick and Okker, however, depict Stowe as more actively involved in the range of editorial duties, and whether or not she served as prime shaper of the periodical's overall content, her writing *about* professional writing in *Hearth and Home* highlights women's complex position in the literary marketplace at that historical moment.

12. See "What Shall the Girls Read?" An example of Stowe's negative attitude toward young ladies' formal education appeared in "How Shall I Learn to Write?" (16 Jan. 1869), where she observed: "The education of the woman stops short at the point where the boy's education really begins. At the age that the boy enters college for an arduous and mature course, the girl comes home and addresses herself to going into company; and the five or six years following, that her brother spends in severe intellectual drill, she fritters away in what is called society" (56). This complaint was echoed in the opening to "What Shall the Girls Read?" where Stowe printed a letter from a "Rose P.," who wondered about what she and her classmates could do for a "course of reading for girls after they leave school" (408). After attacking the limited learning available to seminary graduates at that time, Stowe outlined such a course.

13. Stowe's position on the need for improving women's education was consistent with her sister Catherine's and with Sarah Josepha Hale's, as expressed in the *Ladies' Magazine* and, later, *Godey's Lady's Book*. Hale initiated her campaign for improved female education very early on and sustained it throughout her long editorship. A few examples from the many pro-education pieces early in her tenure include "Female Education," "How Ought Woman to Be Educated," and the "Female Seminaries" series appearing in 1833.

14. This would not be the first time Stowe was accused of unfeminine writing, of course. Some of the most vitriolic critiques of *Uncle Tom's Cabin* attacked her on this very point. Stowe's awareness that revealing details of Lord Byron's illicit relations could well produce a similar complaint against her may help explain why she wanted to devote focused time to writing her defense of his wife (Hedrick 1994, 356–57).

15. In 1892, at a reunion of the seminary, Brace was remembered in a major address. (Both Catherine and Harriet had worked there in the 1820s, and John Brace had later served as principal in the early 1830s.) The speaker praising Brace's contribution to female pedagogy was Isabella Beecher Hooker, another of Harriet's sisters, and the majority of Hooker's talk was actually a reading of Stowe's words about her former teacher, as written for the familially composed biography of Lyman Beecher years earlier. References to pages from this talk are cited within the body of the essay as "Hartford." Quotations from Hooker's speech about Brace represent *her* quoting of Stowe.

16. Stowe's support of gendered topics and locations for writing, then, appears here to be quite different from one Joyce Warren has recently identified with Sara Parton (Fanny Fern). Warren argues that Fern "preferred a paper that was intended for both sexes, she said, because it put her 'on the same level as the men in the house.' The *Ledger* was such a paper" (1992, 59), with Fern enjoying an unusual free rein since her male editor never altered her writing (64).

17. See, in this regard, Hedrick's insightful discussion of "The *Atlantic* and the Ship of State" in her biography of Stowe, especially her description of the magazine's perceived mission (1994, 288), her explanation that "women were not full-fledged members of the *Atlantic* club" (289), and her treatment of the infamous dinner purportedly arranged "for" Stowe but actually carried out in ways that reinforced the increasingly masculinized slant of both the periodical and its view of literature's place in national culture (290–91).

18. Stowe erases (or at least obscures) social class differences here, just as she does racial ones elsewhere in her writing for *Hearth and Home*. In one of her pieces on girls' proper reading choices, for instance, she observes: "[I]f a girl, when she leaves school, will be resolute and determined, especially for the first few weeks, she may form such a habit of regular reading as will be of the greatest possible use to her. . . . I recommend that you take some one particular country; and since we are of Anglo Saxon origin, it had better be England. But as we are also partly French in our origin, and as English history for a great many hundred years consists almost entirely in the quarrels between the French and the English, you will do well to take the French history along with it (1869h, 408)." In this case, Stowe imagined all young ladies having the seminary experience her purported correspondent "Rose" did, as well as the chances for continued home study not as available to working-class girls. Similarly, her references to the "Anglo Saxon" and "French" background that "we" share with her reflect not only a view of who her audience is—white European-American females—but also her tendency to equate that audience with all (who really matter) in womankind.

19. The *Mayflower* anthology was originally published in 1842 by *Harper's*. According to the introduction written for an 1896 reissuing of some of its contents in *Stories, Sketches and Studies*, Stowe's early magazine writing marks her as already "an active litterateur" by the early 1840s but one for whom financial rewards were still "meagre" (1896, vii). Thus, the 1842 *Mayflower* anthology had only "a modest reception, and a short life" until her blockbuster novel prompted an 1855 republication by Phillips and Sampson (vii).

20. See Hedrick's comment that Stowe originally predicted to editor Gamaliel Bailey that her submission would "run 'through three or fours numbers,'" and would take the form of "a series of sketches" (1994, 208).

21. See Brodhead, chapter 3, "Manufacturing You into a Personage." Stowe's discussions of Hawthorne in her series on authorship provide one example of what Brodhead describes as "writers' cultural identities [being] created and sustained by an interlocking network of literary agencies in the nineteenth century, agencies that were themselves being fashioned at the same time as those authors' writings" (1986, 58).

22. The combination of her restraining and authorizing advice echoes what Nicole Hoffman has described as Hale's stance toward women readers. Hoffman

observes: "Paradoxically, the ideas her publications promulgated were both constraining and enabling to that readership" (1990, 51).

## WORKS CITED

Adams, John R. (1989). *Harriet Beecher Stowe*. Boston: Twayne.

Albertine, Susan. 1995. Introduction to *A Living of Words: American Women in Print Culture*, ed. Susan Albertine, xi–xxi. Knoxville: University of Tennessee Press.

Brodhead, Richard H. 1986. *The School of Hawthorne*. New York: Oxford University Press.

Hedrick, Joan D. 1994. *Harriet Beecher Stowe: A Life*. New York: Oxford.

Heininger, Mary Lynn Stevens. 1986. *At Home With a Book: Reading in America, 1840–1940*. Rochester, NY: Strong Museum.

Hoffman, Nicole Tonovich. 1990. "Legacy Profile: Sarah Josepha Hale." *Legacy* 7: 47–55.

Mott, Frank Luther. 1930. *A History of American Magazines: 1741–1850*. Cambridge: Harvard University Press, 1930.

Okker, Patricia. 1995. *Our Sisters Editors: Sarah J. Hale and the Tradition of Nineteenth-Century American Women Editors*. Athens: University of Georgia Press.

Robbins, Sarah. 1997. "Gendering the History of the Antislavery Narrative: Juxtaposing *Uncle Tom's Cabin* and *Benito Cereno, Beloved* and *Middle Passage*." *American Quarterly* 49 (3): 531–73.

Stowe, Harriet Beecher. 1855. *The Mayflower and Miscellaneous Writings*. Boston: Phillips, Sampson.

———. 1869a. "Can I Write?" *Hearth and Home*. 9 January, 40–41.

———. 1869b. "How Shall I Learn to Write?" *Hearth and Home*. 16 January, 56.

———. 1869c. "Faults of Inexperienced Writers." *Hearth and Home*. 23 January, 72.

———. 1869d. "How May I Know That I Can Make a Writer?" *Hearth and Home*. 30 January 88.

———. 1869e. "How To Treat Babies." *Hearth and Home*. 6 February, 104.

———. 1869f. "Growing Things." *Hearth and Home*. 6 March, 168.

———. 1869g. "The Cheapness of Beauty." *Hearth and Home*. 20 March, 200.

———. 1869h. "What Shall The Girls Read?" *Hearth and Home*. 19 June, 408.

———. 1869i. "The Woman Question." *Hearth and Home*. 7 August, 520.

———. 1896. *Stories, Sketches and Studies*. Cambridge, MA: Riverside Press.

———. 1993. *The Harriet Beecher Stowe Reader*, ed. Cynthia Reik. Hartford, CT: Stowe-Day Foundation.

Streitmatter, Rodger. 1995. "Josephine St. Pierre Ruffin: Pioneering African-American Newspaper Publisher." In Albertine, 1995, 49–64.

Walker, Alice. 1983. "In Search of Our Mothers' Gardens." In *In Search of Our Mothers' Gardens*, ed. Alice Walker, 241–43. New York: Harcourt.

Warren, Joyce W. 1992. *Fanny Fern: An Independent Woman*. New Brunswick, NJ: Rutgers University Press.

Wilson, Christopher P. 1985. *The Labor of Words: Literary Professionalism in the Progressive Era*. Athens: University of Georgia Press.

# The "Least Drop of Oil"

## Locating Narrative Authority in Harriet Beecher Stowe's *The Minister's Wooing*

*Christiane E. Farnan*

The perceived absence of narrative authority in Harriet Beecher Stowe's *The Minister's Wooing* (1859) has served as a frustrating puzzle for Stowe critics eager to prove the regional novel, as Lawrence Buell so declares, to be "unjustly overshadowed" (1978, 260) by *Uncle Tom's Cabin*. Buell's proclamation is made despite lamenting Stowe's alleged "miscellaneous ensemble" of "tour-de-force-like essays on the New England kitchen . . . thumbnail biographies of secondary characters . . . and genre sketches of ministerial teas and quilting bees" (269). He argues that the novel lacks an organized narrative world presented by an authoritative narrative voice—a voice the character of the historical Calvinist minister Samuel Hopkins, rather than Stowe's overt, heterodiegetic narrator—could have provided. To Buell, Hopkins embodies the "vital center" (264) of *The Minister's Wooing*, who should have served as the voice of Stowe's Newport novel because of his historical authoritative prominence in the eighteenth-century Newport community. Thus, despite his admiration for Stowe's writing, Buell ultimately views *The Minister's Wooing* as a failed novel.

Buell was among the first of those early critics who reintroduced Stowe to readers as the author of valuable nineteenth-century American novels other than *Uncle Tom's Cabin*, but he was not the last to search for evidence of an authoritative textual voice in *The Minister's Wooing*. Nor was he the last to attempt to locate the source of narrative authority in the voice of a white, privileged male—that could even exist beyond the narrated world. Dorothy Baker, for example, argues that Stowe constructed *The Minister's Wooing*'s narrator as a participant in an ongoing dialogue with the professional, educated, male narrative voice of Oliver Wendell Holmes's *Atlantic Monthly* column "The Professor at the Breakfast Table" and that the narrator's authority stems from this association (2000, 27–38). Christopher Wilson also attributes the narrator's authority to extratextual sources; he argues that *The Minister's Wooing*'s abolitionist and anti-Calvinist arguments are authorized through Stowe's allusions to William Shakespeare's *The Tempest* and Charles Dickens's *Hard Times* (1985, 554–77).

These intriguing and seemingly logical theories are difficult to resist because the female voices emitting from the novel are marginalized female voices, voices not traditionally associated with nineteenth-century New England figures of social, political, or religious authority: Miss Prissy, a middle-aged gossipy dressmaker; Candace, a slave woman stolen from Africa in her teens; Mrs. Marvyn, a near-mad grieving mother; Mary, a young devout girl coerced into betrothal. Miss Prissy's courageous words bring Dr. Hopkins to his senses and save Mary from a loveless marriage; Candace gains her manumission by voicing her desire for freedom; Mrs. Marvyn denounces the dark determinist core of Calvinism that renders marriage and child-rearing a deadly torment; and Mary's public prayer reveals the transformative grace of New Testament forgiveness to a community frozen in fear of a vengeful Old Testament God. The textual voice of *The Minister's Wooing* continually reveals the antislavery, anti-Calvinist ideologies and values of the Newport community through female characters who operate from supposed positions of powerlessness.

For the purposes of this essay's search for a textual voice through which authority is conveyed in *The Minister's Wooing*, I will refer to narratologist Susan Sniader Lanser's model of the "communal" narrative voice, which she developed in her study *Fictions of Authority: Women Writers and Narrative Voice*.[1] Lanser points to the correlation between a narrator's "discursive authority" and his or her conformity to "dominant social power" (1992, 6). A narrator's authority is rooted in "the intellectual credibility, ideological validity, and aesthetic value" conferred upon him or her by the reader. Whether or not the reader cedes to the narrator's quest for authority, Lanser argues, greatly depends upon the narrator's status, acts of self-representation (6), or on how the narrator aligns or does not align him- or herself with broad patriarchal authority. At first glance, Stowe's heterodiegetic narrator's alliance with marginalized female voices in *The Minister's Wooing* casts doubts upon her ability to maintain traditional authority in the narrative as she never relies upon the powerful, threatening, patriarchal structure of Calvinism to support her own position. It is therefore not surprising that identifying an authoritative narrative voice in *The Minister's Wooing* has proved difficult for critics in the last twenty-five years. I suggest that critics have recognized the powerful existence of Stowe's narrative voice but have been unable to isolate and categorize the voice successfully because this particular voice speaks for the entire Newport community, not merely from an individual speaker's point of view. The narrative voice practices the empathetic narration techniques that Judith Fetterley and Marjorie Pryse identified and analyzed in many nineteenth-century regional short stories and novels, yet moves beyond an empathetic relationship with regional characters to a symbiotic narrative voice whose identity and ideologies meld with the identity and ideologies of a community. I argue that in *The Minister's Wooing* Stowe created that type of authoritative textual voice that Lanser calls "communal": a narrative mode characterized by "a spectrum of practices that articulate either a collective voice or a collective of voices that share narrative authority" and related primarily to "marginal and suppressed communities" (1992, 21).

Stowe's narrative voice in *The Minister's Wooing* can be defined as communal because it meets the three central requirements identified by Lanser. First, the narrative authority of *The Minister's Wooing* is "invested in a definable community and textually inscribed . . . through the voice of a single individual who is manifestly authorized by [the] community" (21). Second, the communal mode in *The Minister's Wooing* is empowered by the "marginal or suppressed" members of nineteenth-century Newport. Third, the communal voice focuses upon female community as a whole rather than on "individual protagonists and personal plots" (1992, 22).

Susan Harris recognizes the connection between authority and community identity in *The Minister's Wooing*. Acknowledging that "[m]uch of the authority assumed by Stowe's narrator comes from the author's own familiarity with the historical issues she engages" (1999, ix), Harris argues that "as a scion of the Beecher dynasty, Stowe saw herself as part of regional history . . . her parents' courtship and marriage . . . were legendary in both familial and regional annals" (xi). Born into a family that made post-Revolutionary New England Calvinist and educational history and she herself a critical member of pre–Civil War educational abolitionist moral activism, Stowe easily created a voice seemingly steeped in post-Revolutionary New England history. The narrative voice has a reciprocal relationship with her own narrative; the source of her authority is the Newport community itself, yet the manifestation of the community's authority stems from the narrator's representation of both herself as a member of the Newport community and of Newport as a valuable community. Carolyn Karcher also points to the power in what she calls "the most experimental of Stowe's novels," arguing that "Stowe's narrator speaks as a member of the community, setting herself on par with the other characters comprising it, and aligning her own art of narration with the domestic arts its female members practice" (2004, 213).

The first two paragraphs of *The Minister's Wooing* illustrate the narrator's refusal to assume the traditional authoritarian voice of the dominant culture. The first paragraph consists of one sentence: "Mrs. Katy Scudder had invited Mrs. Brown and Mrs. Jones and Deacon Twitchel's wife to take tea

with her on the afternoon of June second, A.D. 17——" ([1859] 1994, 1).
Dorothy Baker rightly describes this line as "a formulaic social announce-
ment placed in a local newspaper" (2000, 29), and the novel opens as
though the narrative voice were reading through a stack of saved clippings,
looking for an item to catch her interest. The voice continues:

> When one has a story to tell, one is always puzzled which end of it to begin at.
> You have a whole crop of people to introduce that *you* know and your reader
> doesn't; and one thing so presupposes another, that, whichever way you turn
> your patchwork, the figures still seem ill-arranged. The small item which I have
> given will do as any other to begin with, as it certainly will lead you to ask,
> 'Pray, who was Mrs. Katy Scudder?'—and this will start me systematically on
> my story. (1)

The manner in which the narrative voice begins *The Minister's Wooing*
provides immediate evidence that the narrator is speaking in the mode
Lanser has defined as "communal." With an abrupt change in style and
direction, the narrator contemplates narrative construction. She begins with
the use of the formal pronoun "one," but switches immediately into the
familiar "you" form of address, thus bonding with both her real and her
imagined readers. As the narrator talks, she begins gently to transform her
straightforward, linear, formal narrative into an open-ended, overlapping,
communal narrative in which she "know[s]" (Stowe [1859] 1994, 1) her
characters. The tale of *The Minister's Wooing* is the tale of a community, so
any community member would serve "as any other to begin with" (1). A
story must start somewhere, so the narrator begins with a character, Mrs.
Katy Scudder, and with an imagined reader that will not passively listen to
"formulaic" narrative, but who will interrupt, ask questions, and propel the
narrative forward.

The reader is guided to ask about Mrs. Katy Scudder; hers is the only first
name given in that opening line. The widow Scudder's life story reintro-
duces the reader to the "forgotten past" culture of the Newport community,
underscores the narrator's knowledge of the historical Newport community,
and also emphasizes the importance of community stories. Through Katy
Scudder, the reader sees Newport as a bustling seaport in which courtship
rituals and efficient housekeeping are not trivialized but debated alongside
Calvinist theology and slavery at the tea table. Horses, boats, moonlit walks
on the shore, spinning, churning, baking, reading, and visiting fill the days
of Newport residents while their minds wrestle with "the doctrine of entire
Disinterested Benevolence" (30). Other stories are presented in a nonlinear
fashion and the communication network of Newport is revealed to consist
of gossip. As the narrator states, gossip "has its noble side to it. . . . Show
me a person who lives in a country village absolutely without curiosity or

interest . . . and I will show you a cold, fat oyster, to whom the tide-mud of propriety is the whole of existence" (192). Neighbors eagerly tell each other's stories over and over again because they care enough to tell them. As the gentle medium for these stories, the narrator draws her own unique brand of narrative authority from her established membership in the Newport community.

The narrator identifies Mrs. Scudder as a confident woman of importance in Newport; not only can she hold her own against wealthier women of higher social standing, it is she who boards the highly esteemed Dr. Hopkins. Declaring Mrs. Scudder a woman of utmost organization and domestic accomplishments, the narrative voice refers to Mrs. Scudder as a woman of "faculty," a New England term as familiar to the Newport community as unconditional submission. So sure and ordered, the woman of faculty

> shall scrub floors, wash, wring, bake, brew, and yet her hands shall be small and white; she shall have no perceptible income, yet always be handsomely dressed; she shall have no servant in the house,—with a dairy to manage, hired men to feed, a boarder or two to care for, unheard of pickling and preserving to do,—and yet you commonly see her every afternoon sitting at her shady parlor-window behind the lilacs, cool and easy, hemming muslin cap-strings or reading the latest new book. (3)

The narrator shares this communal knowledge of the woman of faculty in general, and Mrs. Scudder in particular, with the reader. Gently, and without even seeming to, the narrator builds her authority on the basis that the reader shares in her own cultural and historical knowledge. Lanser argues that for a narrator to be granted authority by the reader, she must prove that the identity she is presenting is "intellectually and morally trustworthy" (1981, 170). In other words, a communal narrator must convince the reader that the information she has gathered came from accurate community sources or first-hand community experiences. Stowe's narrator smoothly achieves this by telling a story that is "fictively true, but not necessarily tied to historical reality" (174) by constructing the reader as a member of the New England history and culture of which the narrator is speaking.

The narrator of *The Minister's Wooing* is overt and heterodiegetic, but she tells the story as though she is a homodiegetic narrator, a first-person narrator who at some point existed within the world of her story. As Lanser points out, the communal "narrators retain the syntax of 'first-person' narrative" even as "their texts avoid the markers of individuality that characterize personal vice and thereby resist the equation of narrator and protagonist" (1992, 241). Urging her imagined readers to recall "personal memories" and "participate in creating the fictional world itself" (Warhol

1989, 37), the narrator continues to meld the imagined reader's memories with her own implied memories. The narrator asks:

> [P]erhaps, Sir, you remember your grandmother's floor, of snowy boards sanded with whitest sand; you remember the ancient fireplace stretching quite across one end, a vast cavern, in each corner of which a cozy seat might be found. . . . Oh, that kitchen of the olden times, the old, clean, roomy, New England kitchen. . . . With all our ceiled houses, let us not forget our grand-mothers' kitchens! (Stowe [1859] 1994, 16–17)

As the storyteller, the narrative voice fleshes out the domestic details of late eighteenth-century Newport and the characters within those domestic spaces, until the narrator becomes the community-authorized spokes-woman of "our grandmothers' kitchens" (17) and "our" Newport. Accord-ing to Lanser, the speaker has even "explicitly define[d] . . . her presumed readership" (1981, 92) by placing the American collective memory in a New England past and bringing her readers, in essence, "back" to Newport with her. Since the reader is constructed as an active and equal participant in the telling of *The Minister's Wooing*, the "overt contact" (1981, 174) between the narrator and the reader transcends the dominant masculine "superior I / inferior you" narrative hierarchy and establishes a welcoming, communal, "powerful we" voice. The narrator establishes herself as the "authoritative mediator" of Newport to the greater community of readers as the Newport community itself is "represented as the very source of her (textual) identity" (Lanser 1992, 241).

Marginalized members of the community, women who stand outside Newport's formal religious and economic hierarchy centered on Dr. Hop-kins and wealthy landowning farmers, but who nonetheless are critical to the functioning of the community, contribute to Stowe's creation of a communal narrative voice as their dialogue triggers transformative change in the community. The narrator's "unequivocal" membership in the New-port community is further supported by her representation of not just the community's history and culture, but also through what Lanser refers to as a "community's discursive practices . . . letters, stories, conversations, gossip" (243). A number of community members disperse their own judg-ments regarding fear, love, slavery, and Calvinism, among other domestic matters, through unregulated direct discourse, in which characters' speech acts are not commented upon by the narrator but nonetheless contribute to the ideologies advocated by the narrator as community representative. In *The Narrative Act*, Lanser writes that the "expression of ideology by any given voice may first of all be explicit on the surface of the discourse or more deeply embedded in the narrator's speech activity" (1981, 216) and ideological expressions delivered through the community's discourse seem to be understood as communally acceptable if the discourse triggers a narrative consequence, such as change in plot, or a narrative event that has a profound impact on the communal narrative.

As O'Harae states, all the main women characters "play an integral part in the narration of the story" and "decide how different events should be interpreted" (2005, 73). Red-and-yellow turbaned Candace, the Marvyn's exotic slave who "crooned . . . strange, wild African legends" (Stowe [1859] 1994, 67) is the first character to assume control of the communal narrative as she contradicts Mr. Marvyn, not only her owner, but a privileged man of considerable education, wealth, and importance, who firmly believes his "slaves do not desire liberty, and would not take it, if it were offered" (102). Candace's speech, once the question is put to her, stands alone in the text, with no narrative judgment, commentary or other explanations for the reader: Candace's words speak for themselves: "Why, look at me. I ain't a crit-ter. I's neider huffs nor horns. I's a reasonable bein',—a woman,—as much a woman as anybody. . . . I want to feel free. Dem dat isn't free has nuffin to gib to nobdy;—dey can't show what dey would do" (102). Candace's direct speech act has specific results; she is immediately manumitted and at once gains self-authority as well as a stronger voice in the community narrative.

Candace speaks twice more with similar revolutionary results. Mrs. Marvyn's hideous grief over the supposed drowning death of her son (and Mary's lover) James serves to highlight Mrs. Scudder's fears for Mary and her motive in coercing her betrothal to Dr. Hopkins. Christopher Wilson argues that "Mrs. Marvyn's crisis, while certainly vivid, is not at all the centerpiece of the plot" (1985, 563), but the narrator makes central use of her agony in the community's ideological shift away from Calvinism. The narrative voice does not soften or mitigate one word of Mrs. Marvyn's violent rage as she envisions the predetermined hell Calvinist doctrine has imposed upon her nonbeliever son. Speaking of something "long repressed," Mrs. Marvyn vents her anger upon a God that wastes "noble minds . . . warm, generous hearts . . . splendid natures" that "are wrecked and thrown away by the thousands . . . every new family is built over this awful pit of despair, and only one in a thousand escapes" (Stowe [1859] 1994, 346). Contradicting what she believes to be the very Word of God himself, Mrs. Marvyn shrieks, "It is *not* right! . . . I can never love God! I can never praise him! I am lost! lost! lost!" (348). Her despair cannot be calmed by her husband, by Dr. Hopkins, by any representative of dominant authority, but it is calmed by another speech of Candace's who declares that someone needs to "talk *gospel* to her" (348).

The scene between Candace and Mrs. Marvyn is presented in long stretches of directly reported dialogue, with only the briefest of references to Mrs. Marvyn's "despairing wildness," and the narrator practically disappears inside Mary, whom she uses as a point-of-view character throughout the scene. Mary, "pale, aghast, horror-stricken" (349) with her own loss and Mrs. Marvyn's nightmarishly clear picture of the evils of the Calvinist God, is unable to comment on the context of Candace's speech. As a black woman whose religious beliefs remain separate from the white Calvinist doctrine, Candace reassures Mrs. Marvyn, "[Christ] knows all about mothers' hearts; He won't break yours" (350). In *The Minister's Wooing*, the rigid lines of Calvinist doctrine drive humans to the absolute limit of suffering, while the maternal image of Christ and the gentle, forgiving New Testament theology serve as salvation from insanity and death. Candace's consoling words—"I'm clar Mass'r James is one o' de 'lect; and I'm clar dar's consid'able more o' de 'lect dan people tink. Why, Jesus didn't die for nothin'—all dat love a'n't gwine be wasted" (350)—are what save Mrs. Marvyn. The narrator's emphasis on Candace's differences from the rest of the community—race, clothes, values—positions Candace as literally "freer" than those community members who are frozen by the dread of the Calvinist God, and Candace begins to "free" the community that manumitted her. Candace's marginal position allows her to assist in the community's spiritual transformation because she alone can console Mrs. Marvyn.

Candace speaks for "reason" as she deplores Mary's upcoming marriage to the considerably older Dr. Hopkins as she declares "*he* [the minister] *outer be told on't!*" (544) once James has returned from the sea, not drowned after all. Urged on by Candace, Miss Prissy enters Dr. Hopkins' study; "I've felt you ought to know it," Miss Prissy bravely tells the Minister. "If [James had] been alive, she'd never given the promise she has,—the promise that she means to keep, if her heart breaks and his too. They wouldn't anybody tell you, and I thought I must tell you; cause I thought you'd know what was right to do about it" (547–48). Miss Prissy's straightforward and highly emotional act takes an equitable part in the community's transformation from the "coldly analytical and elitist" system of Calvinism to "one which stressed democratic egalitarianism, intuitive emotion and communal selflessness" (Berkson 1980, 256). Miss Prissy's speech, again another example of a character's direct, reported dialogue with no narrative commentary, prompts Dr. Hopkins to release his young betrothed from her promise and frees Mary to wed James. Mary and James Marvyn, both proponents of the "loving kindness of the Lord" (Stowe [1859] 1994, 552), become the center of a reborn Newport community.

Stowe's communal voice depicts Newport as a potential utopia in which women and men unite and equally participate in the rejection of slavery and the transformation of Calvinism. *The Minister's Wooing* disrupts the systematic social, political, economic, and educational division by gender. Joan Hedrick argues that the novel reflects "the emergence of a non-judgmental and non-hierarchal value system that is implicitly at odds with authoritarian methods of [Stowe's] father" (1988, 309). Women are not shut out of political activism in *The Minister's Wooing* and men are equal participants in domestic affairs, yet it is clear that it is a female community that has enacted the transformation, enfolding the men. Susan Harris writes, "[b]y the end of the novel . . . the text-based, male-centered creed has been modified by a new authority, emanating from the women's community with Mary Scudder at its center: this authority is intuited rather than learned, premised on love rather than logic, achieved through community rather than isolation" (1999, xiii). Indeed, Mary's movement to the "center" of the women's community is orchestrated by the speech acts of Candace, Mrs. Marvyn, and Miss Prissy, for without their intercessions, Mary would be unhappily married to Dr. Hopkins and the entire community would still be frozen in the dread to which Mrs. Marvyn gives voice.

In her analysis of the communal mode, Lanser emphasizes the importance of the community over individual character, and in *The Minister's Wooing*, the "personal project" turns to "communal ends" (1992, 248) as the women's objective to save Mary becomes tied into the female community's objective to save themselves and transform Newport. The deep impact of Mrs. Marvyn's words upon Mary is painful, but the community as a whole benefits from Mary's temporary pain. True to the communal mode, the needs and desires of the individual character are secondary in regards to the requirements of the community. "She felt," reveals the narrator from within Mary's unconscious, "as if the point of a wedge were being driven between her life and her life's life;—between her and her God" (Stowe [1859] 1994, 343–45). The concrete image that Mary is forced to acknowledge is that of James in hell, and this image erases all possibilities of Mary's own chances at a "blessed" eternity. For the first time in her life, Mary questions Dr. Hopkins's teachings: "She had been taught that the agonies of the lost would be forever in sight of the saints, without abating in the least their eternal joys; nay, that they would find in it increasing motives to praise and adoration. Could it be so?" (350–51). Mary's crisis forces her to rethink and rewrite her individual spirituality, for she has come face to face with what the Calvinist belief system does to mothers: it forces them to protect themselves psychologically by distancing themselves emotionally from their children lest they suffer like Mrs. Marvyn.

After months of solitude and deep thought, Mary emerges a new woman, a spiritual leader of the community, during a weekly prayer meeting. The narrator assumes access to the communal consciousness (Lanser 1981, 180) as she recalls, "[The women] who heard her had the sensation of rising in the air, of feeling a celestial light and warmth descending into their souls" (Stowe [1859] 1994, 366). This "light and warmth" are the result of both the subject matter and the presentation of Mary's prayer. Using words the women felt were "winged angels," Mary

> spoke of a love passing knowledge—passing all love of lovers or mothers,—a love forever spending, yet never spent,—a love ever pierced and bleeding, yet ever constant and triumphant, rejoicing with infinite joy to bear in its own

body the sins and sorrows of a universe,—conquering, victorious love, rejoic-
ing to endure, panting to give, and offering its whole self with an infinite
joyfulness for our salvation. (366)

"Always a silent girl," Mary's "hour of utterance" arrives "in a praying circle of women of the church." Mary's prayer in the church serves
as an extension of Candace's words to Mrs. Marvyn. Miss Prissy cries,
"[T]hat prayer seemed to take us all right up and put us down in heaven"
(366–67). Surrounded by supportive women, Mary presents God not as
the angry, vengeful Lord Almighty, but as the maternal Christ, who bears
humans the greatest possible love, greater than even that of "lovers or
mothers" because of his absorption of human suffering. Through this
prayer, Mary founds a source of narrative power among women, presents
a new "collective vision" (Lanser 1992, 249) for a glorious new Newport
and brings tears to even Dr. Hopkins eyes.

Unfortunately, it also brings a proposal from Dr. Hopkins, a proposal
embraced by the "matrons and maidens" of the community as they call
"do tell" and "have you heard" to each other "at the spinning-wheel, in the
green clothes-yard, and at the foamy wash-tub" (Stowe [1859] 1994, 415).
The character of James, believed to no longer exist in the community story
of Newport, is fondly remembered, but "What a minister's wife [Mary'd]
be," Miss Prissy declares, speaking for "all the ladies coming out of prayer
meeting" (400). The communal discourse temporarily supports Mrs. Scudder's coercion of Mary into a loveless marriage with a man twice her age.
Psychologically tormented by three dead children with eternal fates unknown, Mrs. Scudder believes there is only one possible end to Mary's story
if she marries Dr. Hopkins: her precious daughter will not suffer the eternal
torments of hell. Calvinism wreaks trauma upon lovers and mothers:

> [A] tremendous, eternal future had so weighed down and compacted the fibers
> of her very soul, that all earthly things were but dust in comparison to it. That
> her child should be one elected to walk in white, to reign with Christ, was her
> one absorbing wish; and she looked on all the events of life only with reference
> to this. The way of life was narrow, the chances in favor of any child of Adam
> infinitely small; the best, the most seemingly pure and fair, was by nature a
> child of wrath, and could be saved only by a sovereign decree, by which it
> should be plucked as a brand from the burning . . . there was the sincerity of
> her whole being in the dread which she felt at the thought of her daughter's
> marriage with an unbeliever. (83)

As Mrs. Scudder presses Dr. Hopkins's proposal on her daughter, she
ignores the clear statement Mary makes regarding the idea of marrying
Dr. Hopkins. While both Candace and Mrs. Marvyn's expression of their
thoughts and desires are made in front of witnesses, Mary's timid refusal

is made only to her mother in the isolated space of her bedroom. Mary's separation from the community is horrible and cold as the narrative voice withdraws completely, no longer using her as a point-of-view character but instead presenting the scene through Mrs. Scudder's eyes.

Mary is quite clear in her feelings on this matter; "I wish he did not want to marry me, mother . . . I liked it a great deal better as we were before" (406). The narrator merely reports the dialogue between the two, and despite the lavish affection Mrs. Scudder bestows on Mary, the result is a stark, painful exchange. Mrs. Scudder convinces Mary that it would give the Doctor "great pain" if Mary refused his offer, insinuating that Mary is responsible for this proposal since she "has allowed [Dr. Hopkins] to act as a very near friend for a long time . . . it is quite natural that he should have hopes that [Mary] loved him" (406). Invoking all of her authoritarian control over her daughter, Mrs. Scudder sacrifices Mary's earthly happiness for her own peace of mind as she forces her into an unwanted engagement.

It takes an enormous amount of community effort and discourse to correct the story of Newport—Candace and Miss Prissy stand at the forefront of the actions that leads Miss Prissy to tell Dr. Hopkins, "[T]he fact is, that James Marvyn and Mary always did love each other, ever since they were children" despite Miss Prissy's fears that the news will put the revered Doctor "into a consumption" (489). This is a powerful point in the communal narrative, for the women of the community assume control over their own destiny. While the narrator tells the story in the communal mode, she has no control over the actual story but must "write only as we are driven" (38); it is Newport's female voices, previously marginalized by slavery, despair, and fear, that propel the narrative.

The narrator's communal mode replaces traditional, patriarchal narrative authority with a maternal, democratic method that provides a model of community-fostered spiritual individualism. The narrator serves as a guide to the story, not as a forceful authoritative omniscient God-figure who puts characters through paces and marches them toward a specific narrative end. Characters gradually learn that attempts to force action in *The Minister's Wooing* are foiled. Miss Prissy, who cannot wait until dawn to try "a new way" of framing a quilt, forces open a bedroom door that "squeaks like a cat . . . enough to raise the dead" (442) and rouses the Scudder household by "knocking down all the pieces of the quilting-frame" (442). What Miss Prissy requires is "the least drop of oil in a teacup, and a bit of quill" (441) to stop the squeak rather than resort to force, but none is at hand. The "least drop of oil," though, is always in the voice of the narrator, who gently and smoothly reveals the story of the community that saves itself. The voice of authority in the novel is the voice of Newport itself; characters in *The Minister's Wooing* create and change their own plots and assist each other in revising a tale of trauma into a story of human loving-kindness.

*The Minister's Wooing* is a triumphant example of a nonoppressive narrative, and Stowe is masterful in constructing a narrative voice in the communal mode that embodies and actively practices the novel's ideologies: community, democracy, and humanity.

The narrator is thus an authoritative yet democratic spokesperson, herself living the story of a small New England town that rewrites its own potentially tragic cultural narrative by shedding a variety of systematic, harshly patriarchal, authoritative belief systems that forced humans to live in terror and fear. *The Minister's Wooing* is filled with horror and heartbreak; harsh and manipulative authority is wielded by those who demand the right to control the lives of others. The Newport community rouses itself to throw off the psychological torment of Calvinism, the inhumanity of slavery, and the heartbreak of forced marriages.

## NOTE

1. In *Fictions of Authority*, Lanser explores "what forms of voice have been available to women" (1992, 15) since the mid-eighteenth century, as women writers met the challenges of creating public narrative modes. Drawing on the argument of her first study, *The Narrative Act* (1981), Lanser explores how female novelists responded creatively to the authorizing conventions that have marked Western, largely white, privileged-class, male literary authority. She ultimately identifies three forms used by women writers in their "quest for discursive authority" (1992, 7): the authorial, the personal, and the communal mode. It is the communal narrative voice that has evaded Stowe critics for so many years because the "dominant culture has not employed communal voice to any perceptible degree, and because distinctions about voice have been primarily on the features of this dominant literature, there has been no narratological terminology for communal voice or for its various technical possibilities" (21).

## WORKS CITED

Baker, Dorothy. 2000. "Harriet Beecher Stowe's Conversation with the *Atlantic Monthly*: The Construction of *The Minister's Wooing*." *New England Quarterly* 28 (1): 27–38.

Berkson, Dorothy. 1980. "Millennial Politics and the Feminine Fiction of Harriet Beecher Stowe." In *Critical Essays on Harriet Beecher Stowe*, ed. Elizabeth Ammons, 244–58. Boston: Hall.

Buell, Lawrence. 1978. "Calvinism Romanticized: Harriet Beecher Stowe, Samuel Hopkins and *The Minister's Wooing*." *ESQ* 24:119–32.

Harris, Susan K. 1998. Introduction to *The Minister's Wooing*, by Harriet Beecher Stowe, vii–xxiii. New York: Penguin.

Hedrick, Joan. 1988. "'Peaceable Fruits': The Ministry of Harriet Beecher Stowe." *American Quarterly* 40 (3): 307–32.

Karcher, Carolyn L. 2004. "Stowe and the Literature of Social Change." In *The Cambridge Campanion to Harriet Beecher Stowe*, ed. Cindy Weinstein, 131–53. Cambridge: Cambridge University Press.

Lanser, Susan Sniader. 1981. *The Narrative Act: Point of View in Prose Fiction*. Princeton, NJ: Princeton University Press.

———. 1992. *Fictions of Authority: Women Writers and Narrative Voice*. Ithaca, NY: Cornell University Press.

O'Harae, Alison. 2005. "Theology, Genre and Romance in Richard Baxter and Harriet Beecher Stowe." *Religion and Literature* 37 (1): 69–87.

Stowe, Harriet Beecher. [1859] 1994. *The Minister's Wooing*. Hartford, CT: Stowe-Day Foundation.

Warhol, Robin. 1989. *Gendered Interventions: Narrative Discourse in the Victorian Novel*. New Brunswick, NJ: Rutgers University Press.

Wilson, Christopher P. 1985. "Tempests and Teapots: Harriet Beecher Stowe's *The Minister's Wooing*." *New England Quarterly* 58 (4): 554–77.

# Kitchen Hierarchies

## Negotiations of American Nationhood in Harriet Beecher Stowe's *Oldtown Folks*

*Maria I. Diedrich*

In the midst of the American Civil War, as the still young republic was tottering under the violent destructiveness of sectional strife, Harriet Beecher Stowe wrote a poem that took recourse to metaphors of powerful natural forces, of natural catastrophe to express the sense of despair that threatened to overwhelm her and the nation as a whole:

> . . . how the waves
> Beat turbulent with terrible uproar!
> Is there no rest from tossing,—no response?
> Where shall we find a haven and a shore?
>
> (Stowe [1862] 1896, 327)

This poem was written during a period in American history when the promise of America was facing its greatest challenge to this day, and Stowe's anxiety almost silenced her, as it also silenced many of the most powerful writers of the day (Masur 1993). Yet Stowe managed to respond creatively to the fierce controversies of the immediate antebellum years, to the horrors of the war, and to the transformations and tribulations of Reconstruction by designing a cycle of novels set in rural New England communities: *The Minister's Wooing* (1859), *The Pearl of Orr's Island* (1862), *Oldtown Folks* (1869), and *Poganuc People* (1878) cover the turbulent decades from the post-Revolutionary to the Jacksonian age. By inviting her readers to re-cover with her the challenges that the founding generation had faced as they took on the task of nation building, by demanding that they remember the trust in God and themselves that had sustained these founders, she hoped to revive in her readers the determination to also embrace the second American revolution in terms of promise. Kathryn R. Kent has convincingly argued that Stowe's New England novels "simultaneously occupy" and critique "two historical-discursive positions" (1997, 41; see also Hedrick 1994, 342; Tang 1998, 85)—the post-Revolutionary and the Reconstruction eras. The article maintains that Stowe moves from her negotiation of a post-Revolutionary past and a Reconstruction present to blueprints of an American future that aim to take the nation beyond the errors of the past and the confusions of the day.

However, the ambivalent response of contemporary critics to these novels documents that this multiple positioning was not understood. The abolitionist poet John Greenleaf Whittier condescendingly associated *Oldtown Folks* with the rapidly emerging women regionalists of the day (Fetterley and Pryse 2003, ch. 3) when he lauded it as "the most charming New England idyl ever written" (quoted in Charles Edward Stowe 1889, 327). The majority of her male critics gleefully seized upon the word "idyl" to turn it against Stowe. Bret Harte complained in the *Overland Monthly* in 1869 that the novel's protagonists were as far removed from "the present civilization as the aborigines" (quoted in May 1991, 78) and Stowe's mode of narration "even more provincial than her subject" (quoted in Hedrick 1994, 346), and Josiah Holland dismissed her as one of the "hearty and homely singers of this blessed early time" (quoted in Spencer 1957, 243). Stowe's rewriting of the early republican era was thus discredited as an elderly woman's nostalgic escapism, her critique of Reconstruction policy and her projections for the nation's future simply ignored. These reviews impacted the reception of this text and Stowe's entire New England cycle for more than a century: they were either given up to oblivion or ridiculed as a woman's sentimental reminiscences in the disguise of historic fiction, "as a convenient bag into which she [Harriet Beecher Stowe] stuffed her rich store of personal and at the same time representative reminiscences of the New England past" (Eakin 1976, 28).

Since the 1970s feminist criticism and gender studies have snatched Stowe's New England novels from oblivion and reaffirmed their place in the American canon. Stowe's narrative is now seen as a female counter-narrative on American nationhood, as a radical, early feminist contribution to contemporary, male-dominated negotiations of national identity in a period of extreme crises. For Dorothy Berkson, Stowe evoked a post-Revolutionary New England setting only to provide her vision of that perfect American nation to be reconstructed out of the war-ravished present with a historical model she considered both respectable and successful; the alternative nation she projected according to Berkson was "anti-materialistic, non-competitive, racially tolerant, and essentially classless" (1980, 245–46). Jane Tompkins stresses Stowe's determination to put "the central affirmations of a culture into the service of a vision that would destroy the present economic and social institutions" (1985, 145) and Jean Fagan Yellin celebrates Stowe as a champion of an "alternative society grounded on egalitarian Christianity" (1986, 101). In short, Stowe affirms the Quaker woman Rachel Halliday's kitchen as the domestic laboratory, in which America's "true women" (Welter 1966, 151–74) test the model of a reconstructed American nation that is gynocentric and matriarchal (Opfermann 2000, 641).

The following analysis will read Stowe's New England cycle, and especially *Oldtown Folks* as a woman's reflections on a social and political context she experienced as challenging in the best and worst sense of the word: there was the violent slavery controversy of the antebellum decades, the devastation of civil war and the regional and racial hatred it had generated. Like most Euro Americans, Stowe was intimidated at the visible presence of millions of free African Americans in Reconstruction America and unable to accept them as American citizens; the United States faced a mass immigration that undermined its traditional demographic and ethnic structure and evoked heated debates over the nation's racial and ethnic identity; the country was rapidly transformed into an industrial nation, its citizens from a predominantly rural to an urban population. This essay will decipher Stowe's regionalist texts in the context of these transformational processes and the anxieties they aroused in the writer. It will also locate the novels within the racial, gendered, and classed discourses, i.e., within the oppressive and exclusive hegemony of the discursive regimes that impacted the world in which Stowe moved and in whose negotiations, constructions, and (to use Foucault's model from *The Order of Discourse* [1974]) ultimate appropriation, though with a difference, she participated as agent and recipient.

Her contemporary male critics ignored that Stowe did not write her regional novels from the restrictive perspective of a woman whose garden fence was her ultimate horizon. In her preface to *Oldtown Folks* she contends: "New England has been to these United States what the Dorian hive was to Greece. It has always been a capital country to emigrate from, and North, South, East and West have been populated largely from New England" (Stowe [1869] 1982, 883). Through her personal biography she participated in this migratory pattern: after a New England childhood and youth, she spent her twenties and thirties in the Midwest, in Cincinnati, the booming frontier town the British traveler Frances Trollope had satirized and immortalized in her *Domestic Manners of the Americans* (1832). Stowe and her family returned to New England only in 1850. After the Civil War she bought property in Florida and commuted between North and South. Moreover, when Stowe began drafting her New England cycle she was not only familiar with large parts of mid-nineteenth-century U.S. territory—she had also made several trips to Europe. Her focus on New

England was thus based on a realm of experience most of her contemporaries would have admired as cosmopolitan. She chose to return to New England not, as Harte and Holland allege, as a provincial, nostalgic recluse but as an experienced national and transatlantic traveler, as a writer eager to speak up and be heard; she opted for New England because it made sense. She used New England regionalism because she felt this approach could "engage the reader's sympathy and identification" (Fetterley and Pryse, 2003, xii). She relied on regional voices to tell a communal history, drawing the readers into this community by addressing them directly as "you" (Karcher 2004, 213).

As early as in *The Minister's Wooing* Stowe celebrates New England as "probably the only example of a successful commonwealth founded on a theory" (Stowe [1859] 1982, 609), and ten years later she revived and redesigned John Winthrop's "city upon a hill" metaphor (Winthrop 1630, 225) when—in a sweeping gesture of patriotic enthusiasm and cultural imperialism—she imagined New England as a model for perfect Christian communities all over the globe, as "the vigorous, germinating seed-bed for all that has since been developed of politics, laws, letters, and theology, through New England to America, and through America to the world" (Stowe [1869] 1982, 1288). For Stowe, the seedbed of this future democratic world order is not the metropolis Boston but—and in that she positioned herself firmly within the physiocratic discourse of the early republic—rural communities, "each a separate little democracy, shut off by rough roads and forests from the rest of the world" (1288). Here, in the calm and relaxed atmosphere of the country, where people produce on their own tract of land whatever they need and where everybody belongs, forms of communal life that include and respect both the free individual as well as her or his responsibility for the whole can germinate. According to Stowe's mediating strategy, these forms of community must be appropriated and redefined by the Reconstruction nation until they can serve as supportive foundation for the more complex structures of the new urban, even industrial United States that were emerging right before her eyes.

Stowe's use of the seedbed metaphor suggests a seed so perfect that you can entrust it with the burden of determining the future; it is a dynamic metaphor that incorporates transformational processes under revised conditions, but it also claims perfection for the original kernel, here the rural community. As the defining components of that model seed Stowe identifies the church and the schoolhouse as the pillars of the public, and the kitchen as the pillar of the private or domestic realm. A close scrutiny of these nuclei, however, reveals the ruptures and tensions that emanate as contemporary conflicting discourses of race, class, gender, ethnicity, and nationhood intersect with Stowe's homogenizing foundation myth and her utopian design of a future America. Constructed by Stowe as loci of national harmony, consensus, and wholeness, they resurface as generators of social borderlines and racial exclusion.

Stowe's first-person narrator in *Oldtown Folks*—the orphan Horace Holyoke who lives on his grandparents' farm, in the Badger household—fondly remembers the service in the Oldtown church as "a complete picture of the population of our village" (Stowe [1869] 1982, 927) and he carefully lists and categorizes all the individuals and groups who gather each Sunday. The reader is informed that women and men of all classes and races or ethnicities—Anglo Americans, Native Americans, and African Americans—that made up these original communities are participating in the event. They are brought together by their desire to worship and by their need to affirm their membership in this closely knit community. Yet once we move beyond Holyoke's unifying reminiscences and decipher the actual social and racial geography of the place, a more conflictual pattern unfolds for which no corrective voice emerges in the narrative. "Social position," Stowe's nostalgic narrator legitimizes a fiercely exclusive and hierarchical praxis, "was a thing marked by lines whose distinctness had not been blurred by the rough handling of democracy" (931).

Within this church community, the status of the individual families and various ethnicities is illustrated by the size and location of their pews and benches, and Stowe evokes positive associations with the British houses to affirm the stability that the hierarchy in this church signifies: close to the pulpit we find the pews of the Anglo-American New England aristocracy—the minister, the entrepreneur, and those members of the British gentry who opted for American citizenship after the Revolution. They constitute the House of Lords, ladies and gentlemen "who wore ruffles round their hands, and rode in their own coaches, and never performed any manual labor" (933).

Next to these pews Stowe places those Anglo Americans who constitute the House of Commons—"men of substance . . . who tilled the earth with their own hands, or pursued some active industrial calling" (933). They are personifications of Crèvecoeur's American farmer, whom Thomas Jefferson provided with mythopoetic dimensions when he glorified them as "the chosen people of God, if ever he had a chosen people" (Jefferson [1780–81] 1955, 165). These are proud and independent citizens, meritocrats like Grandfather Badger from whose class the Oldtown magistrates—the justice of peace, the deacons, the sheriff—are recruited.

People without landed property, which alone would provide them with economic autonomy and the right to political participation, form the lowest order in the Anglo-American sociopolitical hierarchy, the pewless folk. In legitimizing their powerlessness and relative poverty Stowe constructs a causality between virtue, wealth, and grace that her village poor have accepted and internalized, and she has them supported by a network of advice and substantial charity from members of the houses that is firmly rooted in the Calvinist stewardship of wealth. In Stowe's Oldtown, peaceful social coexistence is guaranteed as all affirm their place and responsibility within the social and racial hierarchy. Stowe thus reimages the American Revolution—in stark contrast to the French Revolution—as a change of political systems that was productive of social harmony; her construct of post-Revolutionary New England denies social strife.

The common denominator of these classes within the Oldtown church is their membership in what Stowe defines and, in the New England cycle tends to idealize, as that Anglo-Saxon race, which Benjamin Franklin had already identified as the only legitimate heirs of a future America when he defined American destiny as white. In that, Stowe's construct of American nationhood is even more racially and culturally exclusive than James Fenimore Cooper's in *The Pioneers* (1823), where Anglo-Saxons, French, and Germans cooperate to build their dynamic New World community. In Stowe's regional novels we encounter members of other European cultures exclusively in the role of tourists; in sending them back to the Old World she affirms the legitimacy of Anglo-American leadership in the New World. National harmony is identified with racial and cultural homogeneity, as Stowe's xenophobic response to the mass migration in the postwar decades further confirms. In *Poganuc People* she takes recourse to flood metaphors to express her anxiety as immigrants from non-Anglo-Saxon countries claim their right to American citizenship. Stowe evokes the fear of the inscrutable "Other" in her readers when she warns them that the post-Revolutionary New England could be a land without demeaning poverty only because it was blessed with people who "were of our own race," while she represents "the pauperized population of Europe" (Stowe [1878] 1987, 318–19) as a racial threat to her racially homogenous American Garden of Eden.

Stowe's church episodes do not deny the presence of racial "Others" in her idealized Oldtown community, but she uses a rhetoric of segregation and exclusion to express her ultimate, though unacknowledged disapproval at their presence. This racial homogenization strategy had already found a more unequivocal articulation in *Uncle Tom's Cabin* (1852): here she transported the novel's fugitive slaves from Rachel's integrated kitchen to Canada and, together with all the other free black protagonists, shipped them back to Africa. On the eve of the Civil War and Emancipation Proclamation she thus not only expelled African Americans from the United States and condemned them to live in a separate and racialized national sphere; as a disciple of what Amy Kaplan defines as "Manifest Domesticity" (1998, 581–606, esp. 593) she also transformed them into black agents of American imperial interests when she had them perform as missionaries of Christian doctrine, of the African "Other's" spiritual regeneration and of genuine Americanness on the black continent. "The idea of African coloni-

zation does not simply emerge at the end of a racist failure of Stowe's political imagination," Kaplan maintains convincingly, "rather, colonization
underwrites the racial politics of the domestic imagination" (1998, 602).

In *Oldtown Folks* Stowe locates blacks at the lowest level in the hierarchy
she affirms for her meeting house. The African Americans, "whose houses
formed a little settlement by themselves" (Stowe [1869] 1982, 930) in Oldtown, are also segregated in church: "a side gallery was appropriated to them"
(929). There is no distancing, critiquing voice in these episodes: the Oldtown
blacks have internalized the caste system, and they are represented as perfectly satisfied with their static position as servants. And where racial hierarchies go unchallenged, neither social nor racial unrest can find nourishment.
Stowe's happy New England blacks "lived on most amicable terms with all
the inhabitants" (930), who, in turn, offer them protection and charity.

And yet, a relegation to the periphery and a servant status that are defined
as permanent is only the surface solution Stowe offers to Reconstruction
America. In a subtle but powerful way the novel takes its contemporary
reader beyond this state of racial truce when it conjures up the racist and
dysgenic topos of African American overreproductiveness (Kent 1997,
49–50): as Stowe's narrator Holyoke enters Aunt Nancy Prime's cottage, he
stumbles over her "skirmishing tribe of little darkies, who had been rolling about the floor" and finally "unite in one coil" (Stowe [1869] 1982,
930). For Horace, these children have no individuality, they are excessive
in number and utterly worthless. Stowe suggests her "solution" to this
"threat" when she has the black mother open a trap door and the black
bodies "disappeare(d) in the hole" (930)—a cruelly inverted reenactment
of the Middle Passage as Stowe's answer her Reconstruction anxieties. The
eugenic bent of her projections is further confirmed by the fact that all the
individualized and positively drawn black characters in the New England
novels serve in white households and remain childless even when married—Candace and Cato in *The Minister's Wooing*, Caesar in *Oldtown Folks*;
blackness promises to die with them in the New World.

At first sight Stowe's Oldtown attributes a privileged position to the novel's Native American protagonists via her church geography: honoring the
historical evidence that the meeting house had originally been a mission
church for Native Americans, the chairs at the very center are still reserved
for their descendants. Yet when Stowe introduces these church members as
"the thin and wasted remnants of what once was a numerous and powerful tribe" (927) she shifts from class and status to the Vanishing Indian
discourse. By placing Native Americans at the center, her Anglo-American
church members do not acknowledge ownership and power; they merely
offer a gesture of respect for a dying nation. These Native Americans cannot
possibly perform as members of the dynamic Oldtown community; they
are anachronisms. Located outside of history, they have museal quality.

Though Stowe constructs the church community in *Oldtown Folks* as her anticipation of an "alternative society grounded in egalitarian Christianity" (Yellin 1986, 101) for a future America, the novel's representational racialized praxis subverts the egalitarian rhetoric and pose. With that, it also perverts the seedbed metaphor and its consensus quality. When we add to that diagnosis the fact that, though present and acknowledged as church members, even the Anglo-American women remain voiceless in Horace's reconstructions of the church gatherings, little of the feminist utopia remains.

It is tempting to justify this exclusivist and hierarchical geography by defining, as Stowe does, the church as a public and thus, in a post-Revolutionary context, as a male-dominated realm that tolerated no mitigating, redeeming factors, no female voices affirming fusion and unity. Yet when we turn from this public realm of the church to the private realm of the kitchen, the dichotomy between homogenizing rhetoric and exclusivist praxis that characterizes the church episodes is even enhanced and empowered through the uncontested matriarchal authority with which Stowe invests the novel's true heroine, Grandmother Badger. The rule of love she exerts over this domestic territory legitimizes its racial exclusiveness.

At first sight, Grandmother Badger's kitchen is a New England version of Rachel Halliday's haven of interracial harmony: Anglo-American women and men of all classes, African Americans, and Native Americans happily submit to the generous old women's matriarchal rule as they gather around the fireplace in her large and hospitable kitchen. Together they talk politics and theology, they gossip, they tell stories, and they eat and drink. According to Edward Tang, Stowe imagined the kitchen as "the one space in all of America where the boundaries between public and private spheres dissolved" (Tang 1998, 95). And yet Stowe persists in submitting her construct of an innocent and informal kitchen community to the same segregationist geography as the church. Again she tolerates only the Anglo-American members of the Houses of Lords and Commons in the privileged space around the fire. Sam Lawson, the prototype of the village loafer, drinks his cider together with black Caesar "on his block of wood in the deep recess of the farther corner" (Stowe [1869] 1982, 944), and the Native American beggar women devour their charity meal "on the table in the corner" (958), that is at places farthest removed from the fire as a locus of status and power.

This hierarchy becomes even more distinct if we consider the scene's communication patterns. Only members of the House of Lords and Commons—under Grandma Badger's regime now women as well as men—participate in the conversation, and they claim for themselves the right to graciously extend the power of word to a few select inferiors. Thus Sam Lawson is invited to speak only because his skill as a storyteller and village gossip entertains them, but leaves their social and intellectual superiority unchallenged. That Stowe never doubts the legitimacy of Sam's placement is confirmed by her decision to attribute the authority of narrator and communal voice not to this wonderfully inventive word-artist but to the socially and morally proper Horace Holyoke. Sam's place in this circle of Republicans is also illustrated by the way they address this mature family man: even the young Harvard student Bill Badger feels free to use the condescending "Sam, my boy" (953) when he plays his jokes on this "Oldtown curiosity" (952), while Sam always relies on the deferential "Mr. Badger" or "Master Bill" (953). Sam is Sam for all, even the children, but he attests to the superiority of their status via the "Master" address.

The peripheral and transitional role of African and Native Americans is illustrated not only in that they are relegated to kitchen corners; they also remain voiceless. While the Anglo Americans in the room never communicate with, address, or invite them to speak, they talk about them as if they had no ears to listen, no minds to understand, no pride to hurt. Thus Grandma Badger comments on the haste in which the beggarly Native Americans gobble down their charity meal "with the appetite of wolves" (958) with a kindly meant yet condescending "[t]he poor creatures don't get a good meal of victuals very often" (958). The fact that Grandmother Badger, whose right to admonish and even punish anybody entering her realm is uncontested, never makes the slightest attempt to perform this white woman's prerogative of teaching the colonized "Other" (Said [1978] 1995, 35) when interacting with the Native American women cannot be read as a gesture of respect for alternative cultural norms; she perceives these women as lost to history as progress and has expelled them from the nation's future.

Equally, Caesar remains in the room when the Badger guests debate the slavery issue, and Grandmother Badger even points to "that great scar on Caesar's forehead" to prove "what slavery comes to" (Stowe [1869] 1982, 961), yet they never ask for his opinion. He remains the pitied object of their abolitionist discourse and the grinning entertainer for their children. As a man without a family of his own he poses no eugenic threat to the republic's racial future, and, like the Native Americans, he will drop out of American history. Stowe's rhetoric of fusion, unity, and wholeness thus relies on what Iris M. Young defines as politics of difference; it emanates as a discourse that "generates borders, dichotomies, and exclusions" (1990, 307).

When Dorothy Berkson idealizes the kitchen in Stowe's New England novels as "the symbolic center for these domestically ideal communities where people gather without social stratification" (1980, 250), her reading relies exclusively on surface phenomena. The world in which Grandma Badger rules, heals, and nourishes is without doubt a perfect illustration of Carroll Smith-Rosenberg's "Female World of Love and Ritual" in which all members are free, but it is certainly not a haven of equality, nor is it a utopian anticipation of a multicultural United States to come (1975, 1–27).

With dissenting voices absent from this domestic realm's affirmed social and racial stratification, Stowe's critique of a Reconstruction society in a state of flux and her projections of a future American nationhood leave the association of whiteness and authority as unchallenged as the social and racial hierarchies of the founding period. The kitchen episodes illustrate the paradoxes Stowe encountered when attempting a redefinition of cultural and social values in a discursive field—here constructions of motherhood and domesticity—that had long been the unchallenged property of male-dominated cultural norms whose racial assumptions she affirmed.

In both Oldtown kitchen and church Stowe thus firmly maintains established social and racial hierarchies while regretfully associating the slightest distancing gesture with "the rough handling of democracy" (Stowe [1869] 1982, 931); still, they are places in which members of different classes and races meet and, in a highly ritualized manner, interact. Yet once we also include the third pillar of Stowe's New England model—the school—into our analysis, no trace of this community of surface interactions remains. The school is defined as a white prerogative; if we add the academy, this privileged white circle of participants becomes even more exclusive: at the academy the children of the Lords and Commons—girls and boys—are already among themselves, and only the men head for college. Stowe celebrates the school as an institution responsible for the moral and intellectual formation of young America and, through them, for the nation's future. In making this school the exclusive realm of Anglo-American boys and girls, without signaling a need for racial and social reform options at a time when ex-slaves were crowding the schoolhouses that abolitionists and the Freedmen's Bureau ran in the Reconstruction South, she left no doubt that the American nationhood she projected into the future subscribed to Benjamin Franklin's whiteness program. The young generation of her upper- and middle-class Anglo-American protagonists are provided with a substantial education, and, as they mature, they leave Oldtown well equipped to deal with historical and social change, but the novel's Native Americans and African Americans are programmatically excluded from this process and thus from American history as progress. What in the kitchen episode seemed like the inability of Stowe as designer of a women's utopia to dream herself beyond her Anglo-American homogenization agenda resurfaces as the determination to defend and cement the power of whiteness.

This reading is confirmed when we look beyond *Oldtown Folks* to the New England cycle as a whole. As she moves from the post-Revolutionary period to the Jacksonian age, Stowe delineates a process of secularization and urbanization that affirms the replacement of authoritarian theocratic structures by more democratic ones and invites the reader to accompany the children of farmers as they climb the social ladder to become attorneys in Boston. However, these changes within a society that embraces dynamic progress have no impact whatsoever on the lives and status of African and Native Americans. The blacks, who in *The Minister's Wooing* gossip and laugh "like so many crows" (Stowe [1859] 1982, 621), differ in no way from Dinah, who serves in the minister's kitchen in *Poganuc People* as late as 1818. Like her namesake Dinah in *Uncle Tom's Cabin* she may be "slow, and somewhat disorderly," but she is also "unfailingly good-natured, and had no dignity to be looked after" (Stowe [1878] 1987, 273). In short, at a time when the Reconstruction United States were struggling to define a place for their new black citizens, Stowe's black cook was clearly born to serve, and she is still happy to serve forty years after the War of Independence.

While she thus freezes blacks in the ahistorical, essentialist stasis of the loyal, grinning serf, Stowe's Native Americans are anachronisms, and she denies them even the blacks' reluctantly granted right to a permanently submissive and peripheral state beyond historical progress. In *Oldtown Folks* they are sentimentalized as a vanishing nation, but in *Poganuc People* they have deteriorated to creatures of the past whom a wise Creator cleansed off the earth, eager to prepare "the room for the Pilgrim Fathers to settle undisturbed" (174).

Stowe is unapologetic in her defense of education for girls and boys as a white prerogative and as a guarantor of white power in the nation's future. The school life she designs for her young Americans is almost utopian in quality. Yet the episodes that focus on education as one of the three pillars of American nationhood also document her determination to introduce a critical and distancing voice into her post-Revolutionary reveries. They prove that she is indeed negotiating a deficitarian past, a conflict-torn present, and a hopeful future, though always under the assumption that hers is an "Anglo-American-only" discourse on educational rights. Whenever she takes up the issue of education in her New England novels, Stowe joins ranks with reformist women like the feminist abolitionists Angelina Grimké and Lydia Maria Child, her sister Catherine Beecher and the British journalist Harriet Martineau in her assault on a nation that denies its white female citizens access to higher education and, through that, the right to active political participation.

The strategy she employs in legitimizing her feminist critique and claims is one of homogenized representation: all her middle- and upper-class Anglo-American female characters are—and here she tolerates no exception—defined by their love of learning and their intellectual faculties. Her New England women refuse to see themselves as members of a weaker sex, as beautiful, but brainless angels of the house. They are active, self-reliant, and intelligent women who not only fulfill their domestic duties in a professional way; they also insist on a routine of intellectual self-formation through reading and learned conversation. Stowe uses the term "faculty" to define these qualities. Grandma Badger is probably the most loveable

representative of this ideal American woman, "Stowe's archetypal matri-
arch" (Berkson 1980, 249). She is a perfect mother figure, professional
housewife, and woman of intellectual autonomy and moral integrity, all
in one. Mother to numberless children, either her own or adopted, she is,
in her grandson Horace's words, "the female ruler" (Stowe [1869] 1982,
1071) whose uncontested authority is based on the triad of her emotional,
moral, and intellectual competence.

The foundations for Grandma Badger's and her companions' intellectual
autonomy are laid by an institution Stowe affirms as a New England invention—the system of coeducation. In *Oldtown Folks* the Cloudland episodes
serve to make her point: in this academy, where girls and boys are submit-
ted to a rigorous intellectual routine by their demanding instructor, neither
male chauvinism nor a female sense of interiority can survive, for "the girl is
valued for something besides her person; her disposition and character are
thoroughly tested, the power of her mind go for something" (1339). Stowe
invites her readers to accompany her adolescent protagonists Tina and
Esther, Harry and Horace as personifications of an ideal Anglo-American
future to an educational sojourn in which Tina's and Esther's intellectual
performance is at least equal to that of their male fellow students—but then
collapses her egalitarian utopia by designing an end to this Cloudland episode that exposes the irresponsibility, even dangerous absurdity of an educational system that stimulates and invigorates women's intellectuality only
to relegate them to the domestic realm. After academy life has affirmed in
them the awareness of their intellectual potential and has empowered them
for a life of intellectual autonomy, Tina and Esther are cynically dumped
into a void where they must passively wait for their disposal on the marriage market. Painfully aware that in the Reconstruction United States the
authority of voice still rests with white men, Stowe has her narrator Horace
Holyoke articulate her bitter *j'accuse*:

> Tina's education was now, in the common understanding of society, looked
> upon as finished. Harry's and mine were commencing; we were sophomores
> in college. She was a young lady in society; yet she . . . had, I must say, quite
> as good a mind, and was fully as capable of going through our college course
> with us as of having walked this far. However, with her the next question was,
> whom will she marry? (1372)

The consequences of woman's exclusion from higher education and her
consequential political disempowerment are devastating not only for individual protagonists like Tina, who is almost destroyed when she escapes
into an unhappy marriage; the nation itself is endangered by this policy,
Stowe argued throughout her career as novelist and essayist: the all-male
successors of the founders, who perceived the nation "as a social family,
in which a hierarchical structure of white men ruling over women, blacks,

and children was the norm" (Sundquist 1986, 19), was driving the United States to the brink of ruin, she had warned as early as 1852 in *Uncle Tom's Cabin*. In *Poganuc People* male intolerance splits the village into hostile factions, and every male pub-Republican has a voice in the nation's decision making while the women, who advocate reconciliation and balance, are condemned to political abstinence. A United States that excludes women from political participation is destined to fail, Stowe insists in her Chimney-corner columns for the *Atlantic Monthly* as well as in her New England cycle, just as a family collapses when it silences the mother:

> I think that a State can no more afford to dispense with the vote of women in its affairs than a family. Imagine a family where the female has no voice in housekeeping! A State is but a larger family, and there are many of its concerns which, equally with those of a private household, would be bettered by female supervision. (Stowe [1868] 1896, 252)

Throughout her oeuvre Stowe strategically positions narratives of male-dominated policy resulting in political stalemate and even violent disruption in opposition to narratives of constructive and intelligent female rule to illustrate that her objective is not merely women's participation in a male public realm that remains structurally unchanged. Via model women like Rachel Halliday and Grandma Badger and the enlightened, intelligent rule they exert over their domestic realm she opts for a reconceptualization and reorganization of that public realm on the principles of educated Anglo-American woman- and motherhood. Only a nation thus redesigned will be able to learn the lessons of the nation's post-Revolutionary past and create a future that spells promise, progress, and unity out of the multifarious challenges the writer and her narrator Horace Holyoke face in their various presences. "My good friends of the American Republic," she has Horace address her more skeptical contemporaries, "if ever we come to have mingled among the senators of the United States specimens of womankind like Tina Percival, we men remaining as we by nature are and must be, will not the general line of politics take a decidedly new and interesting turn?" (Stowe [1869] 1982, 1371).

Stowe indeed makes her narrator's "mind as still and passive as a looking-glass" (883) when conjuring up memories of a post-Revolutionary past, but when she does so she has already relocated him in Boston, with its factories, its international harbor, and its growing slums, and she leaves no doubt that, much as he and his wife Tina may mourn the disappearance of their rural Elysium, as children raised in Grandma Badger's kitchen and educated in the Cloudland academy they are morally and intellectually empowered to deal with this complex urban environment, with industrialization and mass migration. Through Harry, the orphan sheltered in the Badger home, and his wife Esther, Stowe even reasserts the transatlantic and potentially global concept of Winthrop's city upon the hill and redefines it in accordance with her and her sister Catherine's dream of "imperial domesticity" (Kaplan 1998, 586), of "colonizing the world in the name of the 'family state' under the leadership of Christian women" (Tompkins 1985, 144) when she asks them to become missionaries of Americanness for the Old World. Like the missionaries in *Poganuc People*, they are "chosen vessels," whom the minister celebrates as people, "commissioned to bear the light of liberty and religion through all the earth and to bring in the great millennial day, when wars should cease and the whole world, released from the thralldom of evil, should rejoice in the light of the Lord" (Stowe [1878] 1987, 197).

Yet it is a model of gynocentric and matriarchal internationhood that Stowe can embrace only because its internal process of democratization—replacing the "half Hebrew theocracy, half ultra-democratic republic" (Stowe [1869] 1982, 885) of *The Minister's Wooing* and of *Oldtown Folks* by the turbulent yet successful 1818 elections of *Poganuc People*—offers broader social mobility to the country's Anglo-American citizens while leaving the basic social hierarchy intact and confirming the nation's racial exclusiveness. In Stowe's precarious presence and projective future the Anglo-American poor still internalize Winthrop's dictum "as in all times some must be rich, some poor, some high and eminent in power and dignity; others mean and in subjection" (Winthrop 1630, 214–15); African Americans still have "no dignity to be looked after," and Native Americans have "wasted" (Stowe [1878] 1987, 174) long since. She still has no recipe for those not "of our own blood and race" (319) whom she blames for introducing the un-American institution of the almshouse to the New World. Fearful of the racial and social implications of her Reconstruction presence, Stowe articulated her yearning for women's participation and a reconceptualized nationhood through a usurpation of established racialized codes of authority and thus left their underlying logic firmly in place. Through her affirmation of an Anglo American bourgeois nation state and of a white middle-class consensus that inexorably spells progress and change for Anglo-Americans only, her texts refuse to critique developments that exclude, render dysfunctional, or even liquidate entire segments of that society.

Via her alternative matriarchal vision of nationhood Stowe moved beyond the stagnant, retrospective escapism with which her critics associated her. In that sense her New England novels can indeed figure as a white woman's oppositional discourse to the situation she faced in both the antebellum and Reconstruction United States. However, Stowe was too deeply entangled in the social and racial discourse of her day to envision a future for her nation that moved beyond established social and racial stratifications. Her religious assumption that all human beings were equal before God did not translate into political strategy and praxis; her personal experience of marginalization as a woman did not immunize her against creating new exclusionary and totalizing discourses (Hartsock 1990, 171). Social and political reconceptualization of American nationhood for her indeed spelt the integration of women in the nation's decision-making processes, but because for Stowe "*women* connotes white, middle-class and American born" (Kent 1997, 43), the community of women thus entitled is as racially and socially hierarchical and exclusive as that of men. Stowe's perfect future United States will continue to harbor the politicizing laborer (Sam), the proud and influential farmer and judge (Badger), the authoritarian minister (Lanthrop), and, perhaps, even the voice- and powerless eternal black serf (Caesar). Her ideal nation differs dramatically from the Reconstruction status quo in that Sam and Hepsie, Grandmother and Grandfather Badger and Lady and Minister Lanthrop will share, on their respective social levels, equal rights to political participation and education, just as Caesar and the black cook Candace will share equality of social stagnation and life at the periphery. Defending the power of whiteness Stowe must firmly refuse to imagine Candace and Grandma Badger, Caesar and Lanthrop interacting in the academy and shaping the nation's destiny as "senators of the United States" (Stowe [1869] 1982, 1371).

## WORKS CITED

Berkson, Dorothy. 1980. "Millennial Politics and the Feminine Fiction of Harriet Beecher Stowe." In Ammons 1980, 245–58.

Eakin, Paul John. 1976. *The New England Girl: Cultural Ideals in Hawthorne, Stowe, Howells and James*. Athens: University of Ohio Press.

Fetterley, Judith and Marjorie Pryse. 2003. *Writing Out of Place: Regionalism, Women, and American Literary Culture*. Champaign: University of Illinois Press.

Foucault, Michel. 1974. *Die Ordnung des Diskurses*. Munich: Carl Hanser Verlag.

Hartsock, Nancy. 1990. "Foucault on Power: A Theory for Women?" In Nicholson 1990, 157–75. New York: Routledge.

Hedrick, Joan D. 1994. *Harriet Beecher Stowe: A Life*. New York: Oxford University Press.

Jefferson, Thomas. [1780–81] 1955. *Notes on the State of Virginia*. Chapel Hill: University of North Carolina Press.

Kaplan, Amy. 1998. "Manifest Domesticity." *American Literature* 70 (3): 581–606.

Karcher, Carolyn L. 2004. "Stowe and the Literature of Social Change." In Weinstein 2004, 203–18.

Kent, Kathryn R. 1997. "'Single White Female': The Sexual Politics of Spinsterhood in Harriet Beecher Stowe's *Oldtown Folks*." *American Literature* 69 (1): 38–65.

Masur, Louis P., ed. 1993. *The Real War Will Never Get in the Books: Selections from Writers During the Civil War*. New York: Oxford University Press.

Opfermann, Susanne. 2000. "Harriet Beecher Stowe." In *Metzler Lexikon Amerikanische Autoren*, ed. Bernd Engler and Kurt Müller, 639-641. Stuttgart: Metzler.

Said, Edward [1978] 1995. *Orientalism*. Harmondsworth, UK: Penguin.

Smith-Rosenberg, Carroll. 1975. "The Female World of Love and Ritual." *Signs: A Journal of Women in Culture and Society* 1:1–29.

Spencer, Benjamin T. 1957. *The Quest for Nationality: An American Literary Campaign*. Syracuse: Syracuse University Press.

Stowe, Charles Edward. 1889. *The Life of Harriet Beecher Stowe Compiled from Her Letters and Journals*. Boston: Houghton Mifflin.

Stowe, Harriet Beecher. [1859] 1982. *The Minister's Wooing*. In *Harriet Beecher Stowe: Three Novels*, ed. Kathryn Kish Sklar, 521–876. New York: Library of America.

———. [1862] 1896. "Consolation: Written After the Second Battle of Bull Run." In *Religious Studies, Sketches and Poems: The Writings of Harriet Beecher Stowe*, 327–28. Boston: Houghton Mifflin.

———. [1868] 1896. "Women's Sphere." In *Household Papers and Stories: The Writings of Harriet Beecher Stowe*, 249–73. Boston: Houghton Mifflin.

———. [1869] 1982. *Oldtown Folks*. In *Harriet Beecher Stowe: Three Novels*, ed. Kathryn Kish Sklar, 877–1468. New York: Library of America.

———. [1878] 1987. *Poganuc People*. Hartford, CT: Stowe-Day Foundation.

Sundquist, Eric J., ed. 1986. *New Essays on "Uncle Tom's Cabin."* Cambridge: Cambridge University Press.

Tang, Edward. 1998. "Making Declarations of Her Own: Harriet Beecher Stowe as New England Historian." *New England Quarterly* 71:77–96.

Tompkins, Jane. 1985. *Sensational Designs: The Cultural Work of American Fiction, 1790–1860*. New York: Oxford University Press.

Welter, Barbara. 1966. "The Cult of True Womanhood." *American Quarterly* 18 (2): 151–74.

Winthrop, John. 1630. "A Model of Christian Charity." In vol. 1 of *The Norton Anthology of American Literature*, ed. Nina Baym, 214–25. New York: Norton.

Yellin, Jean Fagan. 1986. "Doing It Herself: *Uncle Tom's Cabin* and Women's Role in the Slavery Crisis." In Sundquist 1986, 85–106.

Young, Iris Marion. 1990. "The Ideal of Community and the Politics of Difference." In Nicholson 1990, 300–23.

# New England *Tempests?*

## Harriet Beecher Stowe's *The Minister's Wooing* and *The Pearl of Orr's Island*

*Monika Mueller*

Harriet Beecher Stowe appropriated themes from Shakespeare's *The Tempest* (1611) for her New England novels *The Minister's Wooing* (1859) and *The Pearl of Orr's Island* (1862). Shakespeare criticism has deemed *The Tempest* Shakespeare's "American play" because of both its possible setting in the Bermudas and its focus on slavery, problematized in the relationship between the exiled Prospero and his slave Caliban. Stowe transposes Shakespeare's themes into her "organic," relatively closed, New England (post-) Puritan society and explores how unsettling social and spiritual phenomena presented by Shakespeare, as, for example, racial alterity and magic, can be addressed within the context of the strictly religious New England society.

In both of her novels, a young couple, Mary and James in *The Minister's Wooing*, and Mara and Moses in *The Pearl of Orr's Island*, emulate the Miranda-Ferdinand relationship from *The Tempest*. Stowe bestows Miranda-like virginal virtue upon her female characters; her male characters are used to explore "dark" issues related with imperialism and slavery. In *The Minister's Wooing*, James's association with the slave Candace puts him—and perhaps even more importantly his mother—in touch with a spirituality that differs from the oftentimes rather arid Puritan spirituality and finally makes him a spokesperson against slavery. In *The Pearl of Orr's Island*, Moses, like the "imperial" characters in *The Tempest*, is associated with egotism, sensuality, and piratical greed, but he is finally redeemed by his stepsister Mara's deep spirituality. Like Mara's friend Captain Kittredge, who has to relinquish his Prospero-like "magic," the foundling Moses has to give up his heathen ways in order to become a full-fledged member of his adoptive society. Both novels indicate that the New England society has no room for either the imperialism or the "calibanism" of Shakespeare's play. The (post-)Puritan society of the New England novels relentlessly and successfully works toward neutralizing alterity by absorbing or at least containing it.

While previous critics, such as Christopher P. Wilson and Joan D. Hedrick, have put emphasis mainly on generic considerations and questions of gender, the focus of my discussion of Stowe's critical engagement with Shakespeare's *The Tempest* in *The Minister's Wooing* and in *The Pearl of Orr's Island* will be on her treatment of racial and social alterity. In the first part of my essay, I will briefly sum up the critical discussion of *The Tempest* as "American" play and I will then show how strategies of resistance to hegemonic power offered by *The Tempest* are adapted by Stowe for her own presentation of "socially acceptable" black resistance in *The Minister's Wooing*. The essay's second part concentrates on *The Pearl of Orr's Island*; it discusses Stowe's adaptation of *The Tempest*'s marriage plot in the novel and shows how she perfects her strategies of containment of ethnic alterity in her attempt to invent a model society for the United States in her New England novels.

Before presenting my own discussion, I will briefly sum up Wilson's and Hedrick's critical insights. In "Tempests and Teapots: Harriet Beecher Stowe's *The Minister's Wooing*," Wilson remarks upon the shared "themes of suffering and redemption, vengeance and mercy, theology and 'art'" (1985, 564) in Shakespeare and Stowe and argues that the main inspiration that Stowe drew from *The Tempest* was to adopt for her novel a worldview "that unveiled the intrinsically poetic and romantic nature of events" (559) and thus helped her reach out beyond "the strictly evangelical tradition that gives *The Minister's Wooing* its distinctive cast" (559). Wilson further notices plot similarities between *The Tempest* and *The Minister's Wooing* in the plot twists about a child supposedly lost at sea (Ferdinand in *The Tempest* and James Marvyn in *The Minister's Wooing*) and the thematizations of treason (the multiple conspiracies against Prospero in *The Tempest* and Burr's political treachery in *The Minister's Wooing*). Moreover, as a sideline to his central argument about the romance plot in *The Minister's Wooing*, he also comments upon Shakespeare's and Stowe's constructions of gender, arguing that Mary, at times "naïve" like Miranda, receives an "education sentimentale" through her involvement in the love plot between the unhappily married young Frenchwoman Virginie de Frontignac and the callous seducer Aaron Burr. Last but not least, Wilson also comments upon similarities in Shakespeare's and Stowe's presentation of race and slavery when he points out that Cato and Candace's resolution to work harder after they have been set free by the Marvyns seems to echo Caliban's promise at the end of the play to tidy up Prospero's living quarters and to be "wise hereafter / And seek for grace" ([1611] 1999, 5.1.295–96) (1985, 566).

Joan D. Hedrick uses the main character Mara's reenactment of her own and Moses's life stories as scenes from *The Tempest* as her point of departure for discussing *The Pearl of Orr's Island* as a failed "sentimental social novel," which ultimately substitutes its initial promise of possible female empowerment through education with mere "sentimental evasions" (2001, xiv). In many ways, Mara's story is the typical story of a creative, intelligent woman in the nineteenth century who finds no outlet for her talents. Like Maggie Tulliver from George Eliot's *The Mill on the Floss*, for example, Mara quickly learns Latin by just listening to her much-less-gifted stepbrother Moses being instructed. But Mara's education stops with young adulthood, and as with many other nineteenth-century heroines, marriage seems to be her only "vocational choice." Having found a copy of *The Tempest*, she begins to conceive of her relationship with Moses in terms of the Miranda-Ferdinand relationship. Unfortunately, Moses cannot follow her flight of the imagination and fails to see "correspondences with his own stormy history" (xv) in *The Tempest*. Hedrick concludes from this rather fatalistically that this type of "incompatibility sets women up for a double contradiction: unable to be active in the world, restricted to the private sphere and marriage, women are bound to men with whom true intimacy is impossible" (xv). Ultimately, Mara's fate again corresponds to that of many other nineteenth-century female protagonists; towards the end of the novel, she dies a "providential death"[1] from consumption and Moses is free to marry the more practical Sally Kittredge. By arguing that Mara might "have wanted to be an artist like Prospero rather than a helper like Miranda" (xiv), Hedrick points to another important thematic parallel between *The Tempest* and *The Pearl of Orr's Island*, which I want to pursue in my reading of the novel: as in Shakespeare's play, a penchant for "imaginary" pursuits is presented as a human need, but New England's (post-)Puritan society does not tolerate them and thus does its best to root them out. Not only are Mara's flights of the imagination curbed, but Captain Kittredge's sailor yarns are likewise banned because they obviously fall short of (biblical) truth value.

In *The Pearl of Orr's Island*, Mara, enchanted by the play's action, thinks that Orr's Island would have been a perfect setting for the play ([1862] 2001, 136). In this context it is interesting to note that quite a few commentators have considered *The Tempest* Shakespeare's "American play," partly due to the fact that Shakespeare possibly modeled the shipwreck of *The Tempest* on a famous incident in the summer of 1609, when an English ship was wrecked against the not-yet-settled Bermuda islands (Vaughan and Vaughan 1999, 6). Caliban's name, which is obviously an anagram for cannibal, also suggests a New World reference because in America the indigenous Caribs were associated with anthropophagy (131). America, however, is not actually mentioned in the play, and the only actual reference to a specific New World location is Ariel's line about being called "up at midnight to fetch dew from the still-vexed Bermudas" ([1611] 1999, 1.2.229–30). The geographical references in the play, such as the information that Prospero and his daughter were put to sea in a nutshell after he was ousted from Milan, suggest that Prospero's island is located in the western Mediterranean (Franssen 2000, 26), and the fact that Caliban's mother is from Algiers would actually make him a North African. Yet from the late nineteenth century on, as Vaughan and Vaughan's survey of the "Americanization" of *The Tempest* shows, mostly North and South American critics have nevertheless associated *The Tempest* with the New World; Sidney Lee, for example, argued that the play documented early Anglo-American history and "that the play's characters epitomize colonization's representative participants" (1999, 99). This tendency to Americanize the characters and to present Prospero as the bringer of culture and Caliban as the epitome of the savage man was then continued by eminent twentieth-century United States critics such as Leslie Fiedler, Leo Marx, and Frank Kermode (Franssen 2000, 24; Vaughan and Vaughan 1999, 105).

With the arrival of New Historicism, Caliban has taken on additional other identities besides this Native American one; various readings have also presented him as a black slave, a European savage, or as an Irish- or a Welshman (Franssen 2000, 26). Trinculo's reference to him as "half a fish and half a monster" ([1611] 1999, 3.2.28)—which is later repeated by Antonio—even moves him out of the realm of the human. One aspect of Caliban's identity that all critics more or less seem to agree upon is that he has served as a screen for projection of European fantasies about savagery and domination (Franssen 2000, 28). Whether or not Caliban actually is one of the first American slaves in English literature, the figure of Caliban is important to a reading of Stowe's novels through the prism of *The Tempest* because he is the play's slave and representative of racial otherness, and slavery and racial alterity are important thematic concerns of most of Stowe's novels.

Of the plethora of readings of *The Tempest* as one of the most important narratives about the beginnings of colonialism, I will single out the observations of Peter Hulme and Imtiaz Habib as particularly well suited for reading Stowe through Shakespeare. Hulme's discussion of the Prospero-Caliban relationship in *Colonial Encounters: Europe and the Native Caribbean* focuses on Prospero's attitudes as a colonizer and on Caliban's attempts to counteract his subaltern position. As Hulme points out, Prospero's magic (which he uses to control and torment Caliban) shows "a precise match with the situation of Europeans in America during the seventeenth century, whose technology (especially of firearms) suddenly *became* magical when introduced into a less technologically developed society" ([1986] 2004, 244). In spite of fearing Prospero's magic with which he physically torments and pinches Caliban, Prospero's slave remains rebellious; he tells Prospero that he has older claims to the island and indicates that he would not mind "to use Miranda" to people it with little Calibans. In the encounter with Stephano and Trinculo that Prospero sets up for Caliban, Caliban readily seizes the part of the treacherous slave that Prospero offers him, thus exposing the psychological makeup of the enslaver and the mechanisms of slavery:

> If *The Tempest's* critics have conceded that much turns on how you define Caliban, Prospero has no doubts: he offers Caliban the part of the treacherous slave with the silent entailment that acceptance . . . will be taken as definition of being. For Prospero this is merely confirmation of what he knows already: Caliban, like Antonio and Sebastian, only has to act according to character. . . . It would be difficult, incidentally, to deny that *The Tempest* here has its finger on what is most essential in the dialectic between colonizer and colonized, offering a parable of that relationship probably never equalled for its compelling logic. (239)

At the end of the play, after Stephano and Trinculo's plot has been thwarted, Caliban seemingly gives in to Prospero, promising to be wise thereafter and seek for grace. While subsequent commentators and appropriators of *The Tempest* might take this just as an indication that Caliban has decided to "lie low" for a while (Franssen 2000, 37), Hulme sees it as an indication of Prospero's success:

> The recognition afforded him by Caliban . . . franks that repression of the island's early history which we have watched the play enact. Caliban repudiates his claims *of his own volition*. The violence of slavery is abolished at a stroke and Caliban becomes just another feudal retainer whom Prospero can "acknowledge mine." This is the wish-fulfilment of the European colonist: his natural superiority voluntarily recognized. ([1986] 2004, 248)

Imtiaz Habib, who aptly describes Caliban as "early modern England's heterogeneously assembled amalgam of its black Other" (2000, 222), offers the image of "crouching" to explain the inconsistencies of Caliban's at times rebellious, at times servile behavior. The "psychological posture of crouching," according to Habib, reflects a "historical attitude of anti-colonial struggle that is in between the assertion of standing up and the resignation of sitting down" (226). In light of this figure, Habib views Caliban's participation in the unsuccessful rebellion against Prospero as a move that shows that "Caliban thus appears to be wanting not to be master himself, but only a better colonial mastership of the island, and in that seeming to preserve his colonizer's ideology while radically critiquing it and basically weakening it, and so indirectly respecting him while taking away the basis of this respect" (234). This position of crouching that, according to Habib, Shakespeare's colonial Other is subjected to seems both physically and psychologically painful. But many postcolonial critics and writers have read it as inscription of possible subversion and have viewed the *The Tempest* as a "foundational master text . . . of modern anti-colonial thought" (207), a text which, as Ania Loomba suggests, "encode[s], or could be altered to indicate, the possibility of subaltern resistance" (1996, 173).

Authored roughly 250 years before Stowe's novels, *The Tempest* can serve as a useful pretext and foil for *The Minister's Wooing*, which presents a different approach to passive resistance as "subaltern crouching." Race is an important concern of all of Stowe's novels, even the ones that are not as obviously concerned with the subject as are her antislavery novels *Uncle Tom's Cabin* and *Dred*. The main theme of *The Minister's Wooing* is of course Stowe's criticism of Calvinist theology; even the narrator somewhat self-critically remarks about the novel's heavily religious content that the readers might "get more theological tea than [they] can drink" ([1859] 1999, 40). As in Stowe's antislavery novels, in *The Minister's Wooing*, the topic of religion is wedded to the topic of racial otherness and the abolition of slavery is also an important plot element. In *Uncle Tom's Cabin*, Stowe presents the main character, Uncle Tom, as a Christ-like figure who dies for the sins of his enslavers; in *The Minister's Wooing*, the black (former) slave Candace is the holder and teacher of the "right religion," a feminized Protestantism that matches Stowe's preference for "God, the 'dear and tender mother,' not God the avenging father" (Fetterley 1993, 124).

Dr. Hopkins's wooing of the young Mary Scudder, which gives the book its title, proves to be unsuccessful; in the course of the novel "Hopkins undergoes a 'courtship' to Christ's example of sacrifice," as Wilson puts it (1985, 557). The novel's other main plotline revolves around the (spiritual) fate of James Marvyn, Mary's true love interest. For a long time, James remains unregenerate, is lost at sea and believed to be dead. Mrs. Marvyn, James's mother, is almost going insane with grief about his possible damnation and Mary also suffers bitterly—since James did not count himself among the elect who had received "evidences" of their salvation, his damnation is indeed very likely, according to the Calvinist belief system. The core statement of the theology devised by Dr. Hopkins—in his double function as historical figure and the parish's minister—does not promise much relief in this situation. As Lawrence Buell explains,

> Hopkins believed that true holiness consists in a special kind of love. His characteristic term for it is "disinterested benevolence," which he defines as "friendly affection to all intelligent beings" or—more abstractly—as "affection for the greatest good of the whole." Christ's voluntary sacrifice as the willing victim of God's wrath is the model of disinterested benevolence. The truly regenerate person is one who would submit unconditionally to the conviction of God's benevolent purposes even if he knew this meant his own damnation. ([1978] 1980, 265)[2]

Needless to say, this theological position does not provide any comfort for the loved ones of a person believed to have died unregenerate. Mrs. Marvyn expresses this to Mary: "Any father, who should make such use of power over his children as they say the Deity does with regard to us, would be looked upon as a monster by our very imperfect moral sense" ([1859] 1999, 206). Comfort ultimately comes from the freed slave Candace, whose theology puts Christ the redeemer at the center of her belief. Thus she tells Mrs. Marvyn:

> Why, de Lord a'n't like what ye tink,—He *loves* ye, honey! Why, jes' feel how I loves ye,—poor ole Candace,—an' I a'n't better'n Him as made me! Who was it wore de crown o' thorns, lamb? . . . He died for Mass'r Jim,—loved him and *died* for him,—jes give up his sweet, precious body and soul for him on de cross! (201)

And later she tells Mary "Honey . . . don't ye go for troublin' yer mind wid dis yer. I'm clar that Mass'r James is one o' de 'lect and I'm clar dar's consid'able more o' de 'lect dan people tink. Why, Jesus didn't die for nothin',—all dat love a'n't gwine to be wasted" (202). While it is unclear here from where—other than from her own convictions based on feeling—Candace gets her evangelical theology, it is quite clear that this New Testament theology that promises grace to everybody is much better suited to comforting a grieving parent than Dr. Hopkins's stern Calvinism.

As Susan K. Harris notices in her introduction to the 1999 edition of *The Minister's Wooing*, Stowe's characterization of Candace is predominantly positive since she is allowed to be "Stowe's mouthpiece for Gospel—a religion of love and comfort—over Calvinism's cold and succorless creed" (xv). Candace, according to Harris, "is a strategically important, extremely positive figure because she articulates the author's own beliefs on the most salient moral and theological issues in the story—slavery and salvation" (xv). Since Candace "had been stolen when about fifteen years of age" (67) from Africa, she is a reminder of the exotic, but she has been fully domesticized in New England and turned into a stereotypical black mammy, who not only is an expert cook, but also loves her masters. As the bearer of entirely positive "civilized virtues," Candace thus does not seem to have much at all in common with Shakespeare's Caliban, who, as Habib reminds us, is a figure "of the colonized native as the wild man" and thus features a number of distinguishing characteristics: "These are . . . dirt and darkness, barbaric religious practices, multifarious bestialities including chiefly cannibalism, and an uncontrolled sexuality manifested more often than not in a casual, socially pervasive nakedness" (2000, 214).

Stowe's Candace is a respectably married matron, who in many ways comes across as the definition of civilized respectability; thus she seems to be the total opposite of this characterization. The reasons for these diametrically opposed renditions of racial otherness can, I think, be found in the fact that while Shakespeare wrote *The Tempest* at the very beginning of European colonialism and thus had quite a bit of imaginative leeway in his depictions, Stowe, writing at the eve of the Civil War, became a witness to the worst of European and American colonial behavior. Outraged by the colonizers' brutal and inhumane behavior, Stowe had made the abolition of slavery in her own country her life's aim and always presented black slaves in a favorable light.

In *The Minister's Wooing*, she has Candace, again functioning as her spokesperson, advance two of her main arguments against slavery. Dr. Hopkins, trying to convince the Marvyns (and of course all other parishoners, too) that slavery is a great moral wrong, asks Candace if the black race should be slaves to the white, and she answers as follows:

> "Ef I must speak, I must, . . . No,—I neber did think 'twas right. When Gineral Washington was here, I hearn 'em read de Declaration of Independence and Bill O' Rights; an' I tole Cato den, says I, 'Ef dat ar' true, you an' I are as free as anybody.' It stands to reason. Why, look at me—I an't a critter. I's neider huff nor horns. I's a reasonable bein', a woman,—much a woman as anybody," she said, holding up her head with an air majestic as a palm tree; "an' Cato—he's a man, born free an' equal, ef dat's any truth in what you read,—dat's all." ([1859] 1999, 104)

Stowe here puts two important arguments in Candace's mouth: The first is that the United States as a postcolonial nation that has just recently achieved independence from Britain, cannot claim that "all men are born free" as long as it condones slavery on its own soil; the second, that a black woman "an't a critter" and thus should not be treated like chattel. This testimonial, while it seems to be stating the very obvious, shows that Stowe's Christian outlook made her side with the evolutionary monogeneticists of her time, who did not believe in the separate species theory of racial difference that some evolutionary biologists advanced and that was used as a justification of slavery on the grounds that African people were not human.[3] (Being referred to as "not human" certainly is a charge that Shakespeare's Caliban who is called a "monster" and a "fish" has to endure.)

Stowe's decision to have Candace argue her case here on the grounds of her own humanity is part of her strategy in her fight against slavery to make black protagonists personally and collectively unassailable. This strategy entails excluding from the "collective African character" any hint at a barbaric nature, and physical or sexual grossness. Stowe actively tried to debunk the stereotypical presentation of Africans as naturally savage and brutal by endowing them with the best "white" qualities such as "natural religiousness" and motherliness. In *A Key to Uncle Tom's Cabin*, she wrote: "The negro race is confessedly more simple, docile, childlike, and affectionate, than other races; and hence the divine graces of love and faith, when in-breathed by the Holy Spirit, find in their natural temperament a more congenial atmosphere" ([1854] 1968, 41).[4] For Stowe, the "natural religiosity of blacks"[5] always ties in with childlikeness.[6] In her books she often describes individual African Americans and also "the race as a whole" as childlike and dependent. Susan Harris also comments upon this in regard to Candace, thus qualifying her positive assessment of Candace's "natural religiosity":

> Stowe can use Candace as she does precisely because the nineteenth-century racial narratives assumed that black people would be more likely than whites to experience holiness through feeling rather than through thought. The bottom lines here are first, that Stowe values emotion over rationalism in religion, and second, that she assumes that African Americans are better at feeling than at thinking. (1999, xv)

While Shakespeare commentators seem quite reluctant to criticize Shakespeare plays "as ideologically retrograde" in his construction of race and gender (Loomba 2003),[7] Stowe critics have engaged in heated critical discussions about her presentation of racial otherness; African American critics in particular have voiced their outrage at her frequent presentation of black men as feminized and avuncular and of small black children as pet-like, and they have also commented negatively on her privileging of light-skinned black characters as more intelligent than dark-skinned ones, and on her exclusive encoding of sexual desire between different races as transgression.[8] Some white female critics, however, as, for example Elizabeth Ammons, have deemed especially her feminization of African American males (Tom in *Uncle Tom's Cabin*; Tiff in *Dred*) a stroke of genius because it allowed her to debunk the stereotype of the black man as rapist (1986, 168).[9]

Stowe obviously was not able to transcend the racial assumptions typical of her nineteenth-century white middle-class background, and she continued to operate from within them throughout her writing career. As an American "postcolonial" who wanted to end the horror of slavery, she felt obliged to elide any references to savagery in her presentation of the racially Other—thus her sanitized presentation of black slaves effectively killed the Caliban in all of her black male characters.[10] While in *The Tempest* Caliban appears both rebellious and servile, the black characters in *The Minister's Wooing* are servile to the point of completely agreeing with their masters'/ employers' ideas about slavery and about theology;[11] their behavior, in fact, almost suggests that they might be suffering from Stockholm syndrome.[12] Even Candace, who is quite outspoken when she is directly asked to comment upon a situation,[13] ultimately always defers to the point of view of her benignant "superiors" ([1859] 1999, 84) (Stowe's term for apparently all the white people that Candace comes in contact with).

Candace's reaction to her newly given freedom does not come as much of a surprise and, to repeat Hulme's observation with a twist, can also be seen "as the wish-fulfilment of the *American master* [European colonizer in the original]: his natural superiority voluntarily recognized" ([1986] 2004, 248). Almost echoing Caliban's promise at the end of *The Tempest* to be "wise hereafter / And seek for grace" ([1611] 1999, 5.1.295–96), Candace says "I want ye all to know . . . dat it's my will an' pleasure to go right on doin' my work jes' de same; an' Missis, please, I'll allers put three eggs in de crullers, now; an I' won't turn de wash-basin down in de sink, but hang it jam-up on de nail; . . . I'll do eberything jes' as ye tells me. Now you try me an' see ef I won't! ([1859] 1999, 104–5).

Thus, the question remains whether or not Candace's behavior can be seen as a type of (post-)colonial "crouching" as described by Habib. While Caliban's way of "crouching" implies secret rebellion, Candace's type of "crouching" at first sight seems to be at best an ambiguous, rather passive, resistance. Prospero has not succeeded in getting Caliban to give up his belief in his mother's God, Setebos, whereas the Puritans seem to have been eminently successful in suppressing African religion by inculcating their Christian faith in Candace and her fellow slaves. Yet the (post-)Puritans' victory at this point might also signify their defeat. Just as Caliban, according to Habib, upsets the colonial mastership by simply wanting it to be a better one, Candace beats her "superiors" at their own game: in having devised a "better theology" that saves rather than scares the sinner, she has bested the colonizer/enslaver at his own game of "civilization."

Stowe's containment of racial alterity through "domestication" has to be seen as part of her attempt to present a model society for the United States (and perhaps beyond) in her New England novels, which portray everyday life in small towns and focus on the "domestic affairs" of religion, race, gender, and class. The communities featured serve as microcosms that reflect social issues that also regard national society at large. A similar project was undertaken by the English novelist George Eliot, a correspondent of Stowe's, whose novel *Middlemarch* is a centerpiece of her project of following cutting-edge scientists and philosophers of her day in comparing society to a natural organism in which human beings function as individual "social organs."[14]

In *The Pearl of Orr's Island* and in *The Minister's Wooing*, Stowe, without explicitly invoking organicism, addresses very similar questions of how the individual fits into a society that is trying to establish a uniquely American identity and to find out how a truly democratic society can be made to function properly. In *The Minister's Wooing* she addresses this venture in a narratorial comment: "New England presents probably the only example of a successful commonwealth founded on a theory, as a distinct experiment in the problem of society. It was for this reason that the minds of its great thinkers dwelt so much on the final solution of that problem in this world" (80). For Stowe, one of the big problems of society was the greed that would turn people into exploitative capitalists or even slaveholders. In *The Minister's Wooing*, Simeon Brown, who had generously contributed to Hopkins's parish, is one of those rapacious slaveholders. Even though Hopkins knows that Brown will withdraw his financial support, he tells him that slavery is "a sin against God" (97). Hopkins sacrifices his own and his parish's financial well-being because he fears that if he does not contribute to solving the biggest problem that his society is facing, namely slavery, the millennium that he, like his fellow Puritans, is waiting for might never come.[15] Moved by humanitarian reasons and religious fear, Hopkins decides to take his stand against the abhorrent practice of slavery: "I believe the time is coming when I must utter my voice: I cannot go down to the wharves or among the shipping, without these dumb creatures look at me so that I am ashamed. . . . I must testify" (85). Yet while Hopkins shows a lot of compassion for the slaves, he himself might be an impediment to democracy, as the narrator describes him as a man whose "soul [was] . . . trained from its earliest years in the habit of thought engendered by monarchy" (247). This lack of democratic spirit is of course also demonstrable in Hopkins's theology of "disinterested benevolence." And the fact that the marriage of Mary and James will ultimately serve as a building block for a democratic society also shows that men like Hopkins belong to an earlier historical time that will have to be overcome to advance society.

By instrumentalizing religion for the benefit of society, Hopkins actually does what his society considers the best remedy for social problems. In Stowe's social organism, religion is both the glue that holds society together and the motor that makes it function. Thus it cannot be above criticism and must also be subject to reform, which, as Stowe suggests, should come about by infusing "the rational, white, masculine" with a dose of "compassionate, feminine, black" feeling.

*The Pearl of Orr's Island* is similarly concerned with questions about how a better society can be built, which character/istic/s are desirable and which ones have to be rooted out. Marriage is obviously one of the foundations of Western society and thus "finding the right match" is of considerable importance to society as well as the individual. In both *The Minister's Wooing* and *The Pearl of Orr's Island*, the female protagonists are compared to Shakespeare's Miranda. In the play, Prospero engineers the marriage of his daughter Miranda to Ferdinand, the son of the King of Naples, which incidentally also ensures his own return to political power. While Shakespeare critics have been able to invest Caliban with a good bit of agency that might not be obvious to a casual reader of the play,[16] Miranda certainly is one of the more passive characters in Shakespeare's work. She passes from the control of a father, who might be using her as exchange object in his power struggle with male rivals (Singh 1996, 200) to the control of a husband whose actions she apparently unquestioningly approves, telling him that even if he cheated at a game, "I would call it fair play" ([1611] 1999, 5.1.174). The only time that she asserts herself is in a speech in which she castigates Caliban for his supposed attempt at raping her—editors of *The Tempest* have found this speech so unlikely coming out of her mouth that they have mistakenly attributed it to Prospero (Franssen 2000, 33).[17] The female protagonists of both *The Minister's Wooing* and *The Pearl of Orr's Island* both have much more agency than Miranda in finding a husband—and this is not only the case because they do not live on an uninhabited island. Mary Scudder's widowed mother initially emulates Prospero's behavior in selecting the much older Dr. Hopkins as a matching husband for Mary, but unlike Prospero, who seems to have mostly his own gain in mind by picking Ferdinand, Mrs. Scudder wants the pious Dr. Hopkins rather than the "unregenerate" James as a spouse for Mary out of concern for Mary's eternal soul. Her attempts are thwarted by the dressmaker Miss Prissy, who tells Hopkins that Mary's heart actually belongs to James, and by Virginie de Frontignac, who is herself unhappily married to a much older man and dresses Mary up as a Miranda awaiting her Ferdinand. Thus, in *The Minister's Wooing*, romance ultimately defeats social control, but this, of course, does not happen before it is proven that James finally counts himself among the elect and thus makes for a proper Puritan husband.

In *The Pearl of Orr's Island*, the protagonist Mara (like Mary, her name is also a variation on Miranda) from childhood on casts herself and her stepbrother Moses in terms of the Miranda-Ferdinand relationship. The match again proves to be problematic, but this time the appropriation seems to comment on the uneven gender relationship presented in the pretext. In that Mara pursues her Moses/Ferdinand without any magical help from outside, she is clearly given more agency than Miranda. The text, by stressing Mara's hybrid being "as a half-spiritual creature—a child of air" ([1862] 2001, 327), indicates that Stowe also wanted Mara to transcend the boundaries of the Miranda figure by adding a bit of an Ariel. As Ferdinand may turn out to be, Moses is a "born ruler"—also in the literal sense, as the plot later on reveals. "As a perfect little miniature of proud manliness" (81), he loves to act like one. The narrator's descriptions of Moses as a boy tend to be rather unfavorable; he puts down Mara for being a girl and thus not being able to go to sea and he constantly refuses to return her affection. And, as Joan Hedrick mentions in her introduction to the novel, he does not see his life story reflected in *The Tempest* and just acts bored, when she recites her favorite passages to him. The narrator comments on the incompatibility of Moses and Mara as follows: "There are two classes of human beings in this world: one class seem made to give love, and the other to take it. Now Mrs. Pennel and Mara belonged to the first class, and little Master Moses to the latter" (104). Even before Moses enters his teenage years, he shows imperial behavior, emulating the Romans and their conquests. Presenting a handful of birds' eggs to Mara, he boasts "the old eagles couldn't beat me" (164), and when Mara interjects that he certainly made the birds feel bad, he just says "No, they're only mad, to think they couldn't beat me. I beat them just as the Romans used to beat folks,—I played their nest was a city, and I spoiled it" (165). At this rather early point in the novel, the narrator implies that Moses and Mara are incompatible and that their story cannot come to a happy ending: "But if ever two children, or two grown people, thus organized are thrown into intimate relations, it follows from the very laws of their being, that one must hurt the other, simply by being itself; one must always hunger for what the other has not to give" (151).

Moses's imperial attitude can apparently actually be traced to his real family of origin. The foundling turns out to be of noble Spanish West Indian origin, but at least the male side of the family is described as dissolute and "of a very low moral standard" (249). According to the narrator, families like his are constantly threatened by devolution because "[i]n ill-regulated families in that region, the care of the children is from the first in the hands of half-barbarized negroes, whose power of moulding and assimilating childish minds is peculiar, so that the teacher has to contend constantly with a savage element in the children which seems to have been drawn in with the mother's milk" (251). Even though there is no evidence that Moses has actually ever been subject to such influences, he seems to be in grave danger of becoming a "Caliban by association." So even though Moses is white, there seems to be a pronounced savage, "half-barbarized negro" element in him that has to be eradicated before he can enter the island community as a full member. (*The Pearl of Orr's Island* is exceptional in that Stowe's narrator does not once mention the redemptive qualities of the black race.)

Moreover, Moses also lacks the civilizing element of "natural religiosity." When he is a teenager, he is still unimpressed by New England Protestantism: "There was no God in his estimate of life—and a sort of secret unsuspected determination at the bottom of his heart that there should be none. He feared religion, from a suspicion that it might hamper some of his future plans" (233). This attitude reveals a dangerous potential, which Moses might actually come to use: Mara soon discovers that he keeps the wrong company. He spends his time with a gang of smugglers who try to convince him of robbing his own grandfather. Afraid of the damage that might be done to Moses's character and salvation if she cannot stop this development, Mara tells her kindly friend, Captain Kittredge, about Moses's problems. Kittredge decides to take Moses on a voyage that will put him on the right path again. The scheme works, and as a young adult Moses appears to have been "civilized" into becoming a productive member of his

Puritan society. He still exhibits traces of immaturity and of his formerly "imperial" behavior but is now able to return Mara's feelings and finally understands that "the winds and waves took me up and carried me to the lonely island where the magic princess dwelt" (324). When Mara calls him Ferdinand, he actually replies, "And you are Miranda" (324). But at this point it is already too late. Mara is fatally ill with consumption and dies shortly after Moses has come back from the sea. After a period of purifying and subduing grief—which finally turns him into the man that Mara wanted him to be—Moses is free to marry Mara's friend Sally Kittredge who is temperamentally much better suited to him.

Stowe's New England novels obviously profit from colorful "Shakespearean" characters like Moses, who does not fit the mold of the stern New England (post-)Puritans, and Captain Kittredge, who tells yarns about his encounters with mermaids and mermen. Many commentators have pointed out that Stowe could not resist seasoning her narratives with hints at romance, magic, and artistry[18]—all phenomena that thrive on forms of "untruthful representation" and thus evoked the natural scorn of Puritan descendants, who were still fighting Satan as the supreme liar and deceiver.[19]

In reference to *The Minister's Wooing*, Christopher Wilson has argued that Stowe's showcasing of feelings evoked by the beauty of God's grace in everyday life, by "pantheistic sentiments," enables "the first step toward a reconciliation with temporal things, for these things are, Stowe thought, imbued with God's romance" (1985, 562). The Frenchwoman Virginie de Frontignac provides the "influence of Catholic beauty and grace" that reinvests Mary's piety with passion ([1859] 1999, 569). Yet, as Wilson points out, the problem that crops up here is that following one's heart, as Virginie suggests, can lead to being seduced by an absolutely corrupt individual like Aaron Burr. Critics Joan Hedrick (as mentioned above) and Judith Fetterley are just as skeptical about Stowe's presentation of the beneficial potential of romance in *The Pearl of Orr's Island*. Like Hedrick, Fetterley argues that romance does not do the female protagonist any good at all; Mara's death "constitutes the final displacement and critique of romance, for Mara dies to escape the loss of self and God that marriage to Moses would entail for both him and her" (1993, 121). She concludes from this rather negatively that "for Stowe romantic love, despite any conventions to the contrary, has no conversionary power and cannot transform difference into something other than danger" (119).

And even if the imagination leads only to fictional pursuits rather than severe romantic disappointment, it remains dangerous because fiction is not fact and thus it represents deception rather than truth. Mara, who, until she is told otherwise, thinks that *The Tempest* is a historical account, is so intrigued by the story and by Prospero's magic that she asks Captain Kittredge about it. Kittredge tells her that *The Tempest* is a play and therefore did not happen, but he nevertheless immediately launches into an account of his own encounters with sorcerers and magicians. Prodded by Mara's remark that Prospero gave up his magic when he had achieved everything he wanted to, he suddenly remembers that he is a Puritan and concedes, "It was pretty much the best thing he could do . . . because the Bible is agin such things" ([1862] 2001, 143). And he immediately also asks his daughter Sally not to tell her mother that he had actually seen a performance of the play in a theater (a Puritan figuration of a den of evil) in London because she "would n't think I 's fit to go to meetin' for six months arter, if she heard on 't" (144). Throughout the narrative, Captain Kittredge catches himself several times telling his yarns in front of adults; usually he only dares to tell his wonderful stories to children who will not immediately pronounce him a lost cause on account of his active imagination. Kittredge's example shows that storytelling remains a risky business in Stowe's New England novels because, like romance, it stubbornly resists containment.

In *The Minister's Wooing* and *The Pearl of Orr's Island*, Stowe appropriates "Shakespearean" plots dealing with romance, magic, patriarchy, imperialism, and racial alterity to negotiate which spiritual tendencies and social elements a changing society like the (post-)Puritan New England can accommodate without jeopardizing its foundational principles. The above discussion has shown that Stowe's narrators—as spokespersons for the more enlightened members of the microcosms of Newport and Orr's Island—seem to be ready to welcome the antipatriarchal tendencies, which will eventually result in more equitable gender relationships. Moreover, both novels condemn imperial behavior, but only *The Minister's Wooing* presents the black race as "civilizing" influence on society at large. While Stowe seems to suggest in her New England novels that the potentially disruptive phenomenon of racial alterity cannot only be contained, but actually even be made productive for societal good, she remains much more ambiguous about "magic" and romance.[20] While the former cannot be rid of its devilish connotations, the latter remains problematic because of its potential for seduction and disillusionment—since both of them have nevertheless proven to be very attractive to human beings, they make for intriguing unresolved tensions in Stowe's fiction.

## NOTES

1. For a discussion of "providential" deaths in nineteenth-century fiction see Carol Christ's article, "Aggression and Providential Death in George Eliot's Fiction" (1976).

2. In this context, Stowe writes about her fictional character Dr. Hopkins: "In calm theological reasoning, he could demonstrate, in the dryest tone, that, if the eternal torment of six bodies and souls were absolutely the necessary means for preserving

the eternal blessedness of thirty six, benevolence would require us to rejoice in it, not in itself considered, but in view of the greater good" ([1859] 1999, 95).

3. Race theory expanded into a field of academic study in the nineteenth century. Eighteenth-century race theory (in spite of its obvious discrimination of Africans) was rather benign because it proceeded from a monogenetic view of human origin, according to which all human beings had a common ancestry and all human races were members of the same species. Racial difference—which was then believed to comprise variations in color, anatomy, intelligence, temperament, and morality— was attributed to environmental differences. During the first half of the nineteenth century, however, scientific opinion on race experienced a paradigm shift from the assumption of a monogenetic to the assumption of a polygenetic human origin. Polygenetic theories maintained that racial difference originated in the separate creation of different human species. In the United States this view was made popular by Josiah Nott, whose theories provided his country with a "scientific" apology for slavery (Young 1995, 1–19).

4. Stowe might have derived her racial views about blacks from lectures delivered in 1837 and 1838 by Alexander Kinmont in Cincinnati, where she lived (Nuernberg 1992, 260).

5. Anthony Appiah notes that this myth of the "naturally religious African" was also common among missionaries who had come back from Africa impressed with the Africans' "natural religiosity" and "the yearning of the native African for a higher religion" (1992, 23). According to Appiah this supposed naturalness of religious worship among Africans was fabricated in the minds of those who observed the behavior of enslaved African Americans through a "racialized" lens (1992, 23).

6. It is interesting to note that throughout her novels dealing with race, Stowe consistently equates women with children and black men—thus, in *Dred*, Harry Gordon, the white character Nina's slave brother, never addresses his wife, Lisette, by her first name, but always calls her "child" instead. From a twenty-first-century point of view one might certainly wonder what kind of self-image Stowe had if she associated women with children. Did she mean to imply that their intelligence was "less developed" than that of white males? If this was the case one could almost exonerate Stowe from the reproach of racial discrimination because in the light of this conviction, she would put herself on par with black males. But by the same token one could, of course, also argue that Stowe's socialization necessarily made her adopt racist and sexist viewpoints.

7. Ania Loomba suggests that Shakespeare remains rather sacrosanct when it comes to being criticized: "Postcolonial critics (again like cultural materialists) are accused of regarding Shakespeare's plays as ideologically retrograde, of 'attacking' Shakespeare, as well as of positing a reductive relationship between text and context. . . . In these attacks on postcolonial readings of *The Tempest* . . . it is the genius of Shakespeare, or at least the all-encompassing nature of his vision (sometimes confused with the vision of Prospero) that is repeatedly at stake" (2003).

8. For criticism of Stowe's depiction of race in *Uncle Tom's Cabin* see James Baldwin ([1949] 1980), Sophia Cantave (2000), Sarah Smith Ducksworth (1992), and Richard Yarborough (1986).

9. Ammons very astutely identified what Stowe accomplished when she created Tom: "Stowe's Tom *is* soft. He personifies the motherly Christ. . . . That Tom is not

classically masculine—that he does not fight for his life but instead puts the lives of others first, that he refuses to meet violence with violence, that he remains compassionate, giving, and emotional to the end—illustrates Stowe's political genius in *Uncle Tom's Cabin*. What better way to inflame the culture against slavery than by characterizing her hero as a stereotypical Victorian heroine: pious, home-centered, self-sacrificing, nonviolent?" (1986, 168).

10. Dred, the eponymous hero of Stowe's second antislavery novel, shows that Stowe was willing to listen to her critics; unlike Uncle Tom, the figure of Dred proves that a purely black character can exhibit masculine valor and intelligence.

11. In chapter 17, "Polemics in the Kitchen," Candace argues with the slave Digo who believes "that slavery was a divine ordinance" ([1859] 1999, 162) because this is what his own minister master believes.

12. In "The Sambo Mentality and the Stockholm Syndrome Revisited," Barbara A. Huddleston-Mattai and P. Rudy Mattai argue that slaves, like the captives in the famous Sweden bank robbery, "were not merely passive and sterile in the transference of the mode of thought of the masters but sought instead to reconstruct perceptually the psyche of the master and occasionally assumed his characteristics, albeit exceeding the behavior exhibited by the master" (1993, 346).

13. Candace's outspokenness is explained by her African origins: "There was a sort of savage freedom about her which they excused in right of her having been born and bred a heathen, and of course not to be expected to come at once under the yoke of civilization" ([1859] 1999, 69).

14. George Eliot's focus on society as an organism is particularly evident in *Middlemarch*, in which she describes the town's microcosm in terms of web imagery. Eliot's notion of social organicism is indebted to her reception of Auguste Comte, Charles Darwin, John Stuart Mill, Herbert Spencer, and her partner, George Henry Lewes, whose social science treatise *Problems of Life and Mind* (1874) was written in the years before the publication of *Middlemarch*. Lewes situates (hu)man's position in the social organism as follows: "Man is no longer to be considered as an assemblage of organs, but also as an organ in a Collective Organism. From the former he derives his sensations, judgments, primary impulses; from the latter his conceptions, theories, and virtues" (1874, 167). And he describes the relation of individual "organic" societies in relation to a social organism as follows: "The organism is evolved. . . . [I]ts organs are groups of minor organisms . . . all sharing in a common substance . . . ; precisely as the great Social Organism is a group of societies, each of which is a group of families, all sharing in a common life,—every family having at once its individual independence and its social dependence through connection with every other" (113–14).

15. In her article "Confronting Antichrist: The Influence of Jonathan Edwards's Millennial Vision," Helen Petter Westra elaborates that Stowe viewed slavery as a dangerous impediment to the advent of the millennium that would precede Christ's second coming (1992, 156). In *The Minister's Wooing*, Hopkins describes the millennium as an ideal state of social being in which labor will be greatly reduced ([1859] 1999, 80).

16. As Jyotsna Singh puts it, "Caliban has come a long way from appearing as the eighteenth-century primitive or the nineteenth-century Darwinian 'missing link' to be accepted as a colonial subject or an embodiment of any oppressed group" (1996, 193).

17. In "Sister Letters: Miranda's *Tempest* in Canada," Diana Brydon discusses how feminist critics have reacted to Miranda's lack of agency and argues that Canadian appropriations of *The Tempest* have presented "models of defiance and leadership that may not take the form of outright rebellion or violent retaliation" (1993, 167).

18. In chapter 8, "Which Treats of Romance," Stowe's narrator suggests that romance is needed to check egotistical, rapacious behavior. Thus, the narrator argues that if in his youth, the capitalist, Mr. Smith, had actually listened to "the descending angel of love . . . Mr. Smith might have become a man instead of a banker" ([1859] 1999, 70).

19. Yet, according to the narrator of *The Minister's Wooing* even "hard old New England divines," like Dr. Hopkins felt the need for artistic creation and became "poets of metaphysical philosophy, who built systems in artistic fervor" ([1859] 1999, 17). This artistic spirit paradoxically caused them to "feel self exhale beneath them as they rose into the higher regions of thought" (17) and their poetical pursuits paradoxically eliminated feeling, as Hopkins's doctrine of "disinterested benevolence" most certainly did.

20. Gillian Brown proposes a more positive reading concerning the integration of Shakespearean "magic" into Stowe's plot. She interprets the scene in which Mara's grandfather has a dream about Jesus picking up the "pearl Mara" from the shore in terms of a merging of Shakespearean and Christian narrative: "Mara's beloved images from *The Tempest* merge into the vision of heavenly ascension; her grandfather's dream subsumes the Shakespearean representation of marvelous events on earth, like the production of pearls, into Christian narrative, which pairs pearls with the gates of heaven" (2004, 91).

## WORKS CITED

Ammons, Elizabeth. 1986. "Stowe's Dream of the Mother-Savior: *Uncle Tom's Cabin* and American Women Writers before the 1920s." In *New Essays on "Uncle Tom's Cabin,"* ed. Eric J. Sundquist, 155–95. Cambridge: Cambridge University Press.

Appiah, Kwame Anthony. 1992. *In My Father's House: Africa in the Philosophy of Culture.* New York: Oxford University Press.

Baldwin, James. [1949] 1980. "Everybody's Protest Novel." In *Critical Essays on Harriet Beecher Stowe,* ed. Elizabeth Ammons, 92–97. Boston: Hall.

Berkson, Dorothy. 1980. "Millennial Politics and the Feminine Fiction of Harriet Beecher Stowe." In *Critical Essays on Harriet Beecher Stowe,* ed. Elizabeth Ammons, 244–57. Boston: Hall.

Brown, Gillian. 2004. "Reading and Children: *Uncle Tom's Cabin* and *The Pearl of Orr's Island.*" In *The Cambridge Companion to Harriet Beecher Stowe,* ed. Cindy Weinstein, 77–95. Cambridge: Cambridge University Press.

Brydon, Diana. 1993. "Sister Letters: Miranda's *Tempest* in Canada." In *Cross-Cultural Performances: Differences in Women's Re-Visions of Shakespeare,* ed. Marianne Novy, 165–84. Urbana: University of Illinois Press.

Buell, Lawrence. [1978] 1980. "Calvinism Romanticized: Harriet Beecher Stowe, Samuel Hopkins, and *The Minister's Wooing.*" In *Critical Essays on Harriet Beecher Stowe,* ed. Elizabeth Ammons, 259–75. Reprint, Boston: Hall.

Cantave, Sophia. 2000. "Who Gets to Create the Lasting Images? The Problem of Black Representation in *Uncle Tom's Cabin*." In *Approaches to Teaching Stowe's "Uncle Tom's Cabin*," ed. Elizabeth Ammons and Susan Belasco, 93–103. New York: Modern Language Association of America.

Christ, Carol. 1976. "Aggression and Providential Death in George Eliot's Fiction." *Novel* 9:130–40.

Ducksworth, Sarah Smith. 1992. "Stowe's Construction of an African Persona and the Creation of White Identity for a New World Order." In *The Stowe Debate: Rhetorical Strategies in "Uncle Tom's Cabin*," ed. Mason I. Lowance Jr., Ellen E. Westbrook, and R. C. De Prospo, 205–35. Amherst: University of Massachusetts Press.

Fetterley, Judith. 1993. "Only a Story, Not a Romance: Harriet Beecher Stowe's *The Pearl of Orr's Island*." In *The (Other) American Traditions: Nineteenth-Century Women Writers*, ed. Joyce W. Warren, 108–25. New Brunswick, NJ: Rutgers University Press.

Franssen, Paul. 2000. "A Muddy Mirror." In *Constellation Caliban*, ed. Nadia Lie and Theo D'haen, 23–42. Amsterdam: Rodopi.

Habib, Imtiaz. 2000. *Shakespeare and Race*. Lanham, MD: University Press of America.

Harris, Susan K. 1999. Introduction to *The Minister's Wooing*, by Harriet Beecher Stowe, vii–xxiii. New York: Penguin.

Hedrick, Joan. 2001. Foreword to *The Pearl of Orr's Island: A Story of the Coast of Maine*, by Harriet Beecher Stowe, vii–xvi. Boston: Houghton Mifflin.

Huddleston-Mattai, Barbara A., and P. Rudy Mattai. 1993. "The Sambo Mentality and the Stockholm Syndrome Revisited: Another Dimension to an Examination of the Plight of the African-American." *Journal of Black Studies* 23:344–57.

Hulme, Peter. [1986] 2004. "Prospero and Caliban." In *The Tempest*, ed. Peter Hulme and William P. Sherman, 233–49. Amended reprint, New York: Norton.

Lewes, George Henry. 1874. Vol. 1 of *Problems of Life and Mind*. London: Trübner.

Loomba, Ania. 1996. "Shakespeare and Cultural Difference." In *Alternative Shakespeares*, ed. Terence Hawkes, 2: 164–91. London: Routledge.

———. 2003. "The Postcolonial Tempest: Response to Peter Hulme's 'Stormy Weather.'" www.emc.eserver.org/1-3/loomba.html.

Nuernberg, Susan Marie. 1992. "The Rhetoric of Race." In *The Stowe Debate: Rhetorical Strategies in "Uncle Tom's Cabin*," ed. Mason I. Lowance Jr., Ellen E. Westbrook, and R. C. De Prospo, 255–70. Amherst: University of Massachusetts Press.

Shakespeare, William. [1611] 1999. *The Tempest*, ed. Virginia Mason Vaughan and Alden T. Vaughan. Walton-on-Thames, UK: Nelson.

Singh, Jyotsna G. 1996. "Caliban versus Miranda: Race and Gender Conflicts in Postcolonial Rewritings of *The Tempest*." In *Feminist Readings of Early Modern Culture: Emerging Subjects*, ed. Valerie Traub, M. Lindsay Kaplan, and Dympna Callaghan, 191–209. Cambridge: Cambridge University Press.

Stowe, Harriet Beecher Stowe. [1854]. 1968. *A Key to Uncle Tom's Cabin*. New York: Arno Press.

Stowe, Harriet Beecher. [1859] 1999. *The Minister's Wooing*, ed. Susan K. Harris. New York: Penguin.

———. [1862] 2001. *The Pearl of Orr's Island*, ed. Joan Hedrick. Boston: Houghton Mifflin.

Vaughan, Virginia Mason, and Alden T. Vaughan. 1999. Introduction to *The Tempest*, by William Shakespeare, 1–138. Walton-on-Thames, UK: Nelson.

Westra, Helen Petter. 1992. "Confronting Antichrist: The Influence of Jonathan Edwards's Millennial Vision." In *The Stowe Debate: Rhetorical Strategies in "Uncle Tom's Cabin*," ed. Mason I. Lowance Jr., Ellen E. Westbrook, and R. C. De Prospo, 141–58. Amherst: University of Massachusetts Press.

Wilson, Christopher P. 1985. "Tempests and Teapots: Harriet Beecher Stowe's *The Minister's Wooing.*" *New England Quarterly* 58:554–77.

Yarborough, Richard. 1986. "Strategies of Black Characterization in *Uncle Tom's Cabin.*" In *New Essays on "Uncle Tom's Cabin,*" ed. Eric J. Sundquist, 45–84. Cambridge: Cambridge University Press.

Young, Robert. 1995. *Colonial Desire: Hybridity in Theory, Culture and Race.* London: Routledge.

# Ecstasy in Excess

## Mysticism, Hysteria, and Masculinity in Harriet Beecher Stowe's *Dred*

*William P. Mullaney*

In *Uncle Tom's Cabin* (1852), Harriet Beecher Stowe describes midnight as "the strange, mystic hour when the veil between the frail present and the eternal future grows thin" ([1852] 1989, 142). In her evocative description, we are immediately drawn to Stowe's Hawthornian reference to the veil, here symbolizing the boundary between worldly existence and the afterlife. In many ways, it could be the same veil that Zenobia draped over the delicate Priscilla, in her role as the Veiled Lady, which enabled her to gaze into the future in Hawthorne's *The Blithedale Romance* (1852). However, the word in Stowe's description on which I would like to focus is "mystic" because it invokes a specific historical and religious phenomenon that traditional Christian-centered readings of Stowe's work tend to overlook. While we may be tempted to read Stowe's use of the adjective from a predominantly modern and secular point of view, as a synonym for *mysterious* or *cryptic*, her acute knowledge of religion and contemporary culture points to more contextualized usage that draws upon the long and strange history of mysticism, especially its controversial appearance during the nineteenth-century revival of spiritualism in the United States. In Stowe's description, the midnight hour is mystical because it occupies the uncertain temporal space between this life and the next, much like the figure of the mystic or Hawthorne's mesmerist-inspired Veiled Lady, whose special gift was believed to be his or her ability to inhabit both the spiritual and material worlds.

In the following essay, I use the figure of the mystic and Stowe's complex understanding of mysticism to explicate her much-maligned novel *Dred: A Tale of the Great Dismal Swamp* (1856), the antislavery follow-up to *Uncle Tom's Cabin*. At the center of the novel is the inscrutable title character, a fictional composite of slave leaders Nat Turner and Denmark Vesey. The character of Dred has most often been dismissed as a failed creation, a throwback to an Old Testament warrior-prophet who seems wildly misplaced in the novel. No critic, however, has attempted to read Dred's seemingly outdated and often emotional religiosity within the larger context of the spiritualist movement, seeing it as both a product of and response to the cultural forces that were driving the movement. By examining Dred specifically as a mystic, we can see how Stowe was drawing upon her knowledge of religious history and contemporary philosophy, specifically transcendentalism, as well as upon popular notions of mysticism as undiagnosed hysteria.

By focusing on Dred as Stowe's attempt to create a nineteenth-century black mystic, much of the novel's ambivalence about the future of slavery and the potential of the black race is revealed. As an ancient figure simultaneously venerated, ridiculed, and feared, the mystic occupies a contested space where the forces of faith contend with rational disbelief. It is my contention that Stowe's representation of black mysticism exploits the confusion surrounding many of the practice's beliefs, especially those relating to sanity and gender. In portraying her slave leader as a mystic, Stowe acknowledges the cultural notion of slaves as fundamentally religious people while simultaneously undermining that notion by emphasizing the uncontrollable and sometimes dangerous nature of the mystic. Because the mystical experience typically involves a loss of control, it was identified at the time as innately connected not only with the weakened female constitution but also with the primitive black temperament. Stowe indicates in the narrative that the character of Dred is based on reported accounts of the nation's most famous slave insurrections, the so-called Vesey conspiracy in South Carolina (1822) and the famous slave revolt in Virginia led by Nat Turner (1831), but the novel reveals that she is not willing to support the idea of black retribution, even if it is couched in divine inspiration. Although Dred is also represented as a nature mystic like the transcendentalists, he is depicted as too primitive, too much a part of the swamp he inhabits, to process his mystical experiences beyond their initial impulses. For all her abolitionist intentions, Stowe could not create a black Thoreau in the wilderness because such an image would be too threatening to her readers.

The odd combination of feminine weakness and masculine brutality within the character of Dred highlights the novel's dizzying gender politics and invites a reconsideration of what Elizabeth Ammons, expressing a commonly held point of view, has called Stowe's radical substitution of feminine and maternal values for masculine ones as presented in *Uncle Tom's Cabin* (1980, 152). In the four years between the publications of *Uncle Tom's Cabin* and *Dred*, an undercurrent of uncertainty seems to have developed in Stowe's abolitionism, one that implies that the woman-centered agenda of the first novel is no longer a feasible strategy to achieve the end of slavery. In *Dred*, it appears that the problem of violence between male slave owners and male slaves had escalated to the point where it could no longer be solved in the kitchens across the country, but Stowe seems at a loss to suggest other possible remedies for the conflict. This confusion regarding the problem of race-slavery exposes significant flaws in Stowe's widely accepted feminist agenda and illustrates how the factor of race further complicates Stowe's already problematic construction of masculinity.

## HYSTERIA AS MYSTICISM

The task of defining mysticism within the larger framework of nineteenth-century spiritualism is fraught with difficulty because of the often overlapping isms of the era, including hypnotism, animal magnetism, and mesmerism, that were intriguing nineteenth-century writers, such as Stowe, Hawthorne, and others. This taxonomic process is further complicated when one includes the equally elusive and contemporaneous concept of transcendentalism, which addressed many of the same concerns.[1] Traditionally, spiritualism is the name given to the larger movement that swept the United States around midcentury and serves as the umbrella term that includes more specialized beliefs, such as mysticism, animal magnetism, and mesmerism; however, it is useful to remember that the term "spiritualism" was first used in a very specific context, namely as a belief system that is organized around the communication with the dead (Barrow 1986, 1). Most historians point to the 1848 Rochester rappings as the birth of the spiritualist movement in the United States, as news of the supernatural feats of two sisters, Margaret and Kate Fox, the nation's first "mediums," spread quickly throughout the country.[2] The movement peaked around 1855, when a skeptical backlash severely quelled spiritualism's popularity but did not succeed in completely eradicating it. Given the populist and commercial appeal of mediums who professed the ability to communicate with the dead, many different varieties of spiritualism popped up across the states, such as the performances of mesmerism that flourished in New England and served as the basis for Hawthorne's *The Blithedale Romance*.

Mysticism is a more difficult practice to define given the term's long history and the fundamental paradox at the heart of the mystical experience. Dating back to ancient Platonic and Oriental philosophy, mysticism, in its most basic sense, has traditionally referred to the mystic's union and identification with a Supreme Being. Although much of that meaning has been retained throughout history, the *Oxford English Dictionary* offers two general and opposing definitions, both of which were in use during the nineteenth century, a fact that highlights the crux of the confusion. In the second CD-ROM edition of the *OED*, mysticism is initially defined as a "belief in the possibility of union with the divine nature by means of ec-static contemplation; reliance on spiritual intuition or exalted feelings as the means of acquiring knowledge of mysteries inaccessible to intellectual apprehension"; however, the second definition notes its pejorative con-notation as "a term of reproach . . . that implies self-delusion or dreamy confusion of thought." In her study of American transcendentalism, Cath-erine Albanese identifies a related conflict at the heart of mystical writing to explain this split; although mystics typically described their experiences as "beyond expression," they would then spend volumes trying to describe these supposedly inexpressible encounters (1977, 153–54). It is as if the in-herent inexpressibility of the experience brings about a compulsive attempt to comprehend it, even though the experience is, by definition, incapable of being fully grasped by the intellect. What differentiates mysticism from other offshoots of spiritualism is its focus on the intense physical reac-tion of the experience, a reaction that signals the mystic's crossing into the spiritual realm. As interest in the study of psychology was also rising during the nineteenth century, the mystical experience, which was usually accom-panied by some bodily manifestation, such as shaking or trembling, often led to doubts about the mystic's sanity. It was becoming an increasing com-monplace notion during the nineteenth century that recognized mystics of antiquity were simply hysterics who went undiagnosed, the most famous example being Saint Teresa of Avila (Mazzoni 1996, 5–7). This alignment of mysticism with hysteria was chiefly organized around representations of female saints, as well as a number of feminized male saints, such as Saint Sebastian. Doctors seeking to develop a medical history for their increasing numbers of hysterical patients found in the mystics a host of recognizable symptoms. For example, Saint Francis of Assisi and Saint Teresa of Avila were retrospectively diagnosed as "undeniable hysterics" by one hysteria expert, while another doctor deemed "many women Saints and Blessed [as] nothing other than simple hysterics" (quoted in Mazzoni 1996, 39).[3] While most spiritualist practitioners at the time had to contend with charges of fakery and doubts about their sincerity, self-proclaimed mystics were also faced with questions regarding their mental health.

The version of hysteria that emerged in the nineteenth century possessed many characteristics that were unique to the era yet retained others that harkened back to antiquity. From its early days in ancient Egypt with the myth of the wandering womb to its dramatic appearance in the lecture halls of J. M. Charcot at the end of the nineteenth century, hysteria has had a long and varied career. Although primarily considered a feminine ill-ness for most of its history, the specific language that developed in the late eighteenth and early nineteenth century around hysteria provided a rich vocabulary of symptoms and cures that authors used to describe the anxiety inherent in nascent American masculinity. In fact, it is precisely because of hysteria's connection to femininity that writers found its language such a useful tool for expressing the undefined and uncertain masculinity of the early republic. By placing the construction of nineteenth-century masculinity within the cultural framework of hysteria, a useful historical context emerges, one in which the crucial connections between the social body of the nation and the gendered bodies of its citizens become more apparent.[4] The medical discourse circulating around hysteria, especially that of the late eighteenth and nineteenth centuries, often implied that hysteria was an illness in response to the debilitating conditions of modern life. Some early American writers inverted this diagnosis in their fiction by exploring hysteria as potentially empowering and liberating for the opportunities of redefining the self that it presented.[5] The works of many authors, such as Stowe and Hawthorne, demonstrate what one critic repeatedly refers to as the "uses of male hysteria" (Goldstein 1991) by specifically seizing upon the opportunities presented by hysteria to redefine the positions of their male characters within the real and figurative families in which they exist.[6]

Mysticism, like hysteria, influenced the American literary imagination for most of the nineteenth century in profound and complicated ways. Some writers, such as Twain, used satire to understand the movement's powerful grip on American culture later in the century, but many American writers at midcentury were not yet ready to deal with the subject in a humorous manner. On the one hand, they saw mysticism's excess as a threat to the spiritual foundation of the nation. On the other hand, its exuberance seemed to energize the public imagination in a positive way.[7] Whichever position these writers held, they, like the mystics, wrote voluminously on the subject. Ralph Waldo Emerson was openly critical of the spiritualist performances of the mediums and their rappings; he referred to them as "coxcombs" and to their prophecies as "Rat-revelation" (1912, 298). Henry David Thoreau was even more critical, referring to spiritualists as "idiots inspired by the cracking of a restless board" and wrote that he would rather invest in an "Immediate Annihilation Company" than believe in a Concord spiritualist (1958, 284). The strong reactions of Emerson and Thoreau were likely owing to their deep beliefs in the similar principles that formed the basis of their transcendental philosophy, which they considered demeaned by the commercialism, sensationalism, and feminization that attended the spiritualist movement. In Emerson's and Thoreau's transcendental mysticism, there seems to be not only an attempt to masculinize and intellectualize what had formerly been an essentially inexplicable feminine experience, but also to normalize and democratize the mystical experience by demonstrating how it could be a part of daily life for anyone, not just a chosen few.[8]

Stowe's relationship with the entire spiritualist movement was as complicated as those of Emerson and Thoreau; however, personal circumstances prevented her from enjoying some of the analytical detachment that her male counterparts enjoyed. In a report to the Congregational Association of New York and Brooklyn in 1853, Charles Beecher, Harriet's brother, publicly announced his belief that demonic agency was a possible explanation for the Rochester rappings. In contrast, not only was Stowe's half sister, Isabella, an active spiritualist, but Stowe's own husband, Calvin, also fancied himself something of a psychic, a belief that Stowe rendered faithfully in the creation of the visionary character in *Sam Lawson's Oldtown Fireside Stories* (1871). Most dramatically, it appears that Stowe was drawn to the spiritualist movement after her son Henry drowned in 1857. In her grief she sought out the assistance of mediums, but they almost always left her disgusted with their rappings and moving tables; however, in letters to Elizabeth Barrett Browning, she wrote of messages she received from her dead son. As her grief subsided, she was able to examine the movement from a less emotional perspective and to understand its broad, national appeal. To her husband she wrote, "One thing I am convinced of—that spiritualism is a reaction from the intense materialism of the present age" (quoted in Fields 1898, 254).

In her letters and a number of articles she wrote for her own paper, the *Christian Union*, Stowe reveals her attempt to reconcile her Christian belief and the widespread appeal of spiritualism. In reply to a letter from Stowe, George Eliot responded to Stowe's characterization of the era: "[Y]our view as to the cause of the 'great wave of spiritualism' which is rushing over America, namely that it is sort of a Rachel-cry of bereavement towards the invisible existence of the loved ones is deeply affecting" (11 July 1896). Although she decried the "spiritual jugglery" of the era, Stowe nonetheless acknowledged the possible existence of mystics: "[T]here are, doubtless, people who, from some constitutional formation can more readily receive the impressions of the surrounding spiritual world. Such were apostles, prophets and workers of miracles" (quoted in Fields 1898, 254). Even though mysticism was at odds with her personal beliefs and posed a larger threat to established religion, Stowe appeared to concede that its popularity indicated that mystics were providing the American people with something that they were lacking, and she felt it an important enough subject to place it at the center of *Dred*, the novel she wrote in the four years after the publication of *Uncle Tom's Cabin*.

By all accounts of *Dred*'s composition, Stowe was keeping to the formula that made *Uncle Tom's Cabin* such a success. Much like the character of Uncle Tom, Dred was going to play a pivotal but supporting role, according to Stowe's original conception of the novel. However, as Stowe's biographers note, the recent turn of national events so inflamed her passion that she thrust the underdeveloped character of Dred to the center of the novel. Within the general dismissal of the novel, it is interesting to note the generally disdainful response to the character of Dred by both Stowe's contemporary reviewers and her modern critics. Negative reaction to Dred was not surprising in the South, where the reviewer from the *Southern Literary Messenger* called him "the most uninteresting and unnatural character in the book"; however, reviews in the North and abroad were not that much more favorable, as one critic called him "an unreal presence" whose death brings relief to the reader and another referred to him as a pale imitation of Uncle Tom who lacked the "grace of suffering" (quoted in Gossett 1985, 302). In the decades since the novel was published, the harsh nature of the criticism remains strong, much of it aimed at the far-fetched and disconnected depiction of Dred, with only an occasional acknowledgment of the original and radical nature of his character. Although Dred is certainly an imperfect creation, this critical dismissal is startling, especially due to the fact that no other major American author had previously attempted to essay the character of an insurrectionary slave.[9]

## DRED AS MYSTIC

From his first appearance in the novel, Dred is an amazing if confusing amalgam of signifiers, and one is immediately struck by the sublimated eroticism of the description:

> He was a tall black man, of magnificent stature and proportions. His skin was intensely black, and polished like marble. A loose shirt of red flannel, which opened very wide at the breast, gave a display of a neck and chest of herculean strength. The sleeves of the shirt rolled up nearly to the shoulders, showed the muscles of a gladiator. The head, which rose with an imperial air from the broad shoulders, was large and massive and developed with equal force both in the reflective and perceptive departments. The perceptive organs jutted like dark ridges over the eyes, while that part of the head which phrenologists attribute to the moral and intellectual sentiments, rose like an ample dome above them. The large eyes had that peculiar and solemn effect of unfathomable blackness and darkness which is often a striking characteristic of the African eye. But there burned in them, like tongues of flame in a black pool of naphtha, a subtle and restless fire, that betokened habitual excitement to the verge of insanity. (Stowe [1856] 1992, 261)

The introduction of Dred in the narrative is marked by a sense of taboo in which Stowe's erotic objectification of the black male body is presented to her female readers. Because Dred is identified as a statue and likened to figures from antiquity, the eroticization of his musculature is safely couched in aesthetic, medical, and historic terms. However, this technique of distancing Dred's sexual and physical power is ultimately insufficient in keeping the danger he represents at bay, so that the passage culminates in a gesture of racial othering that taps into widespread cultural fears about slaves. A look into Dred's eyes reveals an "unfathomable blackness" and "restless fire that betokened habitual excitement to the verge of insanity," so what began as a regal and imposing depiction degenerates into a racial stereotype steeped in fear, a progression that defines Stowe's rendering of Dred's character throughout, especially regarding his mystical nature.[10] Dred's strangeness is then magnified when he begins to speak, as his language is neither that of an African nor that of a Southern slave, but rather the fiery speech of an Old Testament prophet: "Therefore, the curse of Meroz is upon thee, saith the Lord. And thou shall bow down to the oppressor, and his rod shall be upon thee; and thy wife shall be for a prey!" (262). Dred's antiquated rhetoric has often served as the final cause of dismissal for critics, leading them to bemoan Stowe's misguided attempt in creating Dred as a Southern Jeremiah. However, careful attention to his sporadic appearances in the novel reveals that Stowe is as interested in creating a contemporary religious figure as she is in summoning the Biblical past.

Soon after his dramatic first appearance in the novel, it becomes clear that Dred is more than an anachronistic void at the center of the narrative. The enigmatic nature of his character stems from Stowe's difficult negotiation between the mystical tradition and more current questions about the connections between mysticism and mental health that form the basis for her conflicted construction of black masculinity. For example, when he comes upon a fugitive slave who has been killed by a hunting dog, Dred seems to be transported to another realm. Stretching his hands to heaven, he screams a prayer to God before falling into a trance: "As Dred spoke, his great black eye seemed to enlarge itself and roll with a glassy fullness, like that of a sleepwalker in an somnambulic dream" (314). Stowe's reference to somnambulism here should remind us of Charles Brockden Brown's *Edgar Huntly* (1799), where sleepwalking was used to illustrate the hysterical tendencies of Edgar and his mysterious friend. What differentiates Stowe's use of sleepwalking from Brown's is her interest in the phenomenon as an outgrowth of religious devotion versus Brown's primarily psychological approach.[11] The narrative later refers to Dred's condition here as his "state of the highest ecstasy," employing language traditionally used to describe the mystic's experience (325).

Dred remains a shadowy presence for the first half of the novel, but any doubt about his mystical nature is swept away with a grand pronouncement at the opening of the second half of the novel, which locates him in "the twilight-ground between the boundaries of the sane and the insane, which the Greeks and Romans regarded with a peculiar veneration" yet, at the same time, places him "under the awful shadow of a supernatural presence" (353). Stowe carefully mines the indeterminacy of the mystic's limbo state, marveling at his divine gift while sympathizing with the burden that accompanies it. Although Stowe implies that it is a failure of contemporary society to acknowledge the "indefinite land" that Dred inhabits during his mystical experiences, the novel itself makes continual references to the "strange and abnormal condition" of Dred (353). So while the narrative voice at times admires the mystic's duality in noting that "[i]t was remarkable . . . how the wandering mystical expression of his face immediately gave place to one of shrewd and practical earnestness" (561), it also tinges the mystical experience with a hint of pathology, noting that it imparts "a singular and grotesque effect to his whole personality" (355). Stowe's depiction of Dred as a mystic reaches its climax in a chapter entitled "Jegar Sahadutha," in which the murder of Hark, a fellow slave, provokes an extreme reaction from Dred and brings him closer to enacting his mission of vengeance. After Dred seemingly considers the un-Christian notion that forgiveness is not always the Lord's work, his body becomes wracked with emotion and demonstrates the physical, as well as psychical, response that is characteristic of the mystical trance:

> As a thunder-cloud trembles and rolls, shaking with gathering electric fire, so his dark figure seemed to dilate and quiver with the force of mighty emotions. . . . He trembled, his hands quivered, drops of perspiration rolled down his face, his gloomy eyes dilated with an unutterable volume of emotion. At last the words heaved themselves up in deep chest-tones, resembling the wild, hollow wail of a wounded lion, finding vent in language to him so familiar, that it rolled from his tongue in a spontaneous torrent, as if he had received their first inspiration. (572)

As part of his trance, Dred mimics the forces of nature, but the emotional groundswell that results is too dangerous, leading Stowe to remind readers of Dred's primitive nature. She seems to be questioning his humanity as well as his sanity; therefore, the mystical trance ultimately produces a regressive effect, leading Dred to span not the material and spiritual worlds but the human and animal worlds.

This questioning of Dred's humanity highlights Stowe's ambivalent treatment of race in the novel, a treatment that is particularly revealed in her presentation of mysticism. Undergirding her alignment of his mysticism and race is the suggestion that the fragile mental constitution of blacks makes them more prone to the emotionalism in religion than whites. Not only does the novel take as truth the assumption that Africans make the best spiritualist subjects, but the novel's inspired depiction of the camp meeting also emphasizes the ease with which the slave participants evolve into a "whirlwind of screaming, shouting and praying" (316). In this section Stowe presents an array of racial attitudes toward the slaves' behavior at the camp meeting from Nina's laissez-faire acceptance to Anne's melancholy discomfort. However, Stowe places the most extensive commentary on the subject in the mouth of the liberal Clayton, who argues for the tolerance of such gatherings because "barbarous and half-civilized people always find the necessity for outward and bodily demonstrations in worship" (317). As he continues, he makes more specific references to the slaves at hand, concluding that they should "let the African scream, dance, and shout, and fall into trances. It suits his tropical lineage and blood as much as our thoughtful inward ways do us" (317). The extreme emotional display at the camp meeting is thus seen as an example of the slaves' inability to express themselves intellectually. Thomas F. Gossett goes so far as to suggest that *Dred* shows signs of Stowe's waning belief in the capacity of blacks for moral and mental improvement (1985, 304).

Stowe's depiction of the emotional black response to the camp meeting invites an interesting comparison between the stereotyping of religious slaves and that of hysterical women. In her feminist study of mysticism, Grace Jantzen notes the correlation between the alleged inexpressibility of the mystical experience and the silencing of women in the public arena. Because this intense connection to spirituality can be positioned as gender related, it can be used to reinforce stereotypes and keep women and spirituality firmly domesticated (1994, 191). We can see how this formulation possesses a special relevance when applied to the figure of a slave mystic because it not only serves to reinforce stereotypes of ignorance and submissiveness but also adds an element of negative feminization to a male mystic, such as Dred.

## DRED AS TRANSCENDENTALIST

In addition to examining how Dred's mysticism is informed by Stowe's knowledge of the conjunction between divine ecstasy and madness, it is also worth exploring how she incorporates transcendentalist aspects into her depiction of Dred's ambiguous mysticism. For example, in a passage worthy of Emerson, Stowe writes of Dred: "Our readers may imagine a human body of the largest and keenest vitality, to grow up so completely under the forces of nature, that it may seem to be as perfectly en rapport with them as a tree" ([1856] 1992, 354). Yet here too, that connection with nature seems more primitive, as Stowe then compares his "savage perfection" to that of a hunting dog plunging into the thicket in "the ecstasy of enjoyment" (354). After earlier comparing him to a lion, Stowe employs another animal analogy here to highlight a key limitation of Dred's mysticism. He apparently lacks what Emerson identified as the imaginative capability necessary for facilitating the mystical experience. According to Emerson, the imagination's contemplation of nature must always lead within: "I go inward until I find Unity universal, that Is [*sic*] before the World was: I come outward to this body a point of variety" (1960, 177). As we saw above, Stowe's view of slaves operates on the principle that they lack the psychical interiority necessary to take the inward journey that Emerson describes. This inability to understand and process his mystical experiences fully also keeps Dred from acting upon his mystical visions, another antithesis to Emersonian mystical theory because, according to Emerson, without action, the mystic fails in his or her role as a conduit between the divine world and the human world.

Dred's failure to act upon his visions is further compounded by his failure to write or reflect on these visions in any attempt to comprehend them. Building on Emerson's notion of the imagination, Thoreau knew that the mystical experience had to be written down and analyzed in order to be valuable:

> Our ecstatic states, which appear to yield so little fruit, have this value at least: though in the seasons when our genius reigns we may be powerless for expression, yet, in calmer seasons, when our talent is active, the memory of those rarer moods comes to color our picture and is the permanent paint-pot, as it were, into which we dip our brush. Thus no life experience goes unreported at last; but if it be not solid gold it is gold leaf, which gilds the furniture of the mind. It is an experience of infinite beauty which we unfailingly draw, which enables us to exaggerate ever truly. (1962, 468–69)

Dred's ecstasy bears little fruit because it does not spur him to action. Stowe stresses Dred's intelligence but depicts him as incapable of processing his mystical experiences beyond their divine impulses. She alludes to the fact that he is a genius, but, paradoxically, she does not grant him any intrinsic means by which his genius can practically express itself.

Central to the understanding of Dred's nature mysticism is his connection to the "Dismal Swamp" as a geographical manifestation of the limbo state he occupies as both a fugitive slave and a mystic. Stowe connects the dark but fertile environment of the swamp to the state of mind of her protagonist. At its most basic level, the swamp is depicted in *Dred* as an area of primitive wildness: "It would seem impossible that human foot could penetrate the wild, impervious jungle" ([1856] 1992, 309). Because the runaway slaves in *Dred* appear to thrive in the swamp, the "human" foot mentioned above is presumably white; moreover, the reference to the swamp as a jungle summons images of Africa and thus serves to explain why the slaves appear so at home in its dark recesses. Much of Stowe's portrait of the swamp draws upon its traditional associations with evil and death, but she also depicts it as a life-sustaining haven, thus playing upon its status as an "ambiguous realm," to use David Miller's term (1989, 77). In his discussion of *Dred*, Miller argues that Stowe's protagonist deserves critical attention "all the more because of the revealing metaphorization of Dred's inner character through swamp imagery" (95). The ambiguity of the swamp operates on two levels in Stowe's characterization of Dred; it expresses his position as a fugitive slave who is neither free nor in bondage, as well as his role as a mystic lodged between the material and spiritual worlds. Most importantly, the moral indeterminacy associated with the image of the swamp strikes at the core of Dred's vacillation between vengeance and forgiveness, a crucial dilemma that the novel never resolves. Finally, for all its claims about the swamp as being "far from unhealthy," the novel falls back upon the connotation of the swamp as a breeding ground of disease and corruption, with Dred as its "parasite" (Boyd 1994, 51). As a threat to the already fragile American body politic, Dred's divinely inspired message of vengeance must clearly be exterminated.

Stowe's representation of the swamp also serves to reveal her fears about the expansion of a black consciousness once released from the bonds of slavery, a consciousness personified in Dred: "It is difficult to fathom the dark recesses of a mind so powerful and active as his, placed under a pressure of ignorance and social disability so tremendous" ([1856] 1992, 557). To combat this fear, the novel makes attempts to retain a belief in the concept of gradual emancipation. Stowe offers Magnolia Grove, the Clayton plantation, as a utopian semidemocracy where slaves are taught to read and makes reference toward the end of the novel to a similarly successful system in Canada. However, the narrative makes it clear that this option is little more than a fading fantasy. On one level the image of the swamp as a place of unruly growth allows Stowe to sustain this fantasy by suggesting that the only thing slaves really require is a touch of cultivation. The "goblin growth" of swamp trees is due to the "slimy depths from which they spring" (616), which causes them to assume an unnatural pattern. Placed elsewhere, the narrative implies, they would surely flourish. However, on another level it is clear that when Stowe is talking about this type of natural growth as a negative process, she is referring specifically to black essential consciousness:

> All sorts of vegetable monsters stretch their weird, fantastic forms among its shadows. There is no principle so awful through all nature as the principle of *growth*. It is a mysterious and dread condition of existence, which, place it under what impediment or disadvantage you will, is constantly forcing on; and when unnatural pressure hinders it, develops in forms portentous and astonishing. The wild, dreary belt of swampland which girds in those states scathed by the fires of despotism is an apt emblem, in its rampant and we might say delirious exuberance of vegetation, of that darkly struggling, wildly vegetating swamp of human souls, cut off, like it, from the uses and improvements of cultivated life. (616)

What is normally presented as a core value of the American character, struggling through adversity, becomes in the above passage a dangerous process of evolution. The imminent danger is not in the process of growth itself, but in unchecked and uncontrolled growth. The image that Stowe would like to substitute for the swamp of wildly growing black souls is one of a garden in which those souls could be tended to and, more importantly, monitored, and one where the gardeners would, of course, be the abolitionists. Yet, the novel belies its belief in this fantasy, especially in its representation of Dred, who has enjoyed some of the luxuries of cultivation yet is still a "vegetable monster" that is "portentous and astonishing."

The last important aspect of the swamp's ambiguity lies in its transgression of gender boundaries, a transgression that coalesces with those we have examined in relation to Dred's mystical nature. The figuration of swamp-as-sanctuary in Dred could reflect Stowe's use of its beneficent, maternal side, as it stands as a site of opposition to patriarchal attempts at controlling "feminine" nature. It is clear, however, that the ambiguity of the swamp prevents it serving the clear, symbolic purpose that the kitchen did in *Uncle Tom's Cabin*. As Richard Boyd notes, the swamp, although a marginal site, like the kitchen in *Uncle Tom's Cabin*, does not provide a similar sense of empowerment (1994, 51). Although the enclave of the swamp is some ways aligned with domesticity, the presence of women is negligible, as the only woman that Stowe mentions as inhabiting the swamp is Dred's unnamed wife, whose sole purpose seems to be to establish Dred's status as a family man. However, like Uncle Tom before him, Dred, although married, is imprinted as feminine, a characteristic that is closely tied to his mystical abilities. Despite his hypermasculinized exterior and athleticism, Dred is feminized by his loss of emotional and bodily control and his inability to act upon his divine revelations, the two features that repeatedly epitomize his mystical experiences. Contrary to the assertively masculine mysticism of Emerson, Dred is infused with a more traditional sense of the mystical nature, which as Christina Mazzoni notes, is fundamentally female and closely tied to hysteria (1996, 5). The androgynous environment of the swamp does not create a stronger, more integrated person but a more fractured one, so that Dred combines within himself the worst extremes of both genders, unchecked masculine aggression and paralyzing feminine passivity.

## DRED AS SLAVE LEADER

By designating *Dred* as "A Tale of the Great Dismal Swamp," Stowe, as we saw above, was calling on her audience's general awareness of the swamp as a hideout for fugitive slaves. Drawing upon factual evidence, she expresses her desire to make the fugitive slave a real presence in the minds of her readers by distinctly imbuing Dred with the attributes of contemporary black figures who were very much in the news. As mentioned earlier, Nat Turner and Denmark Vesey inspired Stowe's depiction of Dred's character, but her final choice of his name could have easily come from Dred Scott, whose famous case was winding its way to the Supreme Court at that time.[12] The allegorical nature of the name also undoubtedly appealed to Stowe, and in the novel she notes its popularity among the slave population, especially "those of great physical force" ([1856] 1992, 273); however, it is also likely that she was exposed to stories of Dred Scott sometime after the case began in 1847 (Aptheker 1990a, 274). Written a year before the Supreme Court decision was handed down in 1857, the single-word title of Stowe's book likely sparked a connection in the public, at least among her antislavery readers.[13] Moreover, Dred Scott's attempt to challenge the legality of slavery bears a certain resemblance to the episode in *Dred* when Milly unsuccessfully challenges in a court of law the right of slaveowners to physically abuse their slaves. Whether or not Stowe was making active reference to the Dred Scott case when naming her protagonist, she turned to two more well-known personalities when creating his character; however by doing so, she places her novel on a narrative path that ultimately confounds the story. On the one hand, she wants to emphasize the moral basis of Turner's and Vesey's struggles for freedom. On the other hand, she is not willing to fully embrace the possibly bloody consequences of that struggle. Because of Stowe's ambivalence, Turner and Vesey are transformed into vague icons in the novel rather than actual heroes, a fact evidenced when Dred himself refers to both of them, first, as symbols of fear for the terror they were able to instill in whites and, second, as models for martyrdom when he considers the possibility of his own death.

Stowe found an intellectual father for her protagonist in the reported life of Denmark Vesey, whose story of an aborted rebellion inspired the novel's insurrectionary impulse yet at the same time allowed Stowe to avoid the potentially tragic consequences of an actual slave revolt.[14] While historical documents indicate that Vesey had a number of children (his wife and children were still enslaved after he had purchased his freedom with lottery winnings in 1800, and Vesey made reference to them in the trial transcript as his motivation for the revolt), there is no indication that any of his sons distinguished themselves as slave leaders after his death. In describing the Vesey case in *Dred*, Stowe effectively quotes excerpts from the official report to add authenticity to her novel, but in essaying the character of Vesey as the father of her protagonist, she was not able to escape the cultural stereotype of overachieving black men as brilliant but unstable. Stowe describes Dred as "gifted with that particular faculty of discernment of spirits which belonged to his father, Denmark Vesey, sharpened into a preternatural intensity by the habit of his wild and dangerous life" ([1856] 1992, 615). In a similar vein, historian William F. Freehling paints Vesey as a threatening tyrant who was able to combine high ideals and ruthless savagery, given to fits of rage and violence (*Trial Record* [1822] 1970, 12).

In the transcript of Vesey's trial, published as "An Official Report of the Trials of Sundry Negroes, Charged with an Attempt to Raise an Insurrection in the State of South Carolina" (1822), Vesey's ability to organize his skilled inner circle is commented on favorably, as is his skill in convincing the general population of the viability of his plan (16).[15] What may have interested Stowe in Vesey's story beyond his expressed dedication to his family and almost military-like organizational ability was his curious past, which she generously plagiarizes. The trial record draws upon a biographical sketch of Vesey, noting his "beauty, alertness and intelligence" as a boy (161). However, despite his apparent superiority, he was returned to his original master because he was "unsound and subject to epileptic fits" (161). In the medical writing of the period, there is striking overlap between hysterical fits and epileptic seizures in terms of patients' symptoms. While we cannot say for certain whether Stowe knew this fact about Vesey's life, her familiarity with the trial transcript makes it plausible. Moreover, her description of Dred's mystical trances, with their trembling, perspiring, and rolling eyeballs, carefully walks the edge between divinity and pathology. The trial record goes on to note that Vesey's "temper was impetuous and domineering in the extreme" and "all his passions were ungovernable" (162). Stowe incorporates this image of recklessness into her protagonist, with special emphasis on his inclination toward violence: "[O]n the slightest rebuke or threat, [he] flashed up with a savage fierceness, which supported by his immense bodily strength, made him an object of dread among the overseers" ([1856] 1992, 274). By tapping into the figure of the mystic, Stowe is able to unite Vesey's extreme emotionalism with Nat Turner's devout religiosity, but, simultaneously and counterproductively, she does little to diminish the cultural stereotype of the black man as intellectually irrational, emotionally unstable, and physically dangerous.

If Denmark Vesey is established in the narrative as Dred's biological father, then Nat Turner can be seen as his spiritual father. Despite the novel's established genealogy of Dred, most critics point to Turner, and not Vesey, as the inspiration for the novel's central character. The inherent drama of Turner's story, with its apocalyptic confession and adventurous tales of escape into the swamp, must have appealed to Stowe. Thus, although Stowe's familiarity with the Vesey rebellion is evident in *Dred*, her knowledge about Nat Turner is equally established, evidenced by numerous references in the text, a footnote from the Turner trial transcript and the inclusion of Turner's "confession" as the first appendix to the novel. Often referred to as the most famous slave revolt in American history,

Nat Turner's rebellion occurred in August 1831 in Southampton County, Virginia, the climax of a three-year period of slave unrest in the South. In the aftermath, the casualty toll stood at 160 (60 whites and 100 blacks). Thirteen slaves and three free black men were arrested, tried, and hanged. Turner himself was not captured for two months, but he was quickly executed after his capture. The rebellion had significant repercussions on both sides of the debate about slavery. Despite her access to more detailed information about Turner, Stowe's choice of Vesey over Turner as the father of her protagonist likely stemmed from her knowledge of her readers' tastes. Her choice of a leader of a thwarted rebellion was less threatening to their sense of security than if she had chosen a man who was actually responsible for the death of white slave owners.

Stowe's inclusion of Turner's confession bespeaks a familiarity with its content, and it is easy to see how the descriptions of the mystical experiences within the confession awed her. Officially titled *The Confessions of Nat Turner, the leader of the late insurrection in Southampton [County], Va. (1831)*, the text is supposedly Turner's personal account of the uprising, as told to Thomas R. Gray, although the coerced nature of its delivery renders some aspects of its authenticity questionable. Turner begins by noting an event from his childhood that "laid the groundwork of that enthusiasm which has terminated so fatally to many, both black and white, and for which I am about to atone at the gallows" (quoted in Aptheker 1990b). As many critics have noted and the above quotation indicates, the mediated nature of the confession makes it difficult to discern the true voice of Turner. However, certain aspects of Turner's life emerge nonetheless, foremost of which is his belief in himself as a religious visionary, an image that undoubtedly resounded with Stowe. The Vesey story may have provided her with the intellectual and emotional foundation for *Dred*, but Turner's story gave her the moral thrust for her fugitive slave's mission and the basis for his mysticism. Like Dred, who soon after his birth was clearly believed to be "born for extraordinary things" (Stowe [1856] 1992, 262), Turner notes that his mother and grandmother sensed his call to greatness from "certain marks on my head and breast" (quoted in Aptheker 1990b, 120). Like his fictional counterpart, Turner is also admired for his intelligence and ability to read, but it is the mystical overtones of Turner's story that become the focus of Stowe's novel. Turner's powers of judgment, "perfected by Divine inspiration," and bolstered by "the austerity of his life and manners," raised the interests of both whites and blacks (121). This awareness of his own greatness made him decide that he must also behave appropriately, so he "studiously avoided mixing in society, and wrapped [himself] in mystery," during which time he committed himself to prayer and fasting. Dred's behavior is strikingly similar—from his asceticism at which he "labored with proud and silent assiduity" (Stowe [1856] 1992, 280) to his embracing of the mysticism. If there is a recurrent theme in Turner's story, it is the multiplicity of visions that Turner relates to Gray. For example, reflecting on scriptural passages while plowing one day, the Spirit spoke to him, which, he notes, "fully confirmed me in the impression that I was ordained for some great purpose in the hands of the Almighty" (quoted in Aptheker 1990b, 121). To fulfill his purpose, he knew that he must break from slavery by exerting his influence over his fellow slaves, influence he achieved by sharing his divine revelations with them.

There is a definite progression in Turner's visions as they become increasingly bloody and death related, a development that Stowe cautiously avoids in her rendition. In a particularly vivid vision, Turner claims to sees "white spirits and black spirits engaged in a battle, and the sun was darkened—the thunder rolled in the heavens, and blood flowed in the streams—and I heard a voice saying, 'Such is your luck, such you are called to see; and let it come rough or smooth, you must surely bear it'" (quoted in Aptheker 1990b, 122). Like Turner, Dred believes he is "the subject of visions and supernatural communications" (Stowe [1856] 1992, 354). In his confession's most extended vision, Turner relates to Gray,

> I looked and saw the forms of men in different attitudes; and there were lights in the sky, to which the children of darkness gave other names than what they really were; for they were the lights of the Savior's hands, stretched forth from east to west, even as they were extended on the cross on Calvary for the redemption of sinners. (quoted in Aptheker 1990b, 123)

After praying for the meaning of a vision of "forms of men in different attitudes," he sees "drops of blood on corn" and "hieroglyphic characters . . . portrayed in blood" (123) appearing on the leaves of the trees, which he reads as an indication that the judgment day had arrived. He was to keep his mission a secret until receiving a sign from heaven that he must rise and slay his enemies with their own weapons (Aptheker 1990b, 123). Contrary to the events in Stowe's novel, the sign from the Lord eventually arrives for Turner; after seeing an eclipse, he organized a band of men to exact their revenge, with the express goal that no one, regardless of their sex or age, was be spared. Turner goes on to explain the strategy of attack with the object "to carry terror and devastation wherever we went" (quoted in Aptheker 1990b, 124). Stowe knew she had to walk a fine line when dealing with the issue of slavery, thus she soft-pedals the bloody mission of Turner and, of course, does not include it in her narrative. As something of a compromise, Stowe paints Dred as a Hamlet figure who is incapable of exacting the vengeance to which he is driven. Like Turner, Dred says that when the Lord directs, they will seek their revenge and "will slay them utterly, and consume them from the face of the earth!" ([1856] 1992, 512). But Stowe backs away from such a violent plan by inserting the voice of Milly into the proceedings, singing a hymn of forbearance, which succeeds in convincing Dred that the hour for revenge has not yet arrived.[16]


## CONCLUSION

Critics have often pointed to Milly as this novel's Uncle Tom or referred to her as Uncle Tom's figurative sister, but the comparison is not completely apt. While she does in fact suffer a series of humiliating indignities and brutal physical punishment at the hands of her masters and functions as the novel's Christian core, her portrait achieves a much harder-edged reality than that of Uncle Tom. However, the fact that Milly is not the central character of the novel or even fares very well at the novel's conclusion points to an important shift in Stowe's gender politics. Stowe had managed to channel all her feminine ideals into Milly's character: compassion, maternal strength, resilience, and religious devotion. But, as Richard Boyd points out, despite her ability to transcend the violence around her, Milly's actions are ultimately ineffectual; at the end, she is quietly running an orphanage, "whose exemplary value seems quite limited" (1991, 28). Milly's humble fate functions as Stowe's concession that the power of motherly love as a social corrective possesses limited political agency. Moreover, if the work of redemption is chiefly represented and accomplished by slaves, women, children, and Quakers, that redemptive work, as portrayed in *Dred*, is largely unsuccessful. Perhaps most surprising of all are Stowe's doubts about the conviction and ability of white women to continue the battle against slavery as illustrated in her depiction of Nina. After a fairly rapid and unconvincing transformation from coquette to abolitionist, Nina's quick death amid the cholera outbreak carries with it an air of defeat and possesses none of the resonance of Little Eva's death in *Uncle Tom's Cabin*.

Seen in this light, the narrative of *Dred* demands a revision of the far-reaching argument posed by Jane Tompkins regarding the sentimental power of *Uncle Tom's Cabin*. Tompkins claims, "the mission [of sentimental fiction] is global and its interests are identical with race" (1985, 146). However, a number of post-Tompkins readings of *Uncle Tom's Cabin* have pointed out the problems of trying to subsume the issues of race under the feminist umbrella of sentimental fiction (Berlant 1998, 635–50). A close reading of *Dred* underscores this need to rethink the goals of that mission and the means by which it is accomplished. It may be politically useful for a feminist critic like Tompkins to align the oppression of women with the enslavement of blacks, as it was originally for Stowe, but even Stowe seems to come to the conclusion in *Dred* that the two battles were fundamentally dissimilar and needed to be waged differently.

In the face of this deterioration of the dream of female power so effectively rendered in *Uncle Tom's Cabin*, Stowe, nonetheless, seems unable to abandon the antimasculinist scorn of the earlier novel, so that no character, male or female, is left to carry on the abolitionist cause in *Dred*. Thomas F. Gossett notes that, while Stowe could not finally imagine a woman leading the fight for abolition in the South, she may have reasoned that "a man with some feminine qualities" (1985, 306) would be able to do so. However, feminized men in the novel do not fare much better than those with the typical masculine attributes that Stowe condemns. Coming under the harshest attack are, of course, the self-serving and hypocritical clergy, but even the reverent and tender Father Cushing is criticized for his "moral effeminacy" and "luxuriant softness" (Stowe [1856] 1992, 502), while the pure and straight-talking Father Dickson is humiliatingly stripped, tied to a tree, and beaten by Tom Gordon's band. Cushing and Dickson can be seen as unfortunate casualties in Stowe's relentless attack on the clergy, but laymen with feminine qualities, such as Clayton, suffer a similar fate. Despite all his noble heroics, Edward Clayton is just another one of Stowe's young, Southern white weaklings (Adams 1963, 70). When Clayton is first introduced in the novel, he is described as having a "hypochondriac temperament" and a "feminine mouth" (Stowe [1856] 1992, 42). During his first encounter with Dred, Clayton's "nervous system strained to the last point of tension by the fearful images that filled his mind," and he had to make "an effort to recall his manhood" (470–71). Then, like Father Dickson, Clayton is badly beaten by Tom Gordon and his men, after which he is rescued by the "unseen hand" of Dred and recuperates in the swamp under Dred's care. The relationship that develops between Clayton and Dred comes the closest in Stowe's fiction to approximating male friendship, a situation made all the more interesting because of its interracial nature: "Dred would sometimes come, in the shady part of the afternoon, and lie on the grass beside him, and talk for hours in a quaint, rambling, dreamy style . . . " (632). Yet the narrative makes sure to note that Clayton's interest in Dred is primarily as "a psychological study" and quickly ends the friendship a few pages later with the untimely death of Dred (632). Because Clayton cannot fill the void left by Dred's death, his departure to Canada can effectively be read as a flight of personal survival rather than as a political gesture.

Although, as a mystic, Dred is more adept than the other male characters at fusing the feminine and masculine sides of himself, he is far from an idealized depiction of manhood. The character of Dred has been read as Stowe's answer to critics on her side of the slavery issue, particularly William C. Nell, a black abolitionist, who publicly took issue with *Uncle Tom's Cabin* for its emphasis on Tom's total submissiveness in the face of oppression, a criticism James Baldwin would take up nearly a century later (Newman 1992, 20). Unfortunately, Dred does not constitute much of an improvement in Stowe's depiction of black men. Despite the description of erotic masculinity that accompanies his first appearance in the novel, Dred ends up supporting David Leverenz's notion that "black men [in Stowe's work] are naturally feminized" (1989, 192). However, unlike Uncle Tom, he depicts a femininity that is dangerous and, at times, pathological; as such, he performs stereotypes of both blackness and femininity. Dred is less submissive and more outwardly manly than Tom, but his loss of bodily control and his subjection to his emotions, not to mention his ultimate passivity, mark him as an even more ineffectual feminine presence.

The impossible bind in which Stowe typically places her male characters (not to mention her slave characters) is symbolized in an episode towards the end of the novel. After a meeting with his fellow fugitives, the importance of Dred's mission inflicts him like a "burning pain" causing him to cry out like Cassandra (Stowe [1856] 1992, 617). These feelings, according to Stowe, are admirable, "for he who is destitute of the element of moral indignation is effeminate and tame" (617). Dred's emotional outburst, like that of heroic Cassandra, is initially praised for its expression of deeply felt protest against the horrors of slavery, but then he is immediately reduced to little more than a compendium of hysterical symptoms, including "sobbings, groanings" and "inarticulate moaning" (619). The insurrection is narrowly averted not only because Stowe tries to remain true to her belief in Christian pacifism and to avoid alarming Northern whites, but also because she was not about to undermine the image of black male docility and replace it with that of bloodthirsty savagery (Newman 1992, 23). Her critique of slavery as a patriarchal institution must necessarily include the defeat of Dred, the Old Testament prophet bent on bloody revenge. His last speech is allowed to be so savage because his death is imminent. For all his initial promise and transgressive potential, the character of Dred ends up recalling a phrase from a sermon by Harriet's father Lyman Beecher: "a mournful fragment of something divine" (Beecher 1961, 56).

## NOTES

1. Lawrence Buell makes the important point that literary transcendentalism, with its hybrid mixture of religion and rhetoric, was only one aspect of a larger movement. However, this form of transcendentalism was rooted in the cultural milieu from which the movement arose, a combination of Boston Unitarianism, English romantic thought, and Platonic mysticism (1973, 15).

2. For a detailed examination of the Rochester rapping, see Cross (1965) and Johnson (1978).

3. In her introduction to the collected lectures of J. M. Charcot, Ruth Harris notes the anticlerical undercurrent in the early history of hysteria, especially Charcot's ac-

tive participation during one of the most fervent periods of anticlericalism in French history (1991, xiii).

4. Evelyne Ender writes, "The stage on which hysteria is played out is thus necessarily double: it faces one way towards a cultural imperative and in the other way towards the most intimate obsessions concerning femininity and masculinity" (1995, 15). For the purposes of this study, I have chosen to focus on the cultural imperatives driving the definition of hysteria in the nineteenth century rather than adopting an ahistorical approach that examines hysteria from a more psychological and theoretical standpoint.

5. Although she relegates male hysteria to a single footnote, Carroll Smith-Rosenberg's writings on the hysterical woman in *Disorderly Conduct* were instrumental in the formation of the thesis for this project, particularly her concept of hysteria as an "option or tactic" chosen by some women in order "to redefine or restructure their place within the family" (1985, 200).

6. Jan Goldstein's work on male hysteria in nineteenth-century France, in which he argues that hysteria was used to subvert the very definitions of gender it was attempting to stabilize, was central to the germination of this project. Using the personal and fiction writings of Gustave Flaubert, Goldstein explores hysteria as a potential "conceptual space for the conversion of gender stereotypes" that, while stigmatizing and repressive to women, if "applied by a man to himself, that same category might disclose radical possibilities" (1991, 134–35).

7. Some have even argued that Emerson, for all his bluster, possessed a certain tolerance for the spiritualist movement based on his recognition of its inherent Americanness and its sign of the nation's cultural interest in life on "the other side."

8. Both men clearly saw a distinction between what they dismissed as spiritual charade and what they considered genuine mysticism. Emerson was clearly devoted to the practice, and his key contribution to American mysticism was the foregrounding of nature as the sign of the divine (Riley 1930, 96–97). However, if there was one aspect of traditional mysticism that Emerson sought to revise, it was the passivity and pure physicality at the heart of the experience (Goldfarb and Goldfarb 1978, 54). In contrast, Thoreau had no problem proclaiming "I am a mystic" and celebrating the ecstasy that accompanies the mystic's encounter with nature: "My desire for knowledge is intermittent; but my desire to commune with the spirit of the universe, to be intoxicated even with the fumes, call it, of that divine nectar, to bear my head through atmospheres and laugh over heights unknown to my feet, is perennial and constant" (1962, 150–51). However, Thoreau's embracing of nature mysticism, like Emerson's, was always analytical and never sentimental, as he always remained "the self-aware, hard-edged, character who despised institutions and refused to pay his taxes" (Grant 1983, 138).

9. Only Frederick Douglass's *Heroic Slave* (1852) and Martin Delany's *Blake; or, the Huts of America* (1859–1862) have a similar character, and neither of these men could be called major fiction writers of the time.

10. A similar effect occurs in the description of Dred's clothing, with his "fantastic" turban and scarlet shawl, which Hedrick claims betokens Stowe's newfound interest in representing African ancestry to her readers; however, Hedrick fails to mention that Stowe follows these details with an assessment of the "outlandish

effect of his appearance," indicating her desire to emphasize the strangeness of Africanness, rather than reality of its heritage (1994, 261).

11. Stowe notes his state of "exaltation and trance," which does not impede his senses but provides them with a "preternatural keenness and intensity," which often accompanies "the more completely developed phenomena of somnabulism" ([1856] 1992, 353).

12. Dred Scott, resident of Missouri, filed suit for his freedom in a circuit court, arguing that his residence in the free state of Illinois, where his master had taken him, had rendered him free, according to a provision of the Missouri Compromise. His petition made its way through the machinery of the federal judiciary until the Supreme Court, through Chief Justice Roger B. Taney, rendered the critically important Dred Scott decision (1857), which opened all federal territory to slavery and denied the citizenship of the negro. Ellen Moers disagrees that Stowe could have been inspired by Dred Scott for the name of her title character, considering that the Dred Scott decision was not handed down until 1857 (1970, 29); however, given Stowe's keen familiarity with abolitionist news, it is not improbable that she was aware of the Dred Scott case as it was making its way through the judicial system.

13. Herbert Aptheker includes the reaction to the Dred Scott decision of members of the Israel Church in Philadelphia, which appeared in the *Liberator* on April 10, 1857 (1990a).

14. Although some of the particulars of the Vesey rebellion are unclear, the basic facts are recorded. Vesey was the leader of an 1820 conspiracy to kill all whites in Charleston, South Carolina, and the surrounding areas. Although the massacre was set for 14 July 1822, a number of setbacks caused plotters to move the date up to 16 June 1822 with simultaneous strikes planned. However, upon approaching the center of Charleston from the countryside, they found the city on a "white alert," with armed people and militia everywhere. The plot had been discovered, and Vesey ordered troops back to the countryside to await further orders. Spies made their way into the ranks, some of those arrested revealed the plot, and the magnitude of the conspiracy was revealed. According to a published report, the city was thrown into a state of mass hysteria. A special tribunal was held over five weeks with charges against 131 blacks. In the aftermath, thirty-eight were released for lack of evidence and ninety-three were tried. Of the men tried, sixty-seven were convicted and over half of those were hanged, including Vesey and the other leaders, whose bodies were left hanging for days.

15. Stowe seems to draw directly upon the Vesey story when Tom Gordon's personal servant uses the cover of a religious meeting to plot his escape; in the trial record, the use of a church in Hampstead by the African congregation for insurrectionary purposes is seen as especially perverted and deserving of censure.

16. There is some evidence that the discussion between Milly and Nina in chapter 16 reimagines Stowe's interview with Sojourner Truth that resulted in Stowe's portrait, "Sojourner Truth, the Lybian Sibyl" in which Stowe records her initial meeting with Truth and remembers her as an effective preacher who speaks with passion, faith, and humor (Foster 1954, 83). The anecdote with which she ends the sketch recalls the crisis as the center of *Dred*: before a large crowd, Frederick Douglass calls for a violent retaliation to end slavery; Truth looks at him and asks, "Frederick, is God dead?" Stowe records that her question brought the house to its

knees ([1863] 1990, 302). However, as the progression of *Dred* indicates, Stowe was realizing that effective anecdotes were no match for grim reality.

# WORKS CITED

Adams, John R. 1963. *Harriet Beecher Stowe*, ed. Sylvia E. Bowman. New York: Twayne.

Albanese, Catherine L. 1977. *Corresponding Motion: Transcendental Religion and the New America*. Philadelphia: Temple University Press.

Ammons, Elizabeth. 1980. "Heroines in Uncle Tom's Cabin." In *Critical Essays on Harriet Beecher Stowe*, ed. Elizabeth Ammons, 152–65. Boston: Hall.

Aptheker, Herbert, ed. 1990a. "The Dred Scott Decision, 1857." In vol. 1 of *A Documentary History of the Negro People in the United States: From Colonial Times through the Civil War*, 392–94. New York: Carol.

———. ed. 1990b. "Nat Turner's Own Story, 1831." In vol. 1 of *A Documentary History of the Negro People in the United States: From Colonial Times through the Civil War*, 119–25. New York: Carol.

Barrow, Logie. 1986. *Independent Spirits: Spiritualism and English Plebians, 1850–1910*. London: Routledge.

Beecher, Lyman. 1961. Volume 1 of *The Autobiography of Lyman Beecher*, ed. Barbara M. Cross. Cambridge, MA: Harvard University Press.

Berlant, Lauren. 1988. "Poor Eliza." *American Literature* 70 (3): 635–68.

Boyd, Richard. 1991. "Models of Power in Harriet Beecher Stowe's *Dred*." *Studies in American Fiction* 19 (1): 15–30.

———. 1994. "Violence and Sacrificial Displacement in Harriet Beecher Stowe's *Dred*." *Arizona Quarterly* 50 (2): 51–72.

Buell, Lawrence. 1973. *Literary Transcendentalism: Style and Vision in the American Renaissance*. Ithaca, NY: Cornell University Press.

Cross, Whitney R. 1965. *The Burnt-Over District: The Social and Intellectual History of Enthusiastic Religion in Western New York, 1800–1850*. New York: Harper and Row.

Eliot, George. 1896. Letter to Harriet Beecher Stowe. 11 July. Beecher-Stowe Collection, Schlesinger Library, Radcliffe College.

Emerson, Ralph Waldo. 1912. Vol. 8 of *The Journals of Ralph Waldo Emerson*, ed. Edward Waldo Emerson and Waldo Emerson Forbes. Boston: Houghton-Mifflin.

———. 1960. Vol. 5 of *The Journals and Miscellaneous Notebooks*, ed. William H. Gilman et al. Cambridge, MA: Harvard University Press.

Ender, Evelyne. 1995. *Sexing the Mind: Nineteenth Century Fictions of Hysteria*. Ithaca, NY: Cornell University Press.

Fields, Annie, ed. 1898. *The Life and Letters of Harriet Beecher Stowe*. Boston: Houghton-Mifflin.

Foster, Charles H. 1954. *The Rungless Ladder: Harriet Beecher Stowe and New England Puritanism*. Durham, NC: Duke University Press.

Goldfarb, Russel M., and Clare R. Goldfarb. 1978. *Spiritualism and Nineteenth Century Letters*. Rutherford, NJ: Fairleigh Dickinson University Press.

Goldstein, Jan. 1991. "The Uses of Male Hysteria: Medical and Literary Discourse in Nineteenth Century France." *Representations* 34: 134–65.

Gossett, Thomas F. 1985. *"Uncle Tom's Cabin" and American Culture*. Dallas: Southern Methodist University Press.

Grant, Patrick. 1983. *Literature of Mysticism in Western Tradition*. London: Macmillan.

Hale, Nathan Jr. 1857. Letter to Edward Everett Hale. 23 April. Hale Papers, Smith College.

Harris, Ruth, ed. 1991. *Clinical Lectures on the Diseases of the Nervous System*, by J. M. Charcot. London: Routledge.

Hedrick, Joan D. 1994. *Harriet Beecher Stowe: A Life*. New York: Oxford University Press.

Jantzen, Grace. 1994. "Feminists, Philosophers and Mystics." *Hypatia* 9:186–206.

Johnson, Paul E. 1978. *A Shopkeeper's Millennium: Society and Revivals in Rochester, New York*. New York: Hill and Wang.

Leverenz, David. 1989. *Manhood and the American Renaissance*. Ithaca, NY: Cornell University Press.

Mazzoni, Cristina. 1996. *Saint Hysteria: Neurosis, Mysticism and Gender in European Culture*. Ithaca, NY: Cornell University Press.

Miller, David C. 1989. *Dark Eden: The Swamp in Nineteenth-Century American Culture*. Cambridge: Cambridge University Press.

Moers, Ellen. 1970. "Mrs. Stowe's Vengeance." *New York Review of Books* 15 (4): 25–32.

Newman, Judie. 1992. Introduction to *Dred: A Tale of the Great Dismal Swamp*, by Harriet Beecher Stowe, 9–30. Halifax: Ryburn.

Riley, Woodbridge. 1930. *The Meaning of Mysticism*. New York: Smith.

Smith-Rosenberg, Carroll. 1985. *Disorderly Conduct: Visions of Gender in Victorian America*. New York: Oxford University Press.

Stowe, Harriet Beecher. [1852] 1989. *Uncle Tom's Cabin, or Life Among the Lowly*. New York: Bantam.

———. [1856] 1992. *Dred: A Tale of the Great Dismal Swamp*, ed. Judie Newman. Halifax: Ryburn.

———. [1863] 1990. "Sojourner Truth, the Libyan Sibyl." In vol. 1 of *The Heath Anthology of American Literature*, ed. Paul Lauter et al., 302–3. Lexington, MA: Heath.

Thoreau, Henry David. 1958. *The Correspondence of Henry David Thoreau*, ed. Carl Bode and Walter Harding. New York: New York University Press.

———. 1962. Vol. 2 of *The Journal of Henry David Thoreau*, ed. Bradford Torrey and Francis H. Allen. New York: Dover.

Tompkins, Jane. 1985. *Sensational Designs: The Cultural Work of American Fiction, 1790–1860*. New York: Oxford University Press.

*The Trial Record of Denmark Vesey*. [1822] 1970. Reprint, with added introduction by John Oliver Killens, of the 1822 edition prepared by Lionel H. Kennedy and Thomas Parker. Boston: Beacon.

# Harriet Beecher Stowe's Marianettes

## Reconstruction of Womanhood in *The Minister's Wooing* and *Agnes of Sorrento*

*Joseph Helminski*

The popularity of anti-Catholic prose, especially in the first half of the nineteenth century, was tremendous. Hundreds of pamphlets, scores of fictional and autobiographical works, and dozens of periodicals devoted themselves to uncovering and excoriating the Roman Catholic menace to Anglo-American culture.[1] Yet, only in the last decade-and-a-half has the literature of nineteenth-century American anti-Catholicism attracted much scholarly attention. Jenny Franchot's *Roads to Rome: The Antebellum Protestant Encounter with Roman Catholicism* (1994) argues that Catholicism was an important "imaginative category" for antebellum Americans, one that voiced the tensions inherent in the construction of white, northern, middle-class American identity. More recently, Susan Griffin has focused on representations of Catholicism in the Victorian period in the United States and Great Britain in *Anti-Catholicism and Nineteenth-Century Fiction* (2004). Both Franchot and Griffin see in such representations the oppositional logic of identity construction at work: the normative Protestant culture defines itself against a reviled Roman Catholicism and in doing so reveals its own limitations and ambiguities. In *Veil of Fear*, Nancy Lusignan Schulz has edited two of the nineteenth-century's most popular and infamous tales in the "escaped nuns" genre: Rebecca Reed's *Six Months in a Convent* (1835) and Maria Monk's *Awful Disclosures of the Hotel Dieu Nunnery at Montreal* (1836). She has also published a history of the destruction of the Ursuline Convent in Charlestown, Massachusetts, in 1834, *Fire and Roses: The Burning of the Charlestown Convent, 1834* (2000).

The most infamous of nineteenth-century anti-Catholic works, *Awful Disclosures of the Hotel Dieu Nunnery at Montreal* was published under the name of Maria Monk and purported to be an account of her imprisonment within a Canadian convent. As much as Monk's account clearly voiced the anti-Catholic sentiment of the period, it also raised troubling questions about the relationship between womanhood and authority. In fact, texts such as Monk's appeared during a period in American culture when women's roles were changing.

Anti-Catholicism in America reached its shrillest pitch during the period 1820–60. Like English anti-Catholics, Americans believed that the Roman Catholic Church was the "whore of Babylon" referred to in the Book of Revelation 17:4–5. Pamphlets, sermons, newspapers, novels, poems, and autobiographies attacking Roman Catholicism circulated widely in antebellum America, particularly as the immigration of Irish Catholics increased in the mid-1840s. Controversy over the use of scripture in New York's public schools also generated propaganda against Catholics who objected to the use of Protestant Bibles in classrooms. In 1844, similar controversies over religion and education sparked a riot in Philadelphia, where the houses of thirty Irish families were burned, as well as two Roman Catholic Churches (Billington 1938, 51). Anti-Catholic tropes in texts such as Reed's and Monk's reenact American anxieties about captivity, anxieties that also surfaced in nonfiction works distributed in New York, Boston, and Philadelphia through the 1820s, 1830s, and 1840s. These anxieties tended to cluster around the figure of the American woman.

This essay explores Harriet Beecher Stowe's female characters within the contexts of the anticonvent tale, represented by Maria Monk's *Awful Disclosures*, "the cult of true womanhood," and the larger discourse of anti-Catholic rhetoric in antebellum America. While the central terms of nineteenth-century womanhood in American Protestant culture—first defined by Barbara Welter as piety, purity, submissiveness, and domesticity (1966, 153)—can be assigned to the heroines of Stowe's *The Minister's Wooing* and *Agnes of Sorrento*, the Marian qualities of these heroines are identified less with the elements of "true womanhood" than with spiritual connection to God and nature. The Marian heroines in Stowe's work, or those characters represented literally or figuratively as Roman Catholic, fail to engage fully in what can be regarded as the stereotypical female function of "true womanhood," that of social reform. Stowe thus creates characters who resist those roles imposed upon them by mainstream Protestant culture, thereby adding to the range of meanings that anti-Catholic tropes could assume.

Stowe's own early life was shaped by Calvinism, but her intellectual and spiritual development drove her away from the Puritan principles of her father and toward Catholicism. Stowe's father, Lyman Beecher, viewed Catholicism as a threat to the identity of America. His vitriolic anti-Catholic sermons on the eve of the burning of the Charlestown, Massachusetts, convent in 1834 undoubtedly fueled an already fiery anti-Catholic anger among American Protestants. In 1835, Beecher published *A Plea for the*

*West,* a book whose purpose it was to raise funds for Lane Theological Seminary in Cincinnati, Ohio. Beecher's book, as well as the seminary he helped to found, served as a hedge against the expansion of Roman Catholicism. In the preface to his book, Beecher waxes metaphorical about the West's promise: "Those who go out to do good at the West . . . should go out and mingle with [the] people . . . and be absorbed in their multitude, as rain drops fall on the bosom of the ocean . . . " (1835, 18). The feminized land must be protected from the encroachment of a Catholic "tide" that is "hostile to free institutions" (50). Beecher's rhetoric reflects the popular prejudice that saw Roman Catholicism as a threat to liberty. Despite Stowe's exposure to such ardent sentiment, ultimately she joined the Episcopal Church, a move that placed her closer to "popery" than was comfortable for many Protestants.[2]

Just as Stowe's conversion to the Episcopal Church places her between mainstream New England Calvinism and Roman Catholicism, her heroines occupy a liminal position between Roman Catholicism and conventional Protestant portrayals of saving womanhood. In *Uncle Tom's Cabin,* for example, Eva St. Clare intercedes with her father on behalf of her slaves, demanding just before her own death that he release them. In this respect she reflects the function of the Roman Catholic figure of intercession, the Virgin Mary. But Eva also reflects the potential power of the "true woman" to reform the patriarchal institution of slavery, as Jane Tompkins and many others have noted.[3] Yet the work of reform remains unfinished after Eva's death, and her own father dies before freeing his slaves. The novel suggests the limits of women's power to reform men and social institutions, and Catholicism thus enables Eva to exceed the culturally constructed role of moral reformer.

## CAPTIVITY AND CATHOLICISM: MONK'S *AWFUL DISCLOSURES*

If *Uncle Tom's Cabin* deploys Catholicism in order to critique women's reforming roles, Maria Monk's *Awful Disclosures* seems bent on attacking Catholicism for removing women from their traditional duties. *Awful Disclosures* was likely penned by the American Nativists George Bourne and Reverend J. Slocum.[4] The escaped nun's tale drew on a long tradition of captivity narratives that included women and Roman Catholicism. Such works describe a young woman's experience of cloistered life as a veritable chamber of horrors. She and her fellow "inmates" are subjected to outrageous disciplines and punishments, and female superiors, at least in American versions of such tales, take on authoritative, masculinized roles. American anticonvent tales are meant to offer proof of the corruptions of the church, but more importantly have a function similar to that of the early American captivity narrative: they portray the capture of the whole culture by hostile others. The narrative reflects the fears that gathered around the popular image of the Catholic Church. In Monk's tale, young women from upstanding Protestant families find themselves placed in virtual slavery and must obey the irrational and menacing dictates of their superiors. The most maligned figures in the text, however, are not priests, but women who have taken holy orders.

Certainly Monk's nuns seem to refuse the qualities of "true womanhood." Their piety is false; their purity is compromised by their secret liaisons with priests; their submission, rather than to the rule of decency, is only to priests and bishops, who are likewise only instruments of Catholic wickedness. Monk's principal teachers at the convent are women who impress upon her the importance of absolute obedience, even to the lustful designs of male clerics: "I must be informed, that one of my great duties was to obey the priests in all things; and this I soon learnt, to my utter astonishment and horror, was to live in the practice of criminal intercourse with them" ([1836] 1962, 47).

William L. Stone, a New York attorney, wrote a refutation of Monk's narrative, which was first published in the *New York Commercial Advertiser*, and in it he establishes his authority as a debunker by establishing his anti-Catholic credentials: "However guilty the Catholics may be in other respects, or in other Countries, as a man of honor and professor of the Protestant faith, I MOST SOLEMNLY BELIEVE THAT THE PRIESTS AND NUNS ARE INNOCENT IN THIS MATTER" (1836, 33). Of Monk herself, Stone writes that she "is an arrant impostor—that she was never a nun, and was never within the walls of the cloister of Hotel Dieu—and consequently that her disclosures are wholly and unequivocally, from beginning to end, untrue . . . " (28).

Stone's pamphlet features an interview with Monk herself, and with Frances Partridge, another woman who claimed to have escaped from the Hotel Dieu nunnery. Stone concludes the pamphlet by casting vague aspersions on Roman Catholicism and denying the charges brought by Monk:

> Far be it from me to contribute in the remotest degree to vindication of the system of popery, in any of its forms, from the charges justly made against it by Luther and the Reformers; nor has my visit to Montreal in any measure weakened my Protestant faith, or diminished my hostility to the manifold corruptions of the Church of Rome. On the contrary, stronger than ever, if possible, is my belief, that the celibacy of the priesthood, and of the female recluses, is contrary to the laws of nature and of God; and I can but attribute the vows and privations voluntarily assumed by the nuns, as the effects of misanthropy or delusion, to which Christianity is unalterably and irreconcilably opposed. (54–55)

The question that begs asking here is why Stone, who is by his own admission adamantly anti-Catholic, would write a pamphlet to establish Monk's work as calumny. Is he simply using Monk's work as an occasion to voice his own anti-Catholic sentiments?

Stone recounts his investigation of the convent where Monk claimed to be a captive, and he focuses especially on the true characters of the nuns and superiors whom he meets. Although Stone takes care to note that he does not advocate "monachism," he finds that the women who were villainized by Monk were in actuality as meek as any domestic woman. His refutation takes particular care to characterize the superiors of the convent as pious, gentle women. He corrects Monk's portrayal of the convent's "abominations" because he cannot believe the behavior that her text imputes to women:

> True the tale was most revolting, and it was not little difficult to bring the mind to believe it possible, that even the most hardened of our species could be guilty . . . of the frightful abominations charged. . . . Still more difficult was it to suppose it possible that woman, gentle woman—who had sought in solitude a protection against the corruptions and temptations of the world—assuming a name indicative of purity as well as its garb—could resign themselves [*sic*] by whole communities, as the ready and willing instruments of lust and murder. (9)

Stone regards womanly purity not only as a virtue but an essential element of feminine nature. For anyone to believe in the truth of Monk's narrative is outrageous, not because the text itself is obviously spun from sensationalistic thread, but because it imposes an impossible character on women.

Although Monk depicts the nuns of the convent as either victims or villains, Stone notes that they actually display "cheerfulness" and even "innocent sportiveness" (26). In his search for the "purgatory," or secret room described in Monk's narrative, the sisters play a trick on him, one that fully restores the perverse enclosure of Monk's convent to the more familiar and conventional domestic enclosure:

> At length we came to a small apartment . . . in which the hired women, seamstresses, spinners, &c., were at work. The door was locked and there was no window, except a square hole cut through the partition deals, high up from the floor. "Ah," I exclaimed; "Miss Weeks what have you here?'" "Nothing"—said she with an arch smile;—"nothing—but—a poor nun doing penance!" "That spinning wheel would be penance enough for many young ladies in our country. But give us the keys." "No," she said; "you must look for yourself." Taking a chair, I thereupon resolved to climb up to the dark hole, and thrusting my head through, discovered that the mysterious cell   was a store room for loaf-sugar hanging around the walls, and a few barrels of family supplies. And this was all the "purgatory" discovered by us. (26)

This scene plays upon the infamous confessional episodes in escaped nun's tales like Monk's, but it is clear from the start that the space Stone has seen is one where women function in domestically productive roles. They sew and spin (evidently more eagerly than American "ladies" do). The dark interiors of Monk's nunnery reveal nothing more, it turns out, than the stuff of domestic labor: "loaf-sugar" and "family supplies." According to Stone, women retain their domestic sensibilities even within convent walls—hence his repeated use of the term "sisters" and description of the barrels as "family supplies."

Stone's refutation disputes the facts of Monk's narrative, even comparing the floor plans of Montreal convents to those reproduced in her book. But most importantly, Stone stabilizes women's roles by denying the notion that women might, under the proper circumstances, behave violently, or engage in "lustful" acts. The sisters of Stone's work are the playful cousins of American "ladies." And their cloister, ultimately, is no different from the enclosure of the family kitchen. The women of the convent behave as they ought to because they are, after all, *women.*

## THE MINISTER'S WOOING:
## CALVINISM AND CRITIQUES OF PATRIARCHY

*Awful Disclosures* and the controversy surrounding it illustrate the importance that nineteenth-century America placed upon womanhood, especially within the discourse of anti-Catholicism. Monk's nuns could be outside the boundaries of "true womanhood" or, in Stone's reply to her text, squarely within it. Although critics have attacked Harriet Beecher Stowe for flat characterization, her portrayals of women are complicated, especially when we consider how she deploys popular discourses about womanhood and Catholicism. The heroines of *The Minister's Wooing* and *Agnes of Sorrento* maintain their decency without clinging to contemporary codes of femininity and thus elide the polarized visions of womanhood offered in popular anti-Catholic writing.

Many scholars have examined the complicated intersections of gender, domesticity, and religion in women's fiction.[5] Few, however, have looked at the recurring appearance of anti-Catholic tropes in such works, or the ways that antebellum writing creates Marian figures of its heroines. John Gatta, in *American Madonna: Images of the Divine Woman in Literary Culture* (1997), has written of how Stowe and other American writers, both male and female, reflect the nineteenth century's "flirtation with the Marian cultus." This "flirtation," he argues, "offered certain Protestant writers symbolic compensation for what might be culturally diagnosed as a deficiency of psychic femininity, or of anima, in America" (3). Gatta's observations demonstrate the presence of an important literary trend. In *Uncle Tom's Cabin*, *The Minister's Wooing* (1859), and *Agnes of Sorrento* (1862), Stowe subtly employs Marian figures and calls on anti-Catholic tropes to portray and critique the cultural work of nineteenth-century domesticity. Just as the popular success of *Uncle Tom's Cabin* owed itself to Stowe's ability "to combine so many of the culture's central concerns in a narrative that is immediately accessible to the general population," the two later novels feature American culture's "concern" with domesticity in terms of the popular image of Roman Catholicism (Tompkins 1985, 135).

*Uncle Tom's Cabin* employs Catholic and anti-Catholic tropes in the production of cultural work that performs the ideological labors of submission on the one hand and resistance on the other. The novel inscribes intersections between gender roles and religious identities in the performance of social change. On the one hand, Stowe's decision to portray the slaveholding St. Clare as Roman Catholic suggests what many Americans had been claiming for decades—that the Church was antiprogressive and authoritarian. On the other hand, Eva, the novel's symbol of spiritual and social redemption, is identified with the Virgin Mary, a stereotypically Roman Catholic figure of grace and intercession. Why would Stowe characterize Eva in such terms? Why, indeed, would she also figure the heroines of *The Minister's Wooing* and *Agnes of Sorrento* in similar ways? In the following readings of the novels, I suggest that it is precisely Stowe's employment of Catholic and anti-Catholic tropes that allowed her to create female heroines who at once live up to the requirements of "true womanhood," but who are also positioned critically in relation to the patriarchal structure of society and religion.

*The Minister's Wooing* effectively establishes and destabilizes the nineteenth century's vision of the woman as reforming angel and submissive domestic. Mary Scudder, like Eva St. Clare, is a girl known for her purity of heart and stalwart piety. She belongs to a long line of New England women who are the very model of middle-class domesticity. Yet, like Eva, Mary is described by the novel's narrator and several of its characters as a blessed virgin. Her religious enthusiasm is also contrasted with the staid and paternal Calvinism of eighteenth-century New England. Mary, along with several of the novel's "marginal" characters, reaches a renewed understanding of the Edwardsean notion of "disinterested benevolence," characterized by selfless devotion to duty. Mary, who invests her religious convictions with natural emotions, ultimately rejects the idea of marriage as contractual duty in her courtship with James Marvyn. She wants to marry for love, and is encouraged to do so by her French Catholic friend, Virginie de Frontignac.

*Agnes of Sorrento*, set in fifteenth-century Italy, draws on the story of Girolamo Savonarola[6] and draws parallels between the democratization of American Christianity and Savonarola's efforts to reform the Catholic

Church. The novel revises a familiar formula of nineteenth-century American fiction. Agnes falls in love with an Italian cavalier but refuses his advances until he will reform his behavior. But it is he who leads her to a belief in religious reform. *Agnes of Sorrento* links religious and social reform and reads the moral progress of America against a backdrop of Roman Catholic corruption. These works, however, also substantially complicate conventional uses of Roman Catholicism in American literature. Stowe's creation of female heroines who are explicitly identified with the Virgin Mary departs notably from the dominant portrait of American womanhood, a portrait that the culture defined in opposition to Roman Catholicism. Eva St. Clare, Mary Scudder, and Agnes of Sorrento each fulfill the elements of "true womanhood"; yet, each character presents a critique of patriarchy that sets her outside of the domestic sphere.

Stowe's fiction reclaims anti-Catholic tropes that had been previously used to criticize transgressions of domesticity. In *The Minister's Wooing*, Stowe writes about women and marriage, Calvinist precepts of salvation, and American slavery by contrasting Roman Catholic and Protestant understandings of marriage, womanhood, and domesticity. The novel, set in post-Revolutionary Newport, features a conflict between devotion to duty and devotion to love. Mary Scudder, the novel's main character, lives with her widowed mother and their boarder, Dr. Hopkins, a Congregationalist minister. Mary falls in love with a young sailor, James Marvyn, who early in the novel is presumed lost at sea. A match is arranged between Mary and Dr. Hopkins, but James reappears. Dr. Hopkins agrees to break his engagement with Mary, and she and James marry. Mary is, by the narrator's account, a beautiful girl, pure of heart and intention:

> There was something in Mary . . . which divided her as by an appreciable line from ordinary girls of her age. From her father she had inherited a deep and thoughtful nature, predisposed to moral and religious exaltation. Had she been born in Italy, under the dissolving influences of that sunny dreamy clime, beneath the shadow of cathedrals, and where pictured saints and angels smiled in clouds of painting from every arch and altar, she might, like fair St. Catherine of Siena, have seen beatific visions in the sunset skies, and a silver dove descending upon her as she prayed; but, unfolding in the clear, keen, cold New England clime, and nurtured in its abstract and positive theologies, her religious faculties took other forms. Instead of lying entranced in mysterious raptures at the foot of altars, she read and pondered treatises on the Will, and listened in rapt attention, while her spiritual guide, the venerated Dr. Hopkins, unfolded to her the theories of the great Edwards on the nature of virtue. (15)

Like Eva, Mary represents both the American ideal of "true womanhood" and the object of Roman Catholic veneration. Much of the novel's conflict centers on Mary's understanding and eventual rejection of the Calvinist notion of "disinterested benevolence." Her characterization as "Catholic" prefigures her rejection of orthodox Calvinism and her paternal legacy. Mary exceeds the terms of "true womanhood" that Stowe associates with the "clime" of New England and Calvinist paternalism.

Perhaps Stowe's personal experience of loss motivated her critique of disinterested benevolence in *The Minister's Wooing*. The death of her son Henry in 1857 by drowning sparked questions about his elect status. The grief of the Stowe family, Joan Hedrick notes, was structured by Calvinist theology, but "Calvinism had long been institutionalized in a clerical structure presided over by men . . . [and] . . . likewise became more and more divorced from the bereavement it was meant to structure" (1994, 276). The formulaic nature of Calvinist belief is exemplified in Samuel Hopkins's theory of disinterested benevolence, which "reduced the mystery of death and salvation to a mathematical formula in which the sufferings of a few were justified by the greater good that came from it . . ." (277). The appearance of Samuel Hopkins in *The Minister's Wooing* seems designed, among other things, to set up a kind of straw man for Stowe's critique of orthodox Calvinism. The novel itself sets Mary's intuitive understanding of God and religion against the structured orthodoxy of the intellectual Hopkins and suggests that true religion is based upon feeling rather than the pure workings of reason.

If Mary questions orthodoxy and the cult of true womanhood, her mother, Katy Scudder, exemplifies these ideals. Like Ophelia in *Uncle Tom's Cabin*, Katy highlights the domestic efficiency characteristic of the middle-class "true woman." Her place, quite literally, is in the kitchen: "The kitchen of a New England matron was her throne-room, her pride; it was the habit of her life to produce the greatest possible results there with the slightest possible discomposure, and what any woman could do, Mrs. Katy Scudder could do *par excellence*" (12). The kitchen of the Scudders's house, indeed, becomes the focal point of action in the novel's first half. It is also the place where we first encounter Mary, who stands suggestively on the threshold:

[T]he gentle Mary stands in the doorway with the afternoon sun streaming in spots of flickering golden light on her smooth pale-brown hair,—a *petite* figure in a full stuff of petticoat and white short gown, she stands reaching up one hand and cooing to something about the appleblossoms,—and now a Java comes whirring down and settles on her finger. . . . (13)

This overdetermined description of Mary paints her as a saint, complete with halo. Mary, who stands at the outer limits of the kitchen, competes with the vision of true womanhood represented by her mother.

Unlike her mother, Mary is rarely described in terms of her domestic abilities. As in *Uncle Tom's Cabin*, where Eva appears to stand for the reforming impulse of womanhood and Ophelia for a pragmatic domesticity, Mary stands as an idealized womanhood that contrasts with the New England woman's "faculty," a term that, Stowe points out in chapter 1,

> is Yankee for *savoir faire*, and the opposite virtue to shiftlessness. Faculty is the greatest virtue, and shiftlessness the greatest vice, of Yankee man and woman. To her who has faculty, nothing shall be impossible. She shall scrub floors, wash, wring, bake, brew and yet her hands shall be small and white; she shall have no perceptible income, yet always be handsomely dressed. . . . (4)

The "true woman," despite her domesticity, retains her middle-class virtue, evidenced by the condition of her skin and the quality of her dress. Yet, the world of possibilities for such a woman appears mean and narrow: for her there is only the possibility of more labor and service to the domestic ideal.

But in the "maiden-like place" of Mary's bedroom, a place "small enough for a nun's apartment," she keeps a modest library that includes "'The Spectator,' 'Paradise Lost,' Shakespeare, and 'Robinson Crusoe,'" as well as a collection of works by Jonathan Edwards and, of course, a Bible (19). Mary is not the novel's heroine because she is marriageable, or an able manager of the household. On the contrary, she is, like her namesake, or a "nun," pure, even otherworldly. Her "faculty" is not of a practical, but of a spiritual and intellectual nature.

After Mary's true love, James Marvyn, is presumed lost at sea, she is encouraged to take the hand of the much older Dr. Hopkins, a man obsessed with the study of scripture and the problem of grace. He is also the novel's main proponent of "disinterested benevolence," a doctrine, Susan Harris notes, "which equated self-love with sin and therefore concluded that true love consisted of absolute selflessness" (1999, x).[7] Katy Scudder, in her single-minded devotion to duty, exemplifies this notion. And Mary, to all appearances, is also selfless, until she learns that James is probably dead at sea and begins to study French with Virginie, the wife of Colonel de Frontignac, hero of the American Revolution. Virginie "had been given him to wife when but eighteen,—a beautiful, generous, impulsive, wilful girl" (Stowe [1859] 1999, 135). Their marriage is one of arrangement and convenience rather than love. Mme. de Frontignac is both worldly—"All the pomp and splendor of high life, the wit, the refinements, the nameless graces and luxuries of the courts, seemed to breathe in invisible airs around her" (173)—and innocent:

> She was strung heroically, and educated according to the notions of her cast and church, piously and religiously. True it is, that one can scarcely call *that* education which teaches woman everything except herself,—except the things that relate to her own peculiar womanly destiny, and, on plea of the holiness of ignorance, sends her without one word of just counsel into the temptations of life. Incredible as it may seem, Virginie de Frontignac had never read

a romance or work of fiction of which love was the staple; the regime of the convent in this regard was inexorable; at eighteen she was more thoroughly a child than most American girls at thirteen. (176–77)

Whatever worldliness Virginie has absorbed has come from her marriage to the colonel. Her convent life, contrary to popular American accounts, was hardly a corrupting one. The younger Mary, in fact, becomes the self-proclaimed protector of Virginie from the further advances of the scoundrel Aaron Burr. Stowe uses Virginie, however, not only to contrast the practical abilities and good sense of American girls with European, but also to critique the enclosures of the domestic space.

But perhaps because of her former enclosure, and her unhappy marriage, Virginie is able to advise Mary on the ways of men and the nature of domestic partnership. When Mary first mentions the possibility of her engagement to Dr. Hopkins, Virginia warns her that:

[I]t is *dreadful* to be married to a good man, and want to be good, and want to love him, and yet never like to have him take your hand, and be more glad when he is away than when he is at home; and then to think how different it would all be, if it was only somebody else. That will be the way with you if you let them lead you into this; so don't you do it, *mon enfant.* (179)

Virginie does not object to marriage per se, but to a loveless union made only out of duty. Her implicit criticism of such marriage arrangements grows out of her own experience but also reflects and indicts traditional notions of marriage and the limits they place upon women.

Karen Tracey has written of the nineteenth century's "double proposal novels," in which female heroines reject but finally accept a marriage proposal from the same suitor. Tracey argues that such novels "reveal complex 'imaginative engagements' with changing nineteenth-century perceptions of courtship, marriage, and women's work" (2000, 13–14). The reappearance of Mary Scudder's original love interest—James—substantially complicates her engagement to Dr. Hopkins. Engagement, like marriage, is a contract, the terms of which Mary is bound to after accepting the proposal of Dr. Hopkins. This is the subject of chapter 35, "Old Love and New Duty":

Some will, perhaps, think it an unnatural thing that Mary should have regarded her pledge to the Doctor as of so absolute and binding a force; but they must remember the rigidity of her education. Self-denial and self-sacrifice had been the daily bread of her life. Every prayer, hymn, and sermon, from her childhood, had warned her to distrust her inclinations, and regard her feelings as traitors. (Stowe [1859] 1999, 294)

Mary's devotion to duty, the narrator suggests, is unnatural. But it is the integral part of her domestic education, a stern code of duty passed down from her New England forebears through Mary's mother, who expresses her relief in this chapter that Mary has decided to continue her engagement.

In contrast to Mary's mother, who promulgates still-dominant views of marriage and women's duty, Virginie calls these views into question. In chapter 27, "The Question of Duty," Virginie questions Mary's continued engagement to Hopkins, whom Virginie refers to as "the priest." Virginie urges Mary to be true to her natural feelings for James, rather than to social obligation. Mary, whose conflicted feelings reveal themselves more clearly in her conversation with Virginie, cries: "Oh, I wish somebody would tell me exactly what is right!" (304). Virginie suggests that she "[g]o down to the dear priest, and tell him the whole truth" (304). This suggestion frames Mary as a potential confessant. Since it is Virginie, the Catholic, who encourages Mary to escape her engagement to Hopkins, Stowe's revision of anti-Catholic tropes makes the infamous scene of confession not one in which woman is endangered but one in which she is saved from her social role in an unhappy marriage.[8] Virginie, then, does not represent the corrupting force of the convent. Rather, she speaks to Mary's attempt to rescue herself from a potential captivity. Roman Catholicism, figured in Virginie, has the power to redeem Mary Scudder.

*The Minister's Wooing* undoes the notion of marriage out of duty rather than love and critiques male prerogatives in a society where women's roles were contained by the space of the kitchen or parlor. Mary's relationship with her true love, James Marvyn, subverts the traditional relationship of men and women in courtship novels, where the man is reformed by the woman, led to the saving words of the Bible after being led to them by the domestic and reforming angel. In a letter, he describes to Mary how he came to have faith in God:

> There was *one* passage in particular [in the Bible], and that was where Jacob started off from all his friends to go off and seek his fortune in a strange country, and laid down to sleep all alone in the field, with only a stone for his pillow. It seemed to me exactly the image of what every young man is like, when he leaves his home and goes out to shift for himself in this hard world. I tell you, Mary, that one man alone on the great ocean of life feels himself a very weak thing. . . . He saw there was a way between him and God, and that there were those above who did care for him, and who could come to him to help him. Well, so the next morning he got up, and set up the stone to mark the place; and it says Jacob vowed a vow, saying, "If God will be with me, and will keep me in this way that I go, and will give me bread to eat and raiment to put on, so that I come again to my father's house in peace, *then* shall the Lord be my God." Now *there* was something that looked to me like a tangible foundation. (297–98)

Although James has been reared, like Mary, in the New England Calvinist tradition, he understands and interprets scripture on his own terms.

Mary, while she may be portrayed as a saintly/angelic intercessor through Stowe's use of Marian imagery, does not transmit the culture of Puritanism to James. Both Mary and James, for that matter, demonstrate an intuitive understanding of religion and spirituality. Dr. Hopkins, on the other hand, is progressive in his resistance to slavery but staid in his regular habit of studying, rather than feeling, the words of scripture.

Stowe's novel vaunts spirit over intellect, and her use of Catholicism emphasizes the notion that religion is one with nature.[9] Mary is consistently identified with the natural world and many of the descriptive passages in *The Minister's Wooing* link Mary's intuitive spirituality with natural phenomena. Mary is, in many ways, the personification of nature. In chapter 17, "Polemics in the Kitchen," Mary is outdoors, surrounded by the sea that "lies shimmering and glittering in deep blue and gold, and the sky above . . . firm and cloudless" (161). She stands both literally and figuratively on the threshold of the kitchen, where she "saw a rather original scene acting" (161). Inside, the black servants Digo and Candace argue over the notion of disinterested benevolence and over the rightness of slavery. Digo argues, along with his master, Dr. Stiles, that slavery is ordained by God. Candace, however, dismisses the idea as nonsense, calling the notion of Providence into question: "Oh, you go 'long wid your Providence! Guess, ef white folks had let us alone, Providence wouldn't trouble us" (162).

Candace's commentary parallels Mary's own movement away from the strictures of Puritanism. Candace, whose role, like that of Mary and other women, is limited to the domestic sphere, implies that the notion of Providence itself limits freedom. Candace rebuts Digo's reliance on his master's claim that there is no such thing as disinterested benevolence by appealing to the greater authority of feeling: "'*Our* Doctor knows dere is,—and why? 'cause he's got it IN HERE,' said she, giving her ample chest a knock which resounded like the boom from a barrel" (162). Candace's argument with Digo constructs the novel's tensions between the authority of nature and the authority of tradition, between freedom and enclosure, and between the open spaces of the outer world and the confining spaces of the domestic world.

The novel's critique of traditional, rational religious piety also parallels the nineteenth-century disestablishment of Congregationalism in New England, and the impact of the Second Great Awakening on religious ideas (Ahlstrom 1972, 637–38). Roman Catholicism was often contrasted with the rational virtues of Calvinism. Certainly Mary's "Catholic" intuition is contrasted with Hopkins's cool, Calvinist reason. In "Calvinism Romanticized: Harriet Beecher Stowe and *The Minister's Wooing*," Laurence Buell has observed that the novel reconciles incompatibilities between sentimentalism and Calvinism. This view is developed further in "Puritanism: Hawthorne versus Stowe," where Buell argues that Mary actually embodies

elements of spiritual vitality in Hopkinsianism. This vision of the novel—as
a reconciliation between the rational force of traditional Puritanism and
the pietistic notion of religion—points to a reconciliation between the
patriarchal culture of eighteenth-century New England and the feminized
culture of the nineteenth. Buell also observes that Mary, like Hester Prynne,
is an instrument "for critiquing theological and social order" (1978b, 126).

At least three broader social and literary changes are suggested in *The
Minister's Wooing*: the shift from America as a patriarchal society to a feminized society; an alteration in women's roles; and, finally, a change in the
function of anti-Catholic tropes. Stowe's subversion of these tropes also
upsets the conventional ideology of women's roles. Many popular fictions
wed notions of domesticity to anti-Catholicism. The American obsession
with Roman Catholic convents, as I suggested earlier, is really conditioned
by a larger concern with the role of women in society. Stowe rights (or
rewrites) the figures of the convent story: the women who are held in the
confines of the New England kitchen are not, like their counterparts in the
nunnery, held captive by the Catholic Church, but instead by a rigid Protestantism. The reform of American society must begin, the novel suggests,
with the reform of its religion and its construction of womanhood.


## *AGNES OF SORRENTO*: RELIGIOUS REFORM AND GENDER

*Agnes of Sorrento* (1862), like *The Minister's Wooing*, critiques the construction of normative gender roles, and performs this critique in part through
the implicit paralleling of fifteenth-century Florentine religious reform and
the decline of Congregationalism in late eighteenth-century New England.
The plot focuses on the relationship between its title character and an Italian cavalier, Agostino. Agnes repels the apostate Agostino's advances, hoping to reform him. It is ultimately Agostino who reforms Agnes, however,
by convincing her to support Savonarola. Agnes, like Mary Scudder, is not
painted in the typical terms of true womanhood. Like Mary, Agnes is pure,
and a reform-minded woman, but she also exceeds the confining roles of
domesticity. Agnes is frequently pictured in the novel's descriptive passages
in pastoral settings. Anna Formichella has argued that *Agnes of Sorrento* is a
novel that continues the domestic project Stowe set up in *Uncle Tom's Cabin*
by its use of a foreign setting, and by associating Agnes not with the kitchen,
but with outdoor spaces. The Italian setting of the novel enables Stowe to
question the link between American nationalism and domesticity (1998,
189). According to Formichella, the most important subversive work of the
novel can be located in Stowe's instrumentalization of Catholic traditions
to weaken male authority. While I agree with Formichella's claim that the
relative neglect of this work has been due in part to a "critical tendency

to look for literary corroboration of the anti-Catholicism we expect from nineteenth-century American culture" (190), I would maintain further that there has been a critical failure to recognize the broader meanings of anti-Catholic tropes in literature, and therefore a tendency to ignore their critical subversion. Critics have not fully appreciated that the common figures of anti-Catholic speech and writing in American culture code more widely recognized cultural characteristics, such as women's roles and their connection to the formation of American identity. Because of this, they have been unable to appreciate the subversion of these figures.

Agnes and Mary challenge established religious authorities; each manages to escape an arranged marriage that would lock her into a loveless union; and both are identified with religious conviction based on spiritual devotion rather than reasoned attachment to duty. Mary is the dutiful daughter of New England Puritanism, and Agnes the chaste Catholic virgin who lives under the watchful eye of her grandmother. If Mary and Agnes do not explicitly challenge conventional religion as the plots of these works progress, they do come to stand for the possibility of resistance. Agnes's chief protector is her grandmother, Elsie, an intensely pious woman. Agnes is the love object of two men in the novel: the cavalier, Agostino, and Padre Francesco, the local priest whose desire for Agnes is represented in the novel by "the lurid glow of Vesuvius" (51). Agnes' grandmother also arranges a match with a local blacksmith.

Agnes, like Mary Scudder, finds herself trapped between devotion to religious duty and her love for an unredeemed man. The Italian setting allows Stowe to critique those elements of Catholicism that she finds most objectionable, but more importantly to interrogate women's roles subtly by using anti-Catholic tropes. In chapter 7, "The Day at the Convent," Agnes laments her inability to influence the cavalier, Agostino: "Ah," she softly sighed to herself, "how little I am! how little I can do! Could I convert one soul! Ah, holy Dorothea, send down the roses of heaven into his soul, that he may also believe!" (74). The setting of this chapter would have alerted most contemporary American readers to the popular tropes employed in descriptions of convent life. As the women of popular "escaped nuns' tales," who are removed from their socially defined roles, in this scene Agnes is removed from a world in which she might effect a moral change in Agostino. Yet, as the novel draws on, Agnes fails to change Agostino's infidel heart, even when she is outside of the convent walls. She learns that he has come into the fold of the reforming Savonarolans quite on his own.

But she is convinced of her responsibility to save Agostino, who has been excommunicated from the church. The more conventionally devout Francesco, by contrast, regularly locks himself in his cell in the Capuchin convent, a prisoner to a faith that insists that his desire for Agnes is sinful. He eventually seeks spiritual renewal in a barefoot climb to the top of Mount Vesuvius, hoping that the mortification of the flesh will purify him. Agnes, meanwhile, asks permission to go on a pilgrimage to Rome. As Agnes prepares for her journey, Agostino is in Florence, which Stowe characterizes strangely as a kind of Old World version of New England: "What the Puritans of New England wrought out with severest earnestness in their reasonings and their lives these early Puritans of Italy embodied in poetry, sculpture and painting" (283). The novel's use of artistic images links American and European religious reform across the centuries. Agnes, who is herself characterized alternately as Puritan and Catholic, makes both a literal and a symbolic journey away from her provincial, Catholic home toward a religious reawakening whose home is Florence.

The novel undoes the association between womanhood and moral rightness in part by making Agnes the unwitting object of conversion to the Savonarolan reform movement. The story of Savonarola and his followers parallels the American democratization of Christianity. Linked to this democratization are the feminization of American culture and the tropes of domesticity and enclosure. But in *Agnes of Sorrento*, Stowe refuses the conventional connection between enclosure and moral decay. As Agnes and her grandmother Elsie make their pilgrimage to Rome, Agostino vows to protect them and has them taken to the mountain fortress that is the headquarters of Savonarola's supporters. Agnes is locked overnight in an opulent bedchamber, where she falls asleep. When she awakes, she reflects on her surroundings:

> With the education she had received, she could look on this strange interruption of her pilgrimage only as a special assault upon her faith, instigated by those evil spirits that are ever setting themselves in conflict with the just. Such trials had befallen saints of whom she had read. They had been assailed by visions of worldly ease and luxury suddenly presented before them, by which they were tempted to deny their faith and sell their souls. (345)

Agnes identifies her elegantly appointed chamber with the "evil" of worldliness. She prays for deliverance: "[H]er soul was stayed on God . . . as truly as if she had been the veriest Puritan maiden that ever worshipped in a New England meeting house" (346). Agnes's prayer asks for deliverance from a familiar scene of captivity. But, as the chapter continues, she learns that her deliverance is *in* her captivity. Unlike Bourne's Louise, Rebecca Reed, or Maria Monk, Agnes has not been taken hostage by a hostile Roman Catholicism. She is being protected, saved by the reformer Agostino and his fellow Savonarolans. Agnes is neither the victim of a dangerous enclosure, nor is she like the American female captive who finds her deliverance through an abiding Protestant faith. She is saved by her confinement and eventual conversion.

As nineteenth-century American Protestantism moved away from the patriarchal strictures of New England Puritanism, it also vilified Roman Catholicism. Savonarola sought what historians have described as a series of democratic changes within the church. Medici rule in Florence ended in 1494. A republic was established, and Savonarolans sought to reconcile republicanism with religion.[10] The resonance between Florentine political and religious reforms and American reforms of the nineteenth century may suggest why Agnes is characterized variously as Puritan and Roman Catholic in the novel. Her pilgrimage marks her movement away from the traditional and confining faith in Roman Catholicism, but her moral development is achieved through a kind of narrative defamiliarization: Agnes's involvement in the Savonarolan religious reform movement is symbolized by her enclosure in the castle. The real enclosure, Agostino assures her, is the religion that she espouses: "I sought to warn you of the dangers of this pilgrimage,—to tell you that Rome is not what you think it is,—that it is not the seat of Christ, but a foul cage of unclean birds, a den of wickedness,— that he they call the Pope is a vile impostor" (351).

Harriet Beecher Stowe's writing has long been identified with the construction, rather than the subversion, of the nineteenth-century's cult of domesticity. However, both *The Minister's Wooing* and *Agnes of Sorrento* show that she extended the conventional devices of the domestic novel to endorse and make subversive use of popular understandings of women's roles. The popular material of anti-Catholic sentiment forms the basic elements of critique in *The Minister's Wooing* and *Agnes of Sorrento*, as it does in *Uncle Tom's Cabin*. Although much of American anti-Catholic writing created a Catholic other in order to confirm the structures and values of mainstream Protestant society, Stowe claims familiar anti-Catholic codes for other purposes. The anti-Catholicism of Stowe's writings refuses the easy equation of the church with threats to domesticity. Instead, her anti-Catholic rhetoric participates in a reformulation of the relationship between "true womanhood" and patriarchy. Her figurations of Mary and Agnes simultaneously participate in antebellum understandings of "true womanhood" and refuse the exclusive association of womanhood with a practical domesticity.

## NOTES

1. Ray Allen Billington's *The Protestant Crusade, 1800–1860: A Study of the Origins of American Nativism* (1938) is still one of the most complete studies of anti-Catholicism in this period of American life.

2. For a discussion of Stowe's changing theological views, see John Gatta, "The Anglican Aspect of Harriet Beecher Stowe" (2000).

3. See Tompkins's chapter on the novel in *Sensational Designs: The Cultural Work of American Fiction, 1790–1860* (1985).

4. See Billington for background information on Bourne and Slocum.

5. The work of Nina Baym, Gillian Brown, and Susan K. Harris stands out in this area. See Baym's *American Women Writers and the Work of History, 1790–1860* (1995) and *Woman's Fiction: A Guide to Novels by and about Women in America, 1820–1870* (1993). By Brown, see *Domestic Individualism: Imagining Self in Nineteenth-Century America* (1990). Harris's *19th Century American Women's Novels: Interpretative Strategies* (1990) also provides a brief history of the critical reception of women's writing among American literary scholars in the introduction.

6. For a discussion of Savonarola's political involvement in Florence see Donald Weinstein, *Savonarola and Florence: Prophecy and Patriotism in the Renaissance* (1970) and Laurence Pollizzotto, *The Elect Nation: The Savonarolan Moment in Florence, 1494–1545* (1994).

7. See Harris's introduction to the Penguin edition of the novel for an excellent discussion of the work and its relation to Calvinist theology.

8. However, this may not be a revision. As I am arguing that Stowe's work is subversive of dominant conceptions of women's roles, I think that it is possible that Stowe adopts anti-Catholic codes in order to show how women can free themselves from the responsibilities associated with the "cult of true womanhood."

9. Roman Catholicism, particularly in American writing, is associated with the precivilized, where Protestantism is often viewed as a "rational" religion. For example, the portrayal of Catholicism in early American captivity narratives conflates the wildness of the Indian with the superstitious rites of the Jesuits.

10. Savonarola's attempts at democratizing the Catholic church are discussed at length in Pollizzotto.

## WORKS CITED

Ahlstrom, Sydney. 1972. *A Religious History of the American People*. New Haven, CT: Yale University Press.

Baym, Nina. 1993. *Woman's Fiction: A Guide to Novels by and about Women in America, 1820–1870*. Urbana: University of Illinois Press.

———. 1995. *American Women Writers and the Work of History, 1790–1860*. New Brunswick, NJ: Rutgers University Press.

Beecher, Lyman. 1835. *A Plea for the West*. Cincinnati: Truman and Smith.

Billington, Ray Allen. 1938. *The Protestant Crusade, 1800–1860: A Study of American Nativism*. Chicago: Quadrangle Books.

Brown, Gillian. 1990. *Domestic Individualism: Imagining Self in Nineteenth-Century America*. Berkeley and Los Angeles: University of California Press.

Buell, Laurence. 1978a. "Calvinism Romanticized: Harriet Beecher Stowe and *The Minister's Wooing*. *Emerson Society Quarterly* 24 (1): 119–32.

———. 1978b. "Puritanism: Hawthorne versus Stowe." *Texas Studies in Language and Literature* 25 (1): 188–203.

Douglas, Ann. 1977. *The Feminization of American Culture*. New York: Anchor.

Formichella, Anna Maria. 1998. "Domesticity and Nationalism in Harriet Beecher Stowe's *Agnes of Sorrento.*" *Legacy: A Journal of American Women Writers* 15 (2): 188–203.

Franchot, Jenny. 1994. *Roads to Rome: The Antebellum Protestant Encounter with Roman Catholicism.* Berkeley and Los Angeles: University of California Press.

Gatta, John. 1997. *American Madonna: Images of the Divine Woman in Literary Culture.* New York: Oxford University Press.

———. 2000. "The Anglican Aspect of Harriet Beecher Stowe." *New England Quarterly* 73 (3): 412–13.

Griffin, Susan M. 2004. *Anti-Catholicism and Nineteenth Century Fiction.* New York: Cambridge University Press.

Harris, Susan K. 1990. *19th Century American Women's Novels: Interpretative Strategies.* New York: Cambridge University Press.

———. 1999. Introduction to *The Minister's Wooing,* by Harriet Beecher Stowe, vii–xxviii. New York: Penguin.

Hedrick, Joan. 1994. *Harriet Beecher Stowe: A Life.* New York: Oxford University Press.

Monk, Maria. [1836] 1962. *Awful Disclosures of the Hotel Dieu Nunnery at Montreal.* Hamden, CT: Archon Books.

Pollizzotto, Lorenzo. 1994. *The Elect Nation: The Savonarolan Moment in Florence, 1494–1545.* Oxford: Clarendon.

Schulz, Nancy Lusignan. 2000. *Fire and Roses: The Burning of the Charlestown Convent, 1834.* New York: Free Press.

———. 1999. *Veil of Fear: Nineteenth-Century Convent Tales.* West Lafayette, IN: Purdue University Press.

Stone, William L. 1836. *Maria Monk and the Nunnery of the Hotel Dieu, Being an Account of a Visit to the Convents of Montreal and Refutation of the 'Awful Disclosures.* New York: Howe and Bates.

Stowe, Harriet Beecher. [1852] 1994. *Uncle Tom's Cabin.* New York: Norton.

———. [1859] 1999. *The Minister's Wooing.* New York: Penguin.

———. 1862. *Agnes of Sorrento.* Boston: Ticknor and Fields.

Tompkins, Jane. 1985. *Sensational Designs: The Cultural Work of American Fiction, 1790–1860.* New York: Oxford University Press.

Tracey, Karen. 2000. *Plots and Proposals: American Women's Fiction, 1850–1890.* Chicago: University of Illinois Press.

Weinstein, Donald. 1970. *Savonarola and Florence: Prophecy and Patriotism in the Renaissance,*

Welter, Barbara. 1966. "The Cult of True Womanhood: 1820–1860." *American Quarterly* 18 (1): 151–74.

# Mapping the Environmental Ethical Dimension in Harriet Beecher Stowe's New England Novels

*Sylvia Mayer*

That Harriet Beecher Stowe's texts—both fictional and nonfictional—participated in the efforts of several nineteenth-century American reform movements has been a commonplace of Stowe scholarship. Her contributions to the temperance movement, to various concerns of the women's movement, and, above all, to American abolitionism have been widely discussed. An analysis of her four New England novels that focuses on the representation of the ethical quality of the human-nature relationship, however, shows her contribution to yet another reform movement whose organizational structures consolidated in the last third of the nineteenth century and culminated during the Progressive Era, but whose concerns had been articulated much earlier. Stowe's New England novels, *The Minister's Wooing* (1859), *The Pearl of Orr's Island* (1862), *Oldtown Folks* (1869), and *Poganuc People* (1878), reveal instances of moral inquiry into the relationship between humans and nonhuman nature thereby contributing to the emerging national discourse of American environmentalism.

This essay addresses the environmental ethical dimension of Stowe's New England novels. As the reemergence of literary ethical criticism since the late 1980s has shown, literary texts—in contrast to systematic or "schematic"[1] moral philosophical texts—can be regarded as a specific mode of moral inquiry because of their imaginative range and formal richness of language. They do not develop one succinct ethical argument but instead create characters and situations that indicate a variety of morally relevant attitudes thereby shedding light on the complexity of the human moral experience. In order to map the environmental ethical dimension of Stowe's four novels, I shall make use of a number of value arguments that lie at the heart of several current environmental ethical positions.

Environmental ethics as a branch of applied ethics emerged in the early 1970s and has by now developed into a wide spectrum of positions. What these diverse positions all share is the expansion of the moral universe to include parts of nonhuman nature or nature as a whole—in contrast to traditional ethical systems that focused exclusively on human interpersonal relations. In her survey *Ethics of Nature*, philosopher Angelika Krebs has developed a taxonomy of value arguments on which different environmental ethical positions are founded. Of importance to my analysis is her basic distinction between anthropocentric and physiocentric arguments that attribute value to nature—either to some of its parts or to nature as a whole. While anthropocentric arguments call for the inclusion of nature into the moral universe because of its value for a good human life, physiocentric arguments call for the inclusion of nature into the moral universe for its own sake. The anthropocentric arguments most important for this analysis are "the instrumental value of nature for the satisfaction of *basic human needs* like health," two aesthetic arguments, namely "the instrumental value of nature for *sensual human delight*" and "the *aesthetic intrinsic value* beautiful and sublime nature has for human beings," and, finally, "the *pedagogic* value of treating nature with care" (1999, 1, emphases in the original). The most important physiocentric arguments include attribution of intrinsic value to "*sentient* nature, especially animals," to "*teleological* nature," i.e., parts of nature such as animals that express intent and purpose, to "all *life* in nature," and—reflecting a religious or theological stance—to nature as divine creation, as representing "*God's order*" (1999, 1, emphases in the original).[2] The use of these arguments as a heuristic means makes it possible to identify attribution of value to the natural world in Stowe's novels and thus to map the environmental ethical dimension of the texts.

Complementing this kind of systematic mapping, the essay in its first part situates Stowe and her New England novels in the history of American environmentalism in the nineteenth century, which manifested itself in a diversity of activist groups and environmental ethical positions. It then briefly addresses the specific religious worldview the novels envision, a worldview on which the various types of value attribution in the texts are based. By focusing on single instances of attribution of value to nonhuman nature, it, finally, shows the layers of environmental ethical positions that the novels develop.

Histories of American environmentalism often put emphasis on the last third of the nineteenth century when the first wave of American environmentalism became noticeable as a political movement. The period saw the emergence of the conservation movement that warned against an indiscriminate use of resources, largely for commercial reasons; of the preservation movement that called for the preservation of "wild" nature, largely, though not exclusively, for recreational and spiritual purposes; and of the humane movement whose diverse groups included animal rights activists and health reformers who responded to the environmentally detrimental effects of rapid industrialization and urbanization such as air, water, and ground pollution.

Especially in the New England states, however, environmental concern had been voiced much earlier. As early as the late eighteenth century, conservationist goals were articulated and measures taken. By then almost two hundred years of agricultural transformation by European colonists who had introduced increasingly market-driven land use practices had caused ecological damages that began to threaten local and regional economies. Richard Judd, for instance, has pointed out that late eighteenth-century communities in Maine, Vermont, New Hampshire, and Massachusetts suffered from large-scale deforestation and concomitant soil erosion and called for conservationist measures. Brian Donahue (1989) and John T. Cumbler (1991) have traced the conflicts about the uses of the waters of the Concord River and the Connecticut River caused by economic transformations since the beginning of industrialization in the early nineteenth century. Judd claims that New England "pioneered a number of conservation ideas for the rest of the nation" (1997, 5). This claim is repeated by environmental historian Robert Dorman, who in his study *A Word for Nature: Four Pioneering Environmental Advocates*, has focused on the history of American environmentalism since the mid-nineteenth century. Dorman defines "environmentalism in a historically cumulative sense, as encompassing all of the different movements of environmental concern that have manifested themselves since the mid-nineteenth century" (1998, xiv). He draws attention not only to the impact of the writing of such well-known figures as Henry David Thoreau who forcefully rethought and redefined the human-nature and culture-nature relationship, but also to the key importance of Vermont's George Perkins Marsh, who in 1864 published *Man and Nature; or, Physical Geography as Modified by Human Action*, "the first comprehensive description in the English language of the destructive impact of human civilization on the environment" (Nash 1989, 38). Marsh was concerned with the "changes produced by human action in the physical conditions of the globe we inhabit" ([1864] 1965, 3)[3] and argued that unrestricted resource use would always lead to irreversible ecological changes that could prove—and had proved—economically and socially detrimental. Mid-nineteenth century New England intellectuals such as Harriet Beecher Stowe would thus be familiar with the very concrete environmental concerns of the region and with the emergence of environmentalist thought; they did, after all, live in what Dorman, too, calls "the birthplace of American environmentalism" (1998, 9).

From an environmental ethical point of view, these early environmentalist efforts were dominated by anthropocentric arguments that focused on the value of nature for a good human life. For the purpose of arguing against unlimited resource use, they on the one hand employed the basic needs argument, stressing the instrumental value of nature for the satisfaction of basic human needs, and, on the other hand, aesthetic arguments, putting emphasis on the value of nature as unique source of sensual and contemplative experience. Anthropocentric arguments also dominated the efforts of those parts of the humane movement that can be regarded as part of early American environmentalism, the health reform movement and the animal rights movement. Responses to environmental problems such as water and air pollution or hazardous hygienic conditions in the workplace—problems all caused by the economically, socially, and ecologically transformative processes of industrialization—also made heavy use of the basic needs argument and called for measures that would ensure a healthy (natural) environment.[4] The two major ethical arguments put forth by the animal rights movement were an anthropocentric one and a physiocentric one. On the one hand, activists made use of the pedagogical argument that asked for the inclusion of animals into the moral universe for the good of the human individual and of human society. They followed John Locke's notion in *Some Thoughts Concerning Education* (1693) that cruelty to animals causes moral corruption of the perpetrator and has far-reaching social effects: "A nation that did not stop cruelty to animals ran the risk of cruelty extending to people, and, ultimately, of decline and decay as a civilization" (Nash 1989, 46). On the other hand, animal rights supporters made use of the physiocentric argument that sentient beings must be included into the moral universe. They granted intrinsic moral value to animals due to their obvious capability to feel—a position that can also be traced back in Anglo-American ethical thought to the seventeenth century, for instance to natural theologians such as Henry More and John Ray.

When in 1868 the Massachusetts branch of the American Society for the Prevention of Cruelty to Animals (ASPCA) was founded, Harriet Beecher Stowe and her brother Henry Ward Beecher became articulate supporters of the cause (Nash 1989, 47; Wagenknecht 1965, 118–22). In 1869 Stowe had already published the essay "The Rights of Dumb Animals" in which her commitment became evident:

> Christianity, which has ameliorated so many sorrows, and raised so many sufferers, has as yet made but small progress toward softening the condition of the poor brute. How many men are there who do not consider that they have the *right* to chase, hunt, and terrify wild animals in their native forests, simply for the excitement of mind and exercise it gives? The agony of terror excited by the chase, the victim's turnings and frantic doublings upon its track, are all part of the interest and excitement of the sport. Is this a Christian or a heathen state of mind? The greatest proof of civilization and true Christianity in Martin Luther, that we have ever heard of, was that . . . when he rode out in the chase for

exercise, he declared that his sympathies were so entirely with the poor hunted animal that he was always wishing and contriving for it to escape. (1869, 24)

Stowe condemns the chase, the hunting and killing of animals solely for human pleasure, by putting forth the physiocentric argument of including animals into the moral universe due to their sentience. To her, the capability of animals to feel, in this case to suffer the "agony of terror" during the chase, demands moral behavior that abstains from this kind of "sport." She clearly rejects the idea of a human "right" to chase. Moreover, the text targets a "Christianity" that had failed to ensure the well-being of animals. Stowe here articulates a stance that in Judeo-Christian environmentalist thought has been called the "stewardship position." In contrast to a theological position that legitimizes human dominion in the sense of unlimited exploitation of nature, the stewardship position insists that nature is given to humans to protect rather than to exploit.[5] The analysis of her New England novels will show repeatedly that the concept of Christian stewardship fundamentally motivates value attribution to the natural world both by the narrators of the novels and by various characters. In fact, it can be argued that the multilayered attribution of value to nonhuman nature in Stowe's novels largely emerges from this fundamentally anthropocentric stance.

Stowe's New England novels are all set in the period of the early American republic and envision a preindustrial, rural region in which a "village-centered republican culture" (Conforti 2001, 146) governs the characters' lives. *The Minister's Wooing* is set in Rhode Island in the 1780s and 1790s; *The Pearl of Orr's Island* in Maine in the 1810s; *Oldtown Folks* in Massachusetts in the 1780s and 1790s; and *Poganuc People* in Connecticut in the 1810s and 1820s. Critics see this temporal and local focus both as a symptom of nostalgia and as a conscious contribution to the discourse of national identity formation shortly before, during, and after the Civil War. Joseph Conforti classifies Stowe's regionalism as a "national regionalism" (2001, 91), and Edward Tang claims: "Through the use of a fictionalized New England past . . . Stowe indirectly confronts the issues of her own times. . . . [S]he saw in those cultural remains material sufficient to forge a collective sense of identity, a shared memory of the past bringing coherence to a future-oriented, democratized society" (1998, 85–86). The moral values the novels propose as a sound basis for personal and national identity formation reflect the central impact of the discourses of sentimentalism and domesticity and are crucially informed by what John Gatta has defined as Stowe's "'feminized' Christianity that stresses the motherly compassion of Jesus, the natural sacramentality of love, and the creative power of spirit and intuition" (2000, 417).

Sentimentalism, domesticity, and the concept of a feminized Christianity function as guides for moral choices and social practices and are of key importance for the emergence of an environmental ethical dimension in the texts. Before turning to textual incidents in which this dimension manifests itself, it is, however, necessary to delineate the concept of nature the four novels privilege. This concept emerges out of the religious worldview the novels ultimately propose, a worldview that puts a benevolent, loving God at its center. In *The Minister's Wooing* and in *Oldtown Folks*, this worldview is most explicitly developed because the religious liberalization of New England, the transition from a stern Calvinism to a more liberal "religion of the heart" (Buell 1986, 188) is a central concern in both novels. Two characters in particular struggle with the implications of Calvinist doctrine, Mrs. Marvyn in *The Minister's Wooing* and Jonathan Rossiter in *Oldtown Folks*. They end up embracing a faith that is based on God's benevolence and love and that conceptualizes nature as God's creation in which he is still able to interfere as a crucial, morally relevant force. The dramatization of the two characters' inner conflict focuses on the experience of suffering, and it involves the juxtaposition of Calvinist doctrine, the tenets of a faith based on love, and contemporary scientific discourse.

The immediate cause for Mrs. Marvyn's struggle with Calvinist doctrine in *The Minister's Wooing* is the assumed death of her son James. She cannot accept the idea that James is doomed to damnation since he did not show conviction of personal conversion. After recovering from her initial shock and despair, she tells Mary Scudder:

> I have thought, in desperate moments, of giving up the Bible itself. But what do I gain? Do I not see the same difficulty in Nature? I see everywhere a Being whose main ends seem to be beneficent, but whose good purposes are worked out at terrible expense by suffering, and apparently by the total sacrifice of myriads of sensitive creatures. I see unflinching order, general good-will, but no sympathy, no mercy. Storms, earthquakes, volcanoes, sickness, death, go on without regarding us. Everywhere I see the most hopeless, unrelieved suffering,—and for aught I see, it may be eternal. . . . The Doctor's dreadful system is, I confess, much like the laws of Nature,—about what one might reason out from them.
>
> There is but just one thing remaining, and that is, as Candace said, the cross of Christ. If God so loved us,—if He died for us,—greater love hath no man than this. . . . If there is a fathomless mystery of sin and sorrow, there is a deeper mystery of God's love. ([1859] 1982, 741–42)

Mrs. Marvyn equates Calvinist doctrine—the "Doctor's dreadful system"— with the "laws of Nature."[6] To her mind, neither can deal tolerably with the apparently ubiquitous experience of suffering, let alone her own pain. She finds comfort only in a faith that rests on the sacrifice of Christ's death, which reveals to her that the meaning of human existence is ultimately grounded in divine love, in "a Being whose main ends seem to be beneficent."

In *Oldtown Folks*, the character of Jonathan Rossiter serves a similar function as the character of Mrs. Marvyn in *The Minister's Wooing*. Rossiter is a teacher and scientist as well as a theologian who can look back on a long row of ancestors who were all prominent New England ministers and theologians. Rossiter is a widely travelled man, and his struggles with the implications of Calvinist doctrine result from having had to observe a high degree of suffering among people in various parts of the world. He is tempted to regard human life as "an inflicted curse" ([1869] 1982, 1295) by a God who can only be understood as "a Being who has never interested himself to care for their [humans'] welfare, to prevent their degradation, to interfere with their cruelties to each other, as they have writhed and wrangled into life, through life, and out of life again" (1295). Rossiter is led to the same conclusion when he tries to make sense of this suffering and "degradation" from a scientific point of view: "After seeing nature, can we reason against any of the harshest conclusions of Calvinism?" (1295). Despite his appreciation of the sciences and his successes as a science teacher at the academy of Cloudland (1288–1307), he is skeptical about the reach of scientific methods: "[T]he laws of nature are an inextricable labyrinth,— puzzling, crossing, contradictory; and ages of wearisome study have as yet hardly made a portion of them clear enough for human comfort" (1100).[7] In the end, Rossiter finds consolation and inner peace in the same faith that Mrs. Marvyn develops. In a letter to his sister Mehitable he writes: "Yes, I believe in Jesus Christ with all my heart, all my might. He stands before me the one hopeful phenomenon of history" (1101).

One of the characters in *Oldtown Folks* that holds this faith right from the beginning is the orphan Harry Percival. And Harry also articulates most clearly the concept of nature that emerges from it. In a comment on a sermon by the local minister Harry rejects the Deist concept of nature as a machine. He assesses this sermon as

one of those cool, philosophical sermons in which certain scholarly and rational Christians in easy worldly circumstances seem to take delight,—a sort of preaching which removes the providence of God as far off from human sympathy as it is possible to be. The amount of the matter as he stated it seemed to be, that the Creator had devised a very complicated and thorough-working machine, which he had wound up and set going ages ago, which brought out results with the undeviating accuracy of clock-work. (1131)

Harry acknowledges the existence of laws of nature, but he insists that they are not inflexible. He tells the narrator, Horace Holyoke:

what if natural laws were meant as servants of man's moral life? What if Jesus Christ and his redeeming, consoling work were the *first* thing, and all things made by him for this end? Inflexible physical laws are necessary; their very inflexibility is divine order; but "what law cannot do, in that it is weak through the flesh, God did by sending his Son in the likeness of sinful flesh." Christ delivers us from slavery to natural law; he comes to embody and make visible the paternal idea; and if you and I, with our small knowledge of physical laws, can so turn and arrange them that their inflexible course shall help, and not hinder, much more can their Maker. (1385)

In this passage, Harry develops the classic position of natural theology as it was propagated, for instance, in William Paley's influential study *Natural Theology; or, Evidences of the Existence and Attributes of the Deity Collected from the Appearances of Nature* (1803). Harry regards nature as God's creation, he grants the existence of natural laws by which nature operates, but he still insists on the capability of the Creator to become actively involved in his creation if need be. Natural laws may be inflexible, but their inflexibility illustrates divine order and is, ultimately, still subject to God's will. The suggestion that "natural laws were meant as servants of man's moral life" marks God as the benevolent moral force that always works through nature—and, in its insistence that natural laws can serve human beings, at the same time expresses the anthropocentric stance on which the novels' environmental ethical dimension is grounded to a large extent.

The idea of a paternal creator God who is capable of interfering with the laws of nature that is developed at such length in *The Minister's Wooing* and in *Oldtown Folks* is echoed in *The Pearl of Orr's Island* and in *Poganuc People*. On one of the first pages of *The Pearl of Orr's Island*, when the narrator introduces the character Mara Lincoln, she remarks: "Life goes on as inexorably in this world as death. It was ordered by THE WILL above that out of these two graves [of Mara's parents] should spring one frail, trembling autumn flower" ([1862] 1896, 8, emphasis in the original). And in *Poganuc People* the narrator insists on the existence of "the Creator's scheme" ([1878] 1977, 95) and later on puts emphasis on the divine creative power: "No artist ever has ventured to put on canvas the exact copy of the picture that nature paints for us every year in the autumn months. There are things the Almighty Artist can do that no earthly imitator can more than hopelessly admire" (225). Taken together, these passages hint at the texts' stance in the debate that followed the publication of Charles Darwin's *On the Origin of Species* in 1859. Stowe's novels take an anti-Darwinist and antimaterialist stance in the sense that they reject the idea of the principle of natural selection as the single motivational force of evolution. Ultimately, the novels thus participate in discourses of the sciences and natural theology on conceptualizations of nature, culture, and the human.

From an environmental ethical point of view, this privileged concept of nature implies both a physiocentric and an anthropocentric stance, announcing immediately the complexity of the environmental ethical dimension of the texts. First, according to Krebs's taxonomy, the texts express a physiocentric argument in that they define nature as divine creation that must be included into the moral universe. Second, an assumption such as the one made by Harry that "natural laws were meant as servants of man's moral life" shows that this basic physiocentric stance is in many instances complemented by other types of attribution of moral value—most of them anthropocentric. Harry's notion of the ultimate superiority of human beings in God's creation is only one example of many in the four novels. Other examples are passages in which Stowe made use of the concept of the Great Chain of Being: The narrator in *The Minister's Wooing* talks about an "ascending scale" ([1859] 1982, 744) of beings in which the human being is positioned above the rest of creation, and in another passage she calls humans "superior beings" (567) in comparison to crickets; in *Oldtown Folks* Grandmother Badger quotes the authoritative figure of Cotton Mather who called humanity "the most precious of all creatures" ([1869] 1982, 1199); and in *Poganuc People* the character Dolly is attributed a "higher nature" ([1878] 1977, 281) than a bird. The remainder of the essay will show that what in the end emerges from this hierarchical concept of creation is a plea for the stewardship position, which acknowledges that any part of this Great Chain of Being fulfills its function and that the destruction of one part also affects all the others.

All four novels envision a New England region characterized by a harsh climate and difficult agricultural conditions that require hard work on the part of farmers. The narrator of *The Minister's Wooing* talks about its "hard soil, unyielding to any but the most considerate culture" ([1859] 1982, 593); the region of Maine in *The Pearl of Orr's Island* is characterized by "rocky soil and harsh winds" ([1862] 1896, 2) and by a "cold, clear, severe climate" (18). Horace Holyoke, the narrator of *Oldtown Folks*, describes the region as "hard, rocky sterile New England" ([1869] 1982, 885), and the narrator of *Poganuc People* refers to "rocky soil and icy hills" ([1878] 1977, 95) that mark the working and living conditions of the region's inhabitants and with which, for instance, the farmer Zeph Higgins has to wrestle with in order to make a living. Such environmental conditions ask for an acute and comprehensive knowledge of the natural world, and, in essence, force humans to acknowledge the value of nature as a resource. In Stowe's novels they make many characters acknowledge its instrumental value for the satisfaction of basic needs such as food, heat, and shelter. The necessity to use nature as a valuable resource respectfully and wisely—as conservationists of the Progressive Era would later call it—becomes evident in the representation of such farmers as Mr. Marvyn in *The Minister's Wooing* and Jacob Badger in *Oldtown Folks* who bear traits of the Jeffersonian yeoman ideal and are thus marked as exemplars of republican virtue. More significantly, however, wise use of natural resources becomes evident in the representation of several female characters in all four novels. They reveal a precise knowledge of nature as a resource, betray a respectful attitude toward it, and use it in a circumspect way. The model households of Katy Scudder and Mrs. Marvyn in *The Minister's Wooing*, of Grandmother Pennel in *The Pearl of Orr's Island*, of Grandmother Badger and Aunt Lois in *Oldtown Folks*, and of Mrs. Cushing in *Poganuc People* all excel in their prudent use of natural resources. When Mrs. Marvyn in *The Minister's Wooing* admonishes her maid: "Dinah, take care, that wood is hickory, and it takes only seven sticks of that size to heat the oven" ([1859] 1982, 590), she reveals accurate knowledge about the efficiency of different types of wood that are used as fuel. Miss Roxy in *The Pearl of Orr's Island* and Miss Persis in *Poganuc People* show comprehensive knowledge of the plant world of their region. Their creation of different types of medicine marks an indispensable factor in the respective house and village economies. In this context the central role that the discourse of domesticity plays in the development of this anthropocentric environmental ethical position becomes particularly visible. The environmentally sound household management of all these characters expands the moral universe of the house to include those parts of nature that are needed for the satisfaction of basic human needs. This, in turn, shows that the discourse of domesticity, which functions as a key factor in the texts' attempt to envision a model nation, contains an environmental ethical dimension.

Mrs. Marvyn's admonition to use firewood wisely can also be linked to a critique that is most comprehensively articulated in *Oldtown Folks*, the critique of the consequences of unlimited deforestation. However, while Mrs. Marvyn's admonition clearly reflects the basic needs argument and positions *The Minster's Wooing* in the context of the conservation movement, the critique developed by Horace Holyoke in *Oldtown Folks* operates with the attribution of value to nature for aesthetic reasons. In chapter 37, "The Minister's Wood-Spell," the problem of the disappearance of the New England old growth forests is addressed. Holyoke remembers that in one year the farmers of the region decided to provide their minister with firewood of a particularly good quality since he "had recently preached a highly popular sermon on agriculture, in which he set forth the dignity of the farmer's life." Holyoke, however, retrospectively criticizes this decision:

> Good, straight shagbark-hickory was voted none too good for the minister. Also the axe was lifted up on many a proud oak and beech and maple. What destruction of glory and beauty there was in those mountain regions! How ruthlessly man destroys in a few hours that which centuries cannot bring again! What an idea of riches in those glorious woodland regions! We read legends of millionnaires [*sic*] who fed their fires with cinnamon and rolled up thousand-dollar bills into lamp-lighters, in the very wantonness of profusion. But what was that compared to the prodigality which fed our great roaring winter fires on the thousand-leafed oaks, whose conception had been ages ago—who were children of the light and of the day,—every fragment and fibre

of them made of most celestial influences, of sunshine and rain-drops, and night-dews and clouds, slowly working for centuries until they had wrought the wondrous shape into a gigantic miracle of beauty? (1345)

Holyoke's critique centers on the destruction of the forest as representative of sublime nature. He castigates the "prodigality" of the farmers, their recklessly wasteful logging, not by developing a wise use—or basic needs—argument. Instead, to him it is the trees' beauty and their very old age that mark, first and foremost, their aesthetic intrinsic value, i.e., the value that derives from their uniqueness as objects not only of human sensual experience but also contemplative experience. Holyoke's lament that most of the trees are gone by the time he tells the story implies a call for the preservation of those trees that are left, a call that becomes explicit a few paragraphs later when he admonishes the farmers of his own time: "[T]hink of your wealth, O ye farmers!—think what beauty and glory every year perish to serve your cooking-stoves and chimney-corners" (1346). Ultimately, Holyoke's critique can be read as textual support for the concerns of the preservation movement. The inclusion of sublime nature into the moral universe is to serve its preservation.[8]

Aesthetic arguments for the inclusion into the moral universe dominate Stowe's New England novels. Attention is again and again drawn to both the instrumental value of nature for sensual human delight and the aesthetic intrinsic value of beautiful and sublime nature for human contemplation. Several characters, but also Stowe's narrators, express their delight to simply experience nature sensually, and they show appreciation of how sensual experience can turn into contemplative, even mystical experience. Especially the latter experience demonstrates that for Stowe, "a response to beauty was integral to religious experience" (Gatta 2000, 421). Most significantly, Stowe creates female characters endowed with a large amount of cultural authority to convey the notion that for aesthetic reasons parts of nature ought to be included into the moral universe. She models her characters Tina Percival in *Oldtown Folks*, Mara Lincoln in *The Pearl of Orr's Island*, and Mary Scudder in *The Minister's Wooing* on three types of figures that were endowed with a high degree of cultural—and moral—authority: on the figure of the Romantic child who is not yet corrupted by civilization but still experiences a direct link to nature and its creator; on the figure of the New England saint who was typologically modelled on the life and death of Christ and largely served the function of bringing about the regeneration of others; and on the figure of the sentimental, domestic heroine who is placed at the center of the American key social unit, the family.[9]

Tina Percival's experiences in nature put emphasis on the distinctive value that sensual experience of beautiful nature has for a good human life. Tina is introduced as a "child, who came from a beauty-loving lineage" ([1869] 1982, 982), and in another passage she is described to be "endowed with an organization exquisitely susceptible to beauty" (1034). In several passages—for example, in the chapter "The Day in Fairy Land" (1025–36)—she is shown as intensely enjoying the colors, forms, and smells of the region's flora. To heighten this effect, the character of Tina is juxtaposed with two other characters, Miss Asphyxia, a farmer with whom the orphan lives for some time, and Miss Mehitable Rossiter, the minister's sister with whom she finally grows up. Both women initially lack the ability to enjoy the beauty of nature:

> Miss Asphyxia had one word for all flowers. She called them all "blows," and they were divided in her mind, in a manner far more simple than any botanical system, into two classes; namely, blows that were good to dry, and blows that were not. Elder-blow, catnip, hoarhound, hardhack, gentian, ginseng, and various other vegetable tribes, she knew well and had a great respect for; but all the other little weeds that put on obtrusive colors and flaunted in the summer breeze, without any pretensions to further usefulness, Miss Asphyxia completely ignored. It would not be describing her state to say she had a contempt for them: she simply never saw or thought of them at all. The idea of beauty as connected with any of them never entered her mind,—it did not exist there. (982)

While Miss Asphyxia is caught in this world without beauty, Miss Mehitable is able to escape it. Through her contact with Tina, Miss Mehitable, whose "tastes were in the world of books and ideas, rather than of physical matters," (951) after a while develops an appreciation of beauty: "Suddenly she awoke as from a dark dream, and found herself sole possessor of beauty, youth, and love" (1083).

Mara Lincoln's experiences in nature also emphasize the unique value that sensual experience of beautiful nature has for human beings. Mara loves flowers. As a child she collects them and makes bouquets to brighten up her grandparents' house ([1862] 1896, 124), and as a young woman she draws and paints almost excessively the flora of the island. Her relationship to nature is characterized by a high degree of attentiveness, knowledge, and love:

> Mara had been all her days a child of the woods; her delicate life had grown up in them like one of their own cool shaded flowers; and there was not a moss, not a fern, not an up-springing thing that waved a leaf or threw forth a flower-bell, that was not a well-known friend to her; she had watched for years its haunts, known the time of its coming and its going, studied its shy and veiled habits, and interwoven with its life each year a portion of her own. (341)

Mara is described as the prototypical New England saint, as part of that "class of lives formed on the model of Christ. . . . They are made, not for a career and history of their own, but to be bread of life to others" (366). The fact that her life and death are ultimately essential for the spiritual regeneration of the village community on Orr's Island, and especially for that of Moses Pennel, endows her with the highest moral authority, including an environmental ethical stance.

Mary Scudder's experiences in nature confirm, but also transcend, the emphasis on sensual experience. They highlight the uniqueness of contemplative and mystical experiences in nature. Before turning to a faith that regards the benevolent, loving God as central, Mary, too, has to struggle with the strict implications of Calvinist dogma. In the following passage she becomes aware of the stark contradiction between the overwhelmingly pleasurable sensual experience of nature and Calvinist dogma that insists on original sin and predestination: "[S]he wondered that the sun could shine so brightly, that flowers could flaunt such dazzling colors, that sweet airs could breathe . . . to cheat the victims from the thought that their next step might be into an abyss of horrors without end" ([1859] 1982, 542). The experience of beautiful nature triggers doubt and leads to the rejection of the theological system she was born into. In another passage her contemplation of nature develops into a mystical experience:

> The sea had become to her like a friend, with its ever-varying monotony. Somehow she loved this old, fresh, blue, babbling, restless giant. . . . Sometimes she would wander out for an afternoon's stroll on the rocks, and pause by the great Spouting Cave, now famous to Newport *dilettanti*, but then a sacred and impressive solitude. There the rising tide bursts with deafening strokes through a narrow opening into some inner cavern, which, with a deep thunderboom, like the voice of an angry sea lion, casts it back in a high jet of foam into the sea.
>
> Mary often sat and listened to this hollow noise, and watched the ever-rising columns of spray as they reddened with the transpiercing beams of the afternoon sun; and thence her eyes travelled far, far off over the shimmering starry blue, where sails looked no bigger than miller's wings; and it seemed sometimes as if a door were opening by which her soul might go out into some eternity,—some abyss, so wide and deep, that fathomless lines of thought could not sound it. She was no longer a girl in a mortal body, but an infinite spirit, the adoring companion of Infinite Beauty and Infinite Love. (715–16)

Mary watches and listens to the sea in a way that stresses a noninstrumental attitude. The sea is not so much an object to observe, but another subject that invites observation and contemplation. Ultimately, it turns from being "like a friend" to a medium of revelation. Sensual—here visual and auditory—perception turns into perceptions of something beyond the empirical realm. By the sea, Mary encounters "Infinite Beauty" and "Infinite Love," both core tenets of the faith she develops. The passage thus strongly suggests that the "Christian home" (870) Mary and James Marvyn are founding in the end rests on an ethical stance that includes beautiful and sublime nature in the moral universe.

The domination of aesthetic arguments for inclusion into the moral universe in the novels and the high significance of contemplative and mystical experience in nature places Stowe's novels in a tradition of American Protestant conceptualizations of nature that draws on the Neoplatonism both of the Puritans and the transcendentalists. As Mark Stoll has argued with respect to the history of American environmentalism, this tradition was continued "by such nineteenth-century nature writers as Thoreau, John Muir, and John Burroughs" and "added a crucial spiritual element to the early environmental movement" (1997, 16). As Stowe's New England novels demonstrate, it would be wrong to focus exclusively on the texts of these by now canonized and widely studied nature writers when it comes to assessing the environmental ethical relevance of textual representation of the human contemplative or mystical experience in nature. Especially New England regionalist writing of the second half of the nineteenth century—a corpus of texts largely, though not exclusively produced by female writers— has contributed strongly to propagating this spiritual element of the early environmental movement (Mayer 2004).

In their representations of New England landscapes, the novels show a realist bent, a striving for verisimilitude when it comes to the local geography and to the local fauna and flora. Moreover, the representation of beautiful nature clearly dominates that of sublime nature. Pastoral landscapes in which places of human habitation—and thus the concept of domesticity—figure prominently clearly dominate wilderness landscapes, especially in *The Pearl of Orr's Island* and in *Poganuc People* where landscape representation plays a quantitatively larger role than in *The Minister's Wooing* and in *Oldtown Folks*. In *The Pearl of Orr's Island*, for instance, we find five rather long passages in which the plant world of the Maine coastal region is represented in detail, in its colors, forms, textures, and smells, putting again emphasis on the unique instrumental value that sensual experience in nature has for human beings.[10] A particularly revealing passage that presents beautiful nature and that foregrounds the significance of the concept of domesticity can, however, be found in *The Minister's Wooing*:

> The summer passed over the cottage, noiselessly as our summers pass. There were white clouds walking in saintly troops over blue mirrors of sea,—there were purple mornings, choral with bird-singing,—there were golden evenings, with long, eastward shadows. Apple-blossoms died quietly in the deep orchard grass, and tiny apples waxed and rounded and ripened and gained stripes of gold and carmine; and the blue eggs broke into young robins, that grew from gaping, yellow-mouthed youth to fledged and outflying maturity. Came autumn, with its long Indian summer, and winter, with its flinty, sparkling snows, under which all Nature lay a sealed and beautiful corpse. Came once

more the spring winds, the lengthening days, the opening flowers, and the ever-renewing miracle of buds and blossoms on the apple-trees around the cottage. (714)

This very lyrical passage describes in detail the ever-returning cycle of the seasons. Since it makes the house, a cottage, the central point of reference, it creates a classic pastoral setting. Emphasis is put on the uniqueness of the sensual experience of beautiful nature since proportion, symmetry, and regularity rule the passage both in terms of content and of style.[11]

The aesthetic category of the sublime surfaces only in very few passages in the novels, for instance in the opening chapter of *The Pearl of Orr's Island*, which focuses on the storm that killed Mara's father, and in a passage like the following one, which puts emphasis on the sublime character of the old growth forest along the Maine coast:

> The little knoll where the cottage stood had on its right hand a tiny bay, where the ocean water made up amid picturesque rocks—shaggy and solemn. Here trees of the primeval forest, grand and lordly, looked down silently into the waters which ebbed and flowed daily into this little pool. Every variety of those beautiful evergreens which feather the coast of Maine, and dip their wings in the very spray of its ocean foam, found here a representative. There were aspiring black spruces, crowned on the very top with heavy coronets of cones; there were balsamic firs, whose young buds breathe the scent of strawberries; there were cedars, black as midnight clouds, and white pines with their swaying plumage of needle-like leaves, strewing the ground beneath with a golden, fragrant matting; and there were the gigantic, wide-winged hemlocks, hundreds of years old. . . . ([1862] 1896, 29–30)

Again, attention is drawn and value attributed to the unique aesthetic experience that nature, here sublime nature, offers human beings. Moreover, at this point it is important to draw attention to a further implication such passages of landscape representation have in an environmental ethical context. The anthropocentrism of this type of value attribution is intensified by the use of the adjective "picturesque." This adjective signals not only a specific aesthetic concept, the appreciation of the visually striking, the painterly, but also the commercial context of nineteenth-century New England tourism to which Stowe's texts ultimately contributed. Attribution of value on the basis of aesthetic arguments that calls for inclusion into the moral universe involves an ambivalence that Lawrence Buell has commented upon with reference to the pastoral—yet, his comments also hold true for the picturesque: "Historically, pastoral has sometimes activated green consciousness, sometimes euphemized land appropriation. It may direct us toward the realm of physical nature, or it may abstract us from it" (1995, 31). Stowe's novels may thus be read as supporting a New England tourism that on the one hand consolidated a new type of appreciation of the natural world and contributed to protection efforts, but on the other hand also put a strain on natural resources and brought about a shaping of place, of landscape, that exclusively followed human aesthetic tastes.

The physiocentric argument of sentience is pivotal for the environmental ethical dimension that emerges in the four novels when it comes to the representation of the relationship between human beings and animals. In several passages the texts suggest that animals as creatures that feel and suffer must be included into the moral universe. At the same time the texts also express the pedagogic, i.e., anthropocentric, argument that cruelty to animals corrupts the human individual and human communities. Again, mostly female characters as figures endowed with high cultural authority serve as models to others; and again the impact of sentimentalism, the concept of domesticity and that of a feminized Christian faith, becomes visible.

Neither Sam Lawson in *Oldtown Folks* nor Mara Lincoln in *The Pearl of Orr's Island* can bear watching animals, their fellow creatures, suffer. Whenever Sam goes fishing he makes sure to kill at once what he catches. He tells Horace Holyoke: "I can't bear to see no kind o' critter in torment. . . . Fish hes their rights as well as any on us" ([1869], 1982, 911). Mara expresses the same feelings in a conversation with Moses. He is about to set out on his first longer fishing trip and does not waste a single thought on the sentience of the animals. To him fish are a resource that must be made use of in as large a quantity as possible. When Mara asks him whether she may accompany him on the trip, he answers: "'Pooh! . . . [Y] ou're a girl; and what can girls do at sea? You never like to catch fish—it always makes you cry to see 'em flop.' 'Oh, yes, poor fish!' said Mara . . . 'I can't help feeling sorry when they gasp so'" ([1862] 1896, 125). The passage establishes a link between concepts of manhood and womanhood and an environmental ethical position. To Moses, empathy for the animals marks an unmanly attitude, he regards acknowledgment of their sentience as a feminine flaw. In another passage this becomes even more pronounced. There Moses steals two eggs from the nest of a pair of eagles. When a fight between him and the birds ensues in the top of the tree, the novel uses war metaphors. Mara "heard a commotion and rattling of the branches, the scream of birds, and the swooping of their wings, and Moses' valorous exclamations, as he seemed to be laying about him with a branch which he had broken off" (161). Moses at last "descended victorious, with the eggs in his pocket" (161). When Mara asks him, "don't you suppose they feel bad?" (162), he responds by lecturing her about the inevitability of fighting and wars. The passage juxtaposes not only a female and a male character, but it also juxtaposes two places conventionally connoted as female—the birds' nest, i.e., a "house"—and male—the battlefield. To Mara the concept of domesticity, which asks for empathy for all inhabitants, must be extended to the bird "family," which is thus included in the moral universe of the house. Moses ultimately learns that a morally viable concept of manhood must rest on the capability to at least empathize with one's fellow creatures. In the end his moral notion of self has become feminized in this respect.

The moral stance that is represented in Mara Lincoln's attitudes and behavior is also embodied by Grandmother Badger in *Oldtown Folks*. She "considered calf-killing as an abominable cruelty, and the parting of calf and cow for a day beforehand as an aggravation" ([1869] 1982, 1046). Grandmother Badger compares the relationship between calf and cow with that of child and mother, and the logical conclusion she draws from this is to no longer eat meat: "folks shouldn't eat creatures at all" (1047) she concludes. Moreover, there are two male characters in *Oldtown Folks* who also reveal this moral stance—Mr. Avery, the minister of Cloudland, and the novel's narrator, Horace Holyoke. Mr. Avery is described as a passionate trout fisher who would never catch more fish than he needs and who betrays utmost respect for a trout's "dignity" (1317). And Horace puts forth the argument of the sentience of living beings when he criticizes Mr. Rossiter's entomological collection. Looking at the collection he suffers with the "luckless bugs impaled on steel pins stuck in thin sheets of cork" that "struggled away a melancholy existence, martyrs to the taste for science" (1295).

The various types of attributing moral value to nonhuman nature that can be found in Stowe's New England novels reveal a multilayered environmental ethical dimension. Propagating the Christian stewardship position, the novels participated in the emerging environmentalist discourse of the second half of the nineteenth century, which argued for the inclusion of at least parts of nature into the moral universe. The dominance of anthropocentric arguments signals the embracing of the goals of the conservation and of the preservation movement. At the same time, the employment of physiocentric arguments, especially the argument of the sentience of animals, shows that the texts also attribute intrinsic value to parts of nature. While the four novels certainly lack the political thrust and polemical explicitness of her antislavery texts, they can still be regarded as part of the history of New England environmentalism. Moreover, Stowe's novels can in this respect be regarded as representative for the contribution of nineteenth-century New England regionalist literature as a whole, a genre that deserves further investigation from an environmentally informed literary and cultural perspective. Ultimately, the environmental ethical dimension of Stowe's texts must be regarded as another component of her attempts to envision models of a morally sound American national character.

## NOTES

1. Martha Nussbaum uses the phrase "schematic philosophy" in *Love's Knowledge: Essays on Philosophy and Literature*. She makes the following point about the relevance of literary texts as sites of moral negotiation and inquiry: "Schematic philosophers' examples almost always lack the particularity, the emotive appeal, the absorbing plottedness, the variety and indeterminacy, of good fiction; they lack, too, good fiction's way of making the reader a participant and a friend; and we have argued that it is precisely in virtue of these structural characteristics that fiction can play the role it does in our reflective lives" (1990, 46). My argument in this essay rests on work of antifoundationalist critics and philosophers such as Nussbaum, David Parker, Charles Taylor, and Richard Rorty. For an extended discussion of the relevance of ethical literary criticism for ecologically oriented literary scholarship, see my essay on another New England regionalist writer: "Literature and Environmental Ethical Criticism: Sarah Orne Jewett's New England Texts" (2006).

2. Angelika Krebs's *Ethics of Nature* is the concluding report of a United Nations project on "Value Systems and Attitudes toward Nature" in which Krebs surveyed the field of environmental ethical thought in the English- and German-speaking world. The taxonomy of value arguments she developed in order to map this rapidly growing field of thought does not only help to gain an overview of various positions but also to clarify the argumentative and evaluative basis for any concern for the environment.

3. For information on Marsh's biography and on the relevance of *Man and Nature and Other Writings* see Lowenthal's introduction to *Man and Nature* (1965, ix–xxviii) and Dorman (1998, 3–45).

4. Important constituents of the health reform movement after the Civil War were the home economic movement and, around the turn of the century, the settlement movement. Stowe and her sister Catharine Beecher contributed to the home economic movement with their influential *The American Woman's Home* (1869).

5. An introduction to the historically competing concepts of "stewardship" and "dominion" is provided by Nash in his chapter "The Greening of Religion" (1989, 87–120), and by Mark Stoll in his chapter "Beauty and Wonder, Dominion and Stewardship" (1997, 11–28).

6. The same equation occurs in several passages of the novel, for instance, in the chapter "Views on Divine Government," which focuses on the religious history of New England Calvinism. Stowe's narrator emphasizes its high intellectual achievement that is, however, accompanied by a striking emotional deficit: "But it is to be conceded, that these systems, so admirable in relation to the energy, earnestness, and acuteness of their authors, when received as absolute truths, and as a basis of actual life, had, on minds of a certain class, the effect of a slow poison. . . . They differ from the New Testament as the living embrace of a friend does from his lifeless body, mapped out under the knife of the anatomical demonstrator;—every nerve and muscle is there, but to a sensitive spirit there is the very chill of death in the analysis" ([1859] 1982, 731).

7. The sciences and the creation of scientific knowledge are by no means only negatively assessed in the novels. Mrs. Marvyn's mathematical capabilities in *The Minister's Wooing* and the teaching of scientific study at the Academy of Cloudland

in *Oldtown Folks* (see, for instance, [1869] 1982, 1288–1307) are positively connotated. Scientific knowledge enhances the experience of the variety, beauty, and dynamics of and in nature. Critique starts at that point when the claim of the sciences transcends the limits of natural theology.

8. Stowe articulated this kind of critique also in one of her New England sketches. In "Deacon Pitkin's Farm" the narrator argues: "Now and then Nature asserts herself and does something so astonishing and overpowering as actually to strike through the crust of human stupidity, and convince mankind that a tree is something greater than they are. As a general thing the human race has a stupid hatred of trees. They embrace every chance to cut them down. They have no idea of their fitness for anything but firewood and fruit bearing. But a great cathedral elm, with shadowy aisles of boughs, its choir of whispering winds and chanting birds, its hush and solemnity and majestic grandeur, actually conquers the dull human race and asserts its leave to be in a manner to which all hearts respond" (1896, 255).

9. For the figure of the New England saint see Buell (1986, 275) and Gatta 1997 (especially the chapters on Hawthorne, Fuller, and Stowe).

10. See the following pages in *The Pearl of Orr's Island* ([1862] 1896): 29–30, 74, 123, 160, 192–94. Similar passages can be found in *Poganuc People* ([1878] 1977, 181–83, 207–09, 220–27).

11. My definition of beautiful nature—as opposed to sublime nature—follows the definition Marjorie Hope Nicholson gives in her classic study *Mountain Gloom and Mountain Glory*. Nicholson quotes the English aesthetician John Dennis: "Beauty was equated with proportion, with order, with regularity, with the rules" (1959, 287–88).

## WORKS CITED

Buell, Lawrence. 1986. *New England Literary Culture: From Revolution through Renaissance*. Cambridge: Cambridge University Press.

———. 1995. *The Environmental Imagination: Thoreau, Nature Writing and the Formation of American Culture*. Cambridge, MA: Harvard University Press.

Conforti, Joseph. 2001. *Imagining New England: Explorations of Regional Identity from the Pilgrims to the Mid-twentieth Century*. Chapel Hill: University of North Carolina Press.

Cumbler, John T. 1991. "The Early Making of an Environmental Consciousness: Fish, Fisheries Commissions and the Connecticut River." *Environmental History Review* 15 (4): 73–91.

Donahue, Brian. 1989. "'Dammed at Both Ends and Cursed in the Middle': The 'Flowage' of the Concord River Meadows, 1798–1862." *Environmental Review* 13:47–67.

Dorman, Robert. 1998. *A Word for Nature: Four Pioneering Environmental Advocates, 1845–1913*. Chapel Hill: University of North Carolina Press.

Gatta, John. 1997. *American Madonna: Images of the Divine Woman in Literary Culture*. New York: Oxford University Press.

———. 2000. "The Anglican Aspect of Harriet Beecher Stowe." *New England Quarterly* 73 (3): 412–33.

Krebs, Angelika. 1999. *Ethics of Nature: A Map.* Berlin: de Gruyter.

Lowenthal, David. 1965. Introduction to *Man and Nature; or, Physical Geography as Modified by Human Action,* by George Perkins Marsh, ix–xxviii. Cambridge, MA: Harvard University Press.

Marsh, George Perkins. [1864] 1965. *Man and Nature; or, Physical Geography as Modified by Human Action,* ed. David Lowenthal. Cambridge: Harvard University Press.

Mayer, Sylvia. 2004. *Naturethik und Neuengland-Regionalliteratur: Harriet Beecher Stowe, Rose Terry Cooke, Sarah Orne Jewett, Mary E. Wilkins Freeman.* Heidelberg: Universitätsverlag Winter.

———. 2006. "Literature and Environmental Ethical Criticism: Sarah Orne Jewett's New England Texts." *Anglia* 124 (1): 101–121.

Nash, Roderick Frazier. 1989. *The Rights of Nature: A History of Environmental Ethics.* Madison: University of Wisconsin Press.

Nicholson, Marjorie Hope. 1959. *Mountain Gloom and Mountain Glory: The Development of the Aesthetics of the Infinite.* Ithaca: Cornell University Press.

Nussbaum, Martha. 1990. *Love's Knowledge: Essays on Philosophy and Literature.* New York: Oxford University Press.

Stoll, Mark. 1997. *Protestantism, Capitalism, and Nature in America.* Albuquerque: University of New Mexico Press.

Stowe, Harriet Beecher. [1859] 1982. *The Minister's Wooing. In Three Novels: Uncle Tom's Cabin; or, Life Among the Lowly, The Minister's Wooing, Oldtown Folks,* 521–876. New York: Literary Classics of the United States.

———. [1862] 1896. *The Pearl of Orr's Island.* Boston: Houghton Mifflin.

———. [1869] 1982. Oldtown Folks. In *Three Novels: Uncle Tom's Cabin, or, Life among the Lowly, The Minister's Wooing, Oldtown Folks,* 877–1468. New York: Literary Classics of the United States.

———. 1869. "The Rights of Dumb Animals." *Hearth and Home* 2:24.

———. [1878] 1977. *Poganuc People.* Hartford, CT: Stowe-Day Foundation.

———. 1896. "Deacon Pitkin's Farm." In *Stories, Sketches and Studies,* 254–93. Boston: Houghton Mifflin.

Tang, Edward. 1998. "Making Declarations of Her Own: Harriet Beecher Stowe as New England Historian." *New England Quarterly* 71 (1): 77–96.

Wagenknecht, Edward. 1965. *Harriet Beecher Stowe: The Known and the Unknown.* New York: Oxford University Press.

# To Market!

## Consuming Women in Harriet Beecher Stowe's *My Wife and I* and *We and Our Neighbors*

*Astrid Recker*

Harriet Beecher Stowe's *My Wife and I* (1871) and its sequel *We and Our Neighbors* (1875) rank, somewhat unjustly as I shall suggest, among the more neglected of her works and have not received a considerable amount of critical attention.[1] Together with *Pink and White Tyranny* (1871), the two novels form what has been called Stowe's "New York trilogy" (Karcher 2004, 204) and offer a representation of urban middle-class life in the second half of the nineteenth century.

In her contribution to *The Cambridge Companion to Harriet Beecher Stowe*, Carolyn L. Karcher acknowledges Stowe as the "chief architect" of a school she calls "literature of social change" (2004, 203). Comprising two "varieties" of fiction, this school consists of "protest literature" and "regional" or "sociological fiction, aimed at capturing a changed or changing way of life by portraying the customs, manners, and personalities that typify it" (204). Both *My Wife and I* and *We and Our Neighbors* clearly belong in the latter category and are classified by Karcher accordingly.[2] Thus, the change in way of life that *My Wife and I* vividly captures is "feminine disestablishment" (Douglas [1977] 1996, 44) and the related emergence of distinct male and female spheres. Affecting primarily northern, white, middle-class women, disestablishment is defined by Douglas as a process in which women's position shifted from that of (domestic) producers in the family economy to that of consumers in an increasingly capitalist society, in which the role of producer was no longer available to them.[3] As I will demonstrate in the following, *My Wife and I* takes issue with disestablishment and its consequences by depicting a developing capitalistic culture, which, by keeping women from being productive in the same manner as men, and by restricting the economic positions available to them, not only renders women increasingly dependent on men but also reduces them to commodities. The primary site of this commodification is, as Karcher notes, "the marriage market" (2004, 215), which comes to serve as the novel's exemplary site of the economic restrictions and limitations placed on women.

Although *We and Our Neighbors* engages with the same phenomenon as its predecessor *My Wife and I*, it does so from a slightly different angle and depicts how women, and in particular the novel's protagonist Eva Van Arsdel (later Henderson), have adapted to this "changed . . . way of life" (Karcher 2004, 204). Even if *We and Our Neighbors* addresses the question of women's rights only in passing and focuses primarily on the home- and match-making efforts of Eva, it nonetheless serves as a valuable and necessary companion to *My Wife and I* because it continues and deepens its examination of the emergence of two distinct "sexual spheres" (Matthaei 1982, 101). Thus, whereas *My Wife and I* concentrates predominantly on the limitations and negative effects resulting from feminine disestablishment, *We and Our Neighbors* investigates the freedoms and opportunities women's new role as homemaker and consumer granted them and hence explores positive rather than only negative aspects of woman's consignment to this role.[4]

Yet, without aiming to contest Karcher's categorization of Stowe's novels, it seems necessary to emphasize that both texts do more than merely "portra[y] . . . customs, manners, and personalities" (204). Thus, although their criticism (of women's limited access to social and political agency, of materialism, consumerism, and commodity culture, among others) is often implicit rather than explicit, *My Wife and I* and *We and Our Neighbors* not only exhibit characteristics of sociological fiction but also carry features of protest literature, which according to Karcher is "aimed at promoting social change by exposing current injustices" (204). In both novels Stowe does not limit herself to a description of the status quo but speaks out against and suggests ways of remedying the injustices that result from the commodification of women in the (marriage) market and their reduction to consumers (especially their coercion to excessive consumerism). Thus, particularly *My Wife and I* exceeds the primarily descriptive mode of sociological fiction to expose and attack the limitations placed on women both before and after their disestablishment.[5] In consequence, it does not do the novels justice to dismiss them along with other works of sentimentalist fiction, which, as critics Gillian Brown and Jane Tompkins explain, have been spurned for lacking "polemical force and literary merit" (Brown 1990, 17) or designated as "apologists for an oppressive social order" (Tompkins 1985, 124).[6]

According to Jackson Lears, another critical voice, sentimentalist literature, by glossing over the "contradictions at the heart of the domestic ideal" (1981, 16), helped to contribute to what he calls "the evasive banality of the official culture" (17). Thus, he argues, "[t]he common pattern of culture involved a denial of the conflicts in modern capitalist society, an affirmation of continuing harmony and progress. Sentimental literature performed the same function as the domestic ideal: both were part of an overall pattern of evasion in the dominant culture" (17). In claiming that "[t]he Victorian domestic ideal . . . was commemorated in the novels of Charles Dickens and Harriet Beecher Stowe" (15), Lears, much like Douglas, dismisses Stowe's sentimentalist novels as mere trivialities. Yet, as I intend to show in the following, the two works to be discussed here are far from denying the conflicts that Lears refers to. Thus, unlike Lears's above claim suggests, both make it very clear that "[i]t was impossible for the home to remain altogether isolated from the market society," and that among the home's primary functions in the (emerging) capitalist society was the socialization of people—men and women alike—for the marketplace (1981, 16). Especially *We and Our Neighbors* depicts women not merely as "submissive helpmates" but as "repositories of moral and cultural authority," balancing its main female protagonist's role very carefully between "prescribed self-effacement and self-reliance" (16). Thus, both *My Wife and I* and *We and Our Neighbors* are not only critical investigations of what Gayle Rubin called the "systematic social apparatus which takes up females as raw materials and fashions domesticated women as products" (1975, 158), but they also probe the circumstances at the roots of the "American antimodernism" investigated by Lears, understood by him as "the recoil from an 'overcivilized' modern existence to more intense forms of physical or spiritual experience" (1981, xv). However, in *We and Our Neighbors* remedy to this state of overcivilization is not sought in escapism, an idealization of "medieval or Oriental cultures" (xv), but realized in the contested site of the home itself. Thus, the market is explicitly not exorcized from the home at the end of Stowe's 1875 novel: as her protagonists move from the excessive consumption depicted and criticized in *My Wife and I* to a pious consumption associated with feminine social agency, the women depicted in the novel are given a means to remedy the injustices laid open in *My Wife and I* without their having to forsake the roles of mothers and wives.

## COMMODIFYING WOMEN

In *My Wife and I*, Stowe highlights the considerable increase of restrictions placed upon women over the course of the market revolution by exposing how women were reduced to consumers and commodities on a patriarchally organized and dominated "free" market in a process of disestablishment. *My Wife and I* opposes established and disestablished women primarily along the lines of a rural-urban divide.[7] On its rural side, Stowe places Harry's cousin Caroline and his mother, who in her son's idealizing account becomes an emblem of the "golden ages" (Stowe [1896] 1967a, 99) before woman's disestablishment. Although restricted in her doings primarily to the domestic sphere, Harry's mother is "actively engaged in the productive activities of feeding, clothing, and equipping the nation" (Douglas [1977] 1996, 49). She is pictured as one of those women whose work was "judged essential" (54) and who thus formed "an important part of a communal productive process under her direction" (48, see Stowe [1896] 1967a, 1–2, 33–41). However, Stowe quickly subverts Harry's idealized depiction of woman's role and status in the "golden ages" of rural New England by juxtaposing it to Caroline's unsentimental account of the possibilities for independent action and development granted her by society. With her matter-of-fact assessment of her own situation in the family economy, and that of other women as well, Caroline manages to undermine and counterbalance Harry's distorted male perspective, which is thus exposed as illusory by Stowe.[8] Like her urban counterpart and later companion Ida Van Arsdel, Caroline is dissatisfied with the prospect of life women of her time faced and seeks to be educated in the medical profession rather than make herself "a bright and shining light of contentment in woman's sphere" (Stowe [1896] 1967a, 105). When Harry, characteristically for his and his culture's view of women, therefore suggests: "[Y]ou, with your beauty and your talents,—I think you might be satisfied with a woman's lot in life," her reply casts a different light on women's life in rural New England than suggested by Harry: "A woman's lot! and what is that, pray? to sit with folded hands and see life drifting by—to be a mere nullity, and endure to have my good friends pat me on the back . . . ?" (105). As she continues her plea, not only the whole measure of her despair, but also the exploitative nature of feminine labor in Harry's "golden ages" become obvious:

> I don't want to wait for a husband to make me a position, I want to make one for myself; I don't want to take a husband's money, I want my own. . . . I want a position, a house and home of my own, and a sphere of independent action, and everybody thinks this absurd. . . . [T]here is nothing I do for my father that a good, smart housekeeper could not be hired to do; but you see that would cost money, and the money that I thus save is invested without consulting me; it goes to buy more rocky land, when we have already more than we know what to do with. . . . I am a servant working for board and clothes, and because I am a daughter I am expected to do it cheerfully; my only escape from this position is to take a similar one in the family of some man to whom, in addition to the superintendence of his household, I shall owe the personal duties of a wife, and *that* way out you may know I shall never take. (106–7, emphasis in original)

This passage explains why Caroline equates a "woman's lot" with idleness, despite the fact that it is filled with housekeeping chores, and thus contradicts Harry's earlier account of his mother, which strongly emphasized her activity. As Caroline's allusion to idleness makes apparent, housekeeping is not what she regards as "a life-work worth doing" (111), a work, that is, in which she can be productive for her own benefit. Thus she considers her current work unproductive because it does not secure her an income and property of her own but is transformed into her father's property. Given these circumstances it is not surprising that Uncle Jacob, suggesting that Harry should marry Caroline if he wants to help her, speaks of Harry's "taking Caroline as if she had been a lot of land up for sale" (117). In the logic of Caroline's father and Uncle Jacob, Caroline is not significantly different from a lot of land—her worth, her market value, is determined by what she yields.

The case of Caroline illustrates that the productive labor women were expected and allowed to perform in the family economy before feminine disestablishment was, notwithstanding the "minimal recognition" it granted them (Douglas [1977] 1996, 55), from their perspective *un*productive because the fruits of their labor were not their own. This is particularly consequential when one considers it from the point of view of Locke's theory of property, which remains utterly important to an understanding of North American conceptions of property and personhood until today. In a famous and well-known passage of his second *Treatise of Government*, Locke writes:

> Though the earth, and all inferior creatures, be common to all men, yet every man has a property in his own person: this nobody has any right to but himself. The labour of his body, and the work of his hands, we may say, are properly his. Whatsoever then he removes out of the state that nature hath provided, and left it in, he hath mixed his labour with, and joined to it something that is his own, and thereby makes it his property. ([1823] 1963, 353–54)

The above passage is "the *locus classicus* of the concept of property in the person" (Pateman 2002, 24), and it is here among others that the concept of possessive individualism originates, which was extensively theorized by C. B. Macpherson in the 1960s. In Macpherson's conception, Pateman explains, "possessive individualism" means that the individual is proprietor of "his own person and capacities," and, for that reason, is free. A vital assumption of Macpherson's argument is that the individual "cannot alienate the whole of his property in his own person, [but] he may alienate his capacity to labour" (29).[9]

As Pateman convincingly argues, however, the latter assumption is merely a fiction "because an individual's powers, capacities, abilities, skills, and talents are inseparable from their 'owner'" (27). It follows, according to Pateman, that if these capacities and abilities "become the subject of contract and [are] marketed as 'services,'" what results is not an exchange of (immaterial) goods, "but the alienation of . . . the right of self-government" (27). Therefore Caroline, who does not have a choice but to perform labor for her father (or for a prospective husband) that is to a considerable extent unfree, is not only dispossessed of the work of her hands, but also deprived of her right to govern herself. If Caroline's father has power over his daughter's capacities like a property owner over land or material goods, he owns her whole person because these capacities cannot be separated from her. In consequence, Caroline—like all women in her position—is subjected to "patriarchy in its purest form," which Basch defines "as the reduction of women to the status of property owned and controlled by men . . . " (1982, 38).

The resulting one-sidedness and lack of reciprocity in (business or exchange) relations between men and women is emphasized repeatedly in *My Wife and I*. Raising the issue of men and women's unequal participation in the marriage market, for example, Caroline points out to Harry that while he, as a man, is free to "go all over the world" in his search for a wife, her own possibilities are infinitely more limited: "[M]y chances are only among those who propose to me. . . . My list for selection must be confined to such of the eligible men in this neighborhood as are in want of wives; men who want wives as they do cooking-stoves, and make up their minds that I may suit them" (Stowe [1896] 1967a, 105). Figuring as goods "on exhibition" (105) for men, women are left with no opportunity to negotiate what they will receive in exchange for themselves, and in the course of the novel it becomes apparent that this is a condition that is considerably aggravated by feminine disestablishment.

This aggravation follows necessarily because in the market society that supersedes the family economy, the concept of self is increasingly "aligned with market relations such as exchange, value, alienability, circulations, and competition" (Brown 1990, 2), all of which are unavailable to women. Unable to produce selfhood of the kind outlined in the doctrine of possessive individualism, deprived of the possibility to make themselves into subjects rather than only objects of the market society, disestablished women have no chance of becoming the equals of men or of participating in the market as their partners. Thus, in contrast to the scope of activities women performed in the rural setting depicted by Stowe, in the urban environments of *My Wife and I*, disestablished women are restricted to unproductive idleness and can hence make an appearance on the market only as consumers—a position that is insignificant from the perspective of possessive individualism. Far from being the frugal and hard-working woman productively involved in "feeding, clothing, and equipping the nation"

(Douglas [1977] 1996, 50) epitomized by Harry's mother, Miss Ellery, the first disestablished woman encountered by Harry in the small town where he receives his college education, for the first time confronts him with "the women of this day" (Stowe [1896] 1967a, 99): "[A]ll for flash and ambition and money," these women are characterized by Harry as "effeminate dolls of fashion—all they want is ease and show and luxury" (99–100). Contrasting the idle world of women with that of men, Harry comes to the conclusion that

> [h]is is a world of patient toil, of hard effort, of dry drudgery, of severe economies; while our young American princesses . . . live like the fowls of the air or the lilies of the field, without a thought of labor, or a care, or serious responsibility of any kind. They are "gay creatures of the element," living to enjoy and to amuse themselves, to be fostered, sheltered, dressed, petted, and made to have "good times" generally. (193–94)

In picturing "the women of this day" primarily as consumers—"vicarious livers" and "parasites" (Douglas [1977] 1996, 73)—Harry adheres closely to the view according to which the "ideal woman . . . [was] to spend money—or have it spent on her—in an economy she could not comprehend" (60). Accordingly, urban women are depicted in *My Wife and I* as "gay tropical birds of fashion" (Stowe [1896] 1967a, 208) whose thoughts and conversations generally circle around costumes and other finery, which are the primary articles consumed by the middle- and upper-class women in the novel. Eva Van Arsdel, her sister remarks, "spends all her money on dress" (185), and Eva herself concedes: "Of course, we belong to the class who live in the enjoyment of 'nothing to wear,' and the first result of a projected entertainment is to throw us all on our knees before Tullegig [their dressmaker, A. R.], who queens it over us accordingly" (366). When an engagement is pronounced, the young women care most about the cost of the engagement ring (193). Accordingly, a husband of the "royal princesses" of New York (213) is primarily required to provide his wife with the means for her excessive consumption, to "keep her in all that elegance and luxury she was fitted to adorn and enjoy" (319). "The lovely creatures," Jim Fellows, one of Harry's colleagues and closest friends, asserts, "are perfectly rapacious in their demands" (213).

At the same time that women are depicted as such rapacious creatures, the narrator and other male characters in the novel emphasize repeatedly that the husbands have no interest in their wives' excessive consumption. Thus Mr. Van Arsdel is described by Harry as "a simple, quiet, silent man, not knowing or caring a bodle about any of the wonders of art and luxury with which his womankind have surrounded him" (194, see also 229). It is the women of Mr. Van Arsdel's household whom Harry designates as the driving forces behind the acquisition of all the luxuries with which their mansion is filled. He does so unaware that this role is urged upon women by "counselors and educators" (Douglas [1977] 1996, 60)[10] and moreover derives directly from their being restricted to entering the market either as consumers or, as will be discussed presently, as commodities. However, Harry not only ignores the real causes for the excessive consumption practiced by the women he encounters in New York but also misrepresents these women as cunning traders on the marriage market. When Miss Ellery, deeply adored by Harry, thus agrees to marry a dull but well-to-do man rather than him, he renders this marriage as an act of Miss Ellery's selling herself to the highest bidder:

> But she sells herself before his eyes, for diamonds and laces, and trinkets and perfumes; for the liberty of walking on soft carpets and singing in gilded cages; and all the world laughs at his simplicity in supposing that, a fair chance given, any woman would ever do otherwise. Is not beauty woman's capital in trade, the price put into her hand to get whatever she needs; and are not the most beautiful, as a matter of course, destined prizes of the richest? (Stowe [1896] 1967a, 70)

In this passage, Harry assigns marriage the character of a business transaction in which the woman uses her beauty "as the coin wherewith to buy the riches and honors of the world" (76). It is crucial to note that in Harry's description, the woman figures in the transaction not merely as commodity, but simultaneously as seller and good to be sold: "*she* sells *herself*," and is hence among the persons who profit from this sale (70, emphasis added). In Harry's version of the transaction, Miss Ellery therefore acts as the self of possessive individualism—she markets her capacities and abilities without, however, alienating her self-governance.[11]

Harry purports to "have become . . . very tolerant and indulgent" toward women doing as Miss Ellery did (Stowe [1896] 1967a, 76). Thus he realized that selling herself is at this time the only way left to a woman to make a (worldly) position for herself and remarks accordingly that

> [t]he world has been busy for some centuries in shutting and locking every door through which a woman could step into wealth, except the door of marriage. All vigor and energy, such as men put forth to get this golden key of life, is condemned and scouted as unfeminine; and a woman belonging to the upper classes, who undertakes to get wealth by honest exertion and independent industry, loses caste, and is condemned by a thousand voices as an oddity and a deranged person. A woman gifted with beauty, who sells it to buy wealth, is far more leniently handled. That way of getting money is not called unwomanly. . . . (76)[12]

At the same time, however, Harry and other male characters in the novel do not tire to point to the baseness of such an act of selling oneself. Accordingly, Harry claims that he "shall never marry for money" and is overly anxious not to appear as a "fortune-hunter," since in his opinion "for a man, with every other avenue open to him, to mouse about for a rich wife . . . is too dastardly for anything" (160). Similarly, Uncle Jacob warns his nephew, about to leave for New York, of becoming one of those writers "who don't care a copper what they write up or what they write down . . ., ready to sell their wit, their genius, and their rhetoric to the highest bidder," and claims that he would "rather see [him] a poor, threadbare, hard-worked, country minister than the smartest and brightest fellow that ever kept his talents on sale in Vanity Fair" (94).

Yet, despite the fact that it is out of the question for the male characters of *My Wife and I* to enter the marriage market as a good for sale, it is clear from the outset that to do so as the buyer is entirely acceptable. In consequence, the men portrayed in the novel primarily treat marriage as an act of purchase, a business transaction in which a costly good is obtained. Uncle Jacob not only ascribes marriage the power to "mak[e] or ma[r] a man," thereby making it comparable to a business enterprise, but also likens Harry's mother to "a pearl of great price" and remarks that "a man might well sell all he had to buy her" (Stowe [1896] 1967a, 47). Similarly Jim ceaselessly refers to marriageable women as (luxury) goods to be possessed—if only one has enough money to purchase them.[13] In his eyes, the women of New York

> go exactly in the line of fine pictures and statuary, and all that. They may be adorable and inspiring, and exalting and refining and purifying, the very poetry of existence, the altogether lovely; but after all, it is only the rich that can afford to keep them. A wife costs more in our day than a carriage or a conscience, and both those are luxuries too expensive for Jim. (215)

Consequently, upon hearing that Harry will marry the well-to-do Eva Van Arsdel, Jim congratulates him in the same manner as if he had successfully completed a business transaction: "Up to '*biz*' after all! Well, you've done a tolerably fair stroke! Those Van Arsdel girls are good for a hundred thousand down, and the rest will come in the will" (411, emphasis in original).[14] And although Harry is somewhat embarrassed to appear like a "fortune-hunter," he himself seems to share his uncle's and Jim's view of women as goods to be purchased and owned, as his references to Eva as her family's "chief treasure" (317) and to the "fabulous joy of possession" to be his indicate (406).[15]

That the view of Eva Van Arsdel as a "chief treasure" is also shared by her family becomes apparent in their attempts to coerce her to marry Wat Sydney, a young man of considerable wealth. It is this intended marriage that serves most prominently in the novel's endeavor to expose the business/capitalist character of marriage and the commodification of women it entails. Faced with the threatening prospect of business failure, the Van Arsdels treat their daughter as a commodity, a product of the expensive education and attire they have invested in her, which they aim to sell profitably to the highest bidder in order to gain the credit to save Mr. Van Arsdel's business and secure their status. Thus, after Eva's mother has learned the disappointing fact that Eva has agreed to marry Harry, she tells her daughter:

> But, then, we had this match in view. We supposed, of course, that it was coming off. And such a splendid settlement on you would help the family every way. Mr. Sydney is a very generous man; and the use of his capital, the credit that the marriage would give to your father in business circles, would be immense. (Stowe [1896] 1967a, 384)

This is the only conceivable use to which Eva can be put in the eyes of her parents and her aunt,[16] who hence try to convince Eva to marry Wat although they are perfectly aware that Eva is not in love with Wat, and that he merely wants her as an ornamental adjunct, a costly accessory to his household. Wat, Ida observes, "wants a wife—a brilliant, attractive, showy, dressy wife, to keep his house and ornament his home" (183). It is hence no coincidence that Ida compares Eva to "conquered territory" (184): just like Caroline, Eva is treated like "a lot of land up for sale" (117), and she is intended to go to the highest bidder "in spite of [her] screams" (159).

As the above quoted examples illustrate, in the society depicted in *My Wife and I*, women do not enter the marriage market as traders or sellers (not even sellers of themselves) but only as commodities, i.e., goods to be purchased and possessed. Serving both as the item and "an emblem of conspicuous consumption" (Douglas [1977] 1996, 59),[17] they are turned into goods that are valuable for their owners primarily because of their public rather than their private meanings, that is, because they can indicate and even enhance his "social-material position" (Dittmar [1992] 1997, 98). Stowe hence demonstrates in *My Wife and I* that (other than Harry imagines) the developing capitalist society that she depicts is designed to exclude women such as Eva or Caroline from participating in it actively as a seller or producer of goods. In consequence, their role in the (marriage) market is restricted to that of a commodity, a costly good for sale, and—particularly in the urban environment that Stowe describes—that of a consumer. From the perspective of men, both roles serve a representative purpose. A wife is thus on the one hand an item of conspicuous consumption, a prestigious commodity that only the wealthy can afford. On the other, she serves a similar purpose through her own "vicarious consumption of goods," characterized by Veblen as the "consumption of food, clothing, dwelling, and furniture by the lady and the rest of the domestic establishment" ([1925] 1949, 68). Thus, to emphasize it once more, the exchanges between men and women depicted in *My Wife and I* lack reciprocity; they are possible only when the partners of the exchange are equals. Since women, however, have to wait for a husband to make them a position, they are never the equals of men and the exchange must necessarily favor the latter. Not only Caroline is keenly aware of this, remarking that she cannot choose but has to wait to be chosen, but also Eva, who despite her considerably more conventional views concerning marriage and the role of women in society repeatedly criticizes the fact that "[i]t is n't my business to speak till I'm spoken to" (Stowe [1896] 1967a, 159), a circumstance that leaves men with a decided advantage over women. While men, Eva observes,

> can make every advance and come nearer and nearer . . ., and then suddenly change the whole footing . . ., [s]he cannot even show that she notices the change, without loss of self-respect. A woman in friendship with a man is made heartless by this very necessity, she must always hold herself ready to change hands and make her chassé to right or left with all suitable indifference whenever her partner is ready for another move in the cotillion. (314)

It is particularly the notion of *changing hands* that renders the above passage a comment on the objectification and commodification of women and thus allows Eva's observations concerning the one-sidedness of communication between men and women to be read also as a reference to women's role in the economic exchanges taking place on the marriage market.

### THE CALL TO IDLENESS AND ADVERTISING SELVES: FE/MALE PARADOXES ON THE VANITY FAIR

However, *My Wife and I* not only criticizes the manner in which women were reduced to commodities and consumers in Stowe's time, it also exposes two paradoxes to which this treatment of women gave rise and voices a need for social change to resolve them. Whereas the first of these paradoxes primarily concerns the behavior expected of commodified women, definable as "conspicuous" or "vicarious leisure" (Veblen [1925] 1949, 65, 75), the second undermines the status of men in that it reduces them from active participants in the (marriage) market to commodities themselves. The first paradox results from patriarchal culture's attempt to justify women's exclusion from all spheres but the domestic by presenting marriage as their calling. *Merriam-Webster's Eleventh Collegiate Dictionary* defines *calling* as "a strong inner impulse toward a particular course of action especially when accompanied by conviction of divine influence," and as "the vocation or profession in which one customarily engages." Similarly, it is described by Anthony Giddens as "refer[ring] basically to the idea that the highest form of moral obligation of the individual is to fulfill his duty in worldly affairs" (1985, xii). Although *calling* thus denotes a secular impulse, it has strong religious undertones and "projects," as Giddens notes, "religious behavior into the day-to-day world" (xii). This also becomes apparent in *My Wife and I*, where Uncle Jacob repeatedly voices the common opinion that "[t]he domestic sphere of wife and mother to which woman is called is *divine and godlike*; it is *sacred and solemn*, and no woman can go higher than that, and anything else to which she devotes herself falls infinitely below it" (Stowe [1896] 1967a, 118; emphasis added). The discussion above suggests that it is indeed women's "highest form of moral obligation" to restrict their activity to the domestic sphere, whereas to venture beyond it is to take a moral and religious fall.[18] Therefore, the paradox that I have mentioned arises from the fact that on the one hand women's fulfillment of their role as wives and homemakers was perceived and presented to them as a religious requirement. At the same time, however, to comply with this obligation the urban women depicted in *My Wife and I* are coerced to lead a life in conflict with religious ideals, especially those of frugality, hard work, and modesty. As part of a culture in which a woman's "attractiveness," as Lillian S. Robinson remarks in a different context, is "a form of social currency that she is required to keep on spending as the price of admission to a matrimonial market" (1994, 351), in order to attract a husband—a necessary ingredient in their becoming devoted mothers and wives—young middle- and upper-class women such as Eva Van Arsdel and her sisters are urged to live a materialistic life of vanity, marked by the excessive consumption of showy dresses, costumes, and finery, as well as idleness.[19] In contrast to men, "these girls," Harry's friend Jim thus explains, "have nothing under heaven to do" (Stowe [1896] 1967a, 169). Accordingly Eva, dwelling on her way of life, laments her unproductiveness:

> Now, I live in a constant whirl—a whirl that never ceases. I am carried on from day to day, from week to week, from month to month, with nothing to show for it except a succession of what girls call "good times." I don't read anything but stories; I don't study; I don't write; I don't sew; I don't draw, or play, or sing, *to any real purpose.* I just go "into society," as they call it. I am an idler, and the only thing I am good for is that *I help to adorn a house for the entertainment of idlers*—that is about all. (172, emphasis added)

The regretful tone of Eva's self-reflections suggests that she is wholly aware of the fact that her idle, utterly unproductive life conflicts with the religious ideals associated with the notion of calling, and that she greatly suffers, given her inability to resolve the paradox that defines the behavior expected of her. Thus she writes in a letter to a former teacher:

> Well, you see, I was confirmed; and . . . I wanted to be good—to live a higher, purer, nobler life than I have lived; and yet, after all, it is I, the child of the Church, that am living a life of folly, and show, and self-indulgence. . . . There's

> Aunt Maria, my godmother, she did the renouncing for me at my baptism, and promised solemnly that I should abjure "the vain pomp and glory of the world, with all covetous desires of the same; that I should not follow, or be led by them"; yet she has never, that I see, had one thought of anything else but how to secure for me just exactly those very things. That I should be first in society, be admired, followed, flattered, and make a rich, splendid marriage, has been her very heart's desire and prayer; and if I should renounce the vain pomp and glory of the world, really and truly, she would be utterly heart-broken. So would mamma. (176)

Through Eva, Stowe points to the conflict that arises as a patriarchal and increasingly capitalist culture attempts to justify its commodification of women and their restriction to the domestic sphere by taking recourse to the religious notion of calling. At the same time that girls and women are told to comply with God's will, they are also expected to contradict all that religion demands of them. Almost perversely it is thus precisely those women that, like Eva's sister Ida, do not want to live an idle and essentially parasitic life, who are designated by the patriarchal culture as odd, deviant, and ultimately unfeminine.

What is more, the restriction of women to an unproductive and hence dependent life also leads to the transformation of marriage from "a sacrifice most awful and holy" (Stowe [1896] 1967a, 70) to a purely economic affair, entered by women "for provision, or station, or support" (118). This is emphasized by the fact that from the outset *My Wife and I* treats marriage primarily in economic terms, and Harry's introductory note sets the novel's tone accordingly with its combination of religious and economic terminology. "Is not," he asks,

> that firm in human nature which stands under the title of MY WIFE AND I, the oldest and most venerable form of Christian union on record? . . . It has been said that "MY WIFE AND I" denoted a selfish, close corporation inconsistent with a general, all-sided diffusive, universal benevolence. . . . They have said, too, that MY WIFE AND I, instead of an indissoluble unity, were only temporary partners, engaged on time, with the liberty of giving three months' notice, and starting off to a new firm. (x–xi)

One result of this secularization of marriage is the second paradox pointed to above—a commodification of men, who themselves become reconceived as marketable goods in need of advertisement. Thus, according to the laws of the (marriage) market depicted in *My Wife and I*, the middle- and upper-class daughter in search of a husband will be married to the man with the highest market value. Rather than basing the "measures and valuations" of a future husband on "the character—the intellect and the heart" (71), it is now his wealth and economic success that become the decisive factors. "[O]ne man," Harry complains after Miss Ellery's decision to marry a wealthier man than him, "is as good as another if he is only rich" (100). In consequence, man's role in the marriage market shifts from buyer to that of a commodity in need of advertisement. Accordingly, the attempts of Eva's mother and aunt to convince her of marrying Wat Sydney have the character of a sales talk. Relating her story in a letter, Eva writes:

> Then mamma and Aunt Maria took up the case and told me that I was a foolish girl to throw away such an offer: a man of good character and standing, an excellent business man, and so immensely rich—with such a splendid place at Newport, and another in New York, and a fortune like Aladdin's lamp! (174)

In the foregoing, Wat has been reduced to an offer—he is, in Eva's words, "the prize of the season—the greatest offer in the market" (174). Similarly, after his engagement to Eva, Harry has to convince his future father-in-law that his market value is, although certainly not equal to that of Wat Sydney, sufficiently high to bring Eva into his possession. In his talk with Mr. Van Arsdel Harry thus advertises himself in terms of his economic and monetary value:

> "Now," said I, determined to speak in the language of men and things, "the case is just this: if a young man of good, reliable habits, good health, and good principles has a capital of seventy thousand dollars invested in a fair paying business, has he not a prospect of supporting a family in comfort? . . . [M]y health, my education, my power of doing literary work are this capital. They secure to me for the next year an income equal to that of seventy thousand dollars at ten per cent. Now, I think a capital of that amount invested in a *man* is quite as safe as the same sum invested in any stocks whatever. . . ."
>
> "And there is something in *this*, too, papa," said Eva . . ., "and that is, that an investment that you have got to take for better or for worse, and can't sell or get rid of all your life, had better be made in something you are sure you will like." (399–400, emphasis in original)

Again the readers witness a conversation that is primarily a sales talk. Harry presents himself entirely in terms of what he is and will be worth, just as one would do with stocks one intended to sell. In this scenario, as Eva aptly observes, Harry figures primarily as an investment that is evaluated according to the profit that it can be expected to yield. Thus, Stowe demonstrates, the practice of commodifying women, designed to exclude them from an active participation in the market as producers, buyers, or sellers of goods, and to restrict them to the performance of conspicuous leisure and consumption, ultimately results in a commodification of men. The only remaining difference between men and women is, therefore, that women can enter the (marriage) market only as commodities or consumers, while men in addition occupy the position of the seller. The goods that they sell, and which they are forced to advertise, however, are they themselves. It follows that Harry is forced to perform an act that he criticized before in Miss Ellery and that, as his reaction implied, he regarded as infinitely beneath him and any other respectable man. In doing so, he becomes precisely the kind of man his uncle Jacob warned him to become—one who keeps "his talents on sale in Vanity Fair" (Stowe [1896] 1967a, 94), and one who has hence alienated his "right of self-government" (Pateman 2002, 27).

## PIOUS CONSUMPTION AND THE
## (RE-)PRODUCTION OF CHRISTIAN HOMES

The fact that Harry has to resort to advertising himself can be interpreted as a sign of weakness that, as Douglas observes, makes him akin to other male characters in mid- to late-nineteenth-century sentimentalist fiction, who "are by nature failures, just as the women are by nature successes" ([1977] 1996, 250). Significantly, it is thus Eva, who invests the little money left her by her grandmother in a house at the end of *My Wife and I*, a fact that seemingly indicates the beginning of a shift of Eva's position from passive to active participation in business transactions—even more so as she buys the house against the advice of her aunt Mary, who tries to coerce her into boarding in order to save this money for the consumption of finery.[20] The impression that Eva's position has changed is strengthened by her becoming, in Harry's words, "a shrewd little trader" (473) with "an aptitude for bargains" (479) as she sets out to furnishing their house. Accordingly, when he remarks on "the enterprises conceived, carried out, and prosperously finished under her hands" (478), Harry's description of Eva's efforts employs economic terminology until then for the most part reserved for the novel's male characters. It would be misleading, however, to suggest that Eva's position had shifted from that of commodity and consumer to that of a trader conducting "real" business, an activity that ultimately remains reserved for men. Accordingly, *We and Our Neighbors* makes apparent that although a shift in Eva's position has occurred, this does not enable her to participate in the market like a man. Eva's becoming a trader does not signal her forsaking the domestic in exchange for a male sphere of activity, and in consequence the male and female spheres remain intact and clearly separated in *We and Our Neighbors*. Of these two distinct spheres, it is Eva's—that of homemaking—which constitutes the focus of the novel: her "business" in *We and Our Neighbors* is primarily "to keep a quiet, peaceable, restful home, where he shall always have the enjoyment of seeing beautiful things" (Stowe [1896] 1967b, 36). Entirely satisfied with this role, Eva becomes—despite her impracticality—what Caroline called "a bright and shining light of contentment in woman's sphere" (Stowe [1896] 1967a, 105) and wholeheartedly adopts the common stance of men and women being "different and 'equal'" (Matthaei 1982, 116) as her following remark evinces:

> I suppose some of the ambitious lady leaders of our time would call it playing second fiddle. Yes, that is it; but there must be second fiddlers in an orchestra, and it's fortunate that I have precisely the talent for playing one, and my doctrine is that the second fiddle well played is quite as good as the first. What would the first be without it?
>
> After all, in this great fuss about the men's sphere and the women's isn't the women's ordinary work just as important and great in its way? For, you see, it's what the men with all their greatness can't do, for the life of them. (Stowe [1896] 1967b, 36–37)

In accordance with the conventions of the domestic ideal, Eva thinks of herself as performing a work that men are perfectly unfit for. However, notwithstanding this conservatism Eva is implicated in a significant shift in that she renounces the excessive, conspicuous consumption that she was urged to perform by her patriarchally inclined "counselors and educators" (Douglas [1977] 1996, 60) and replaces it with consumption of a different form, namely "pious consumption" (Merish 2000, 90). Emerging in the early nineteenth century, by the 1820s the "new ideal of 'pious consumption,' promoted by an array of theological, philosophical, and literary discourses, had . . . legitimized and increased cultural and economic investment in domestic material and consumer 'refinement'" (90). According to Merish, the basis for this legitimization, which overturned "traditional and civic humanist sanctions against luxury," was the idea—promoted among others by tastemaker A. J. Downing—that

> an aesthetically pleasing domestic environment presents an "unfailing barrier against vice, immorality, and bad habits." For Downing, "a good house (and by this I mean a fitting, tasteful, and significant dwelling) is a powerful means of civilization": it exerts a "moral influence" and "elevates" character, resulting in the "refinement" of sensibility and manners. . . . (15)

Such pious consumption, Stowe suggests throughout *We and Our Neighbors*, can bring about the social change needed to resolve the two paradoxes exposed in *My Wife and I*. It is assigned this capacity because it endows women with a form of social agency enabling them to renounce their passive role as consumers and to replace it, despite their restriction to the domestic sphere, with that of an active producer—not of material goods but of a new social order.

Eva's renunciation of excessive consumption of luxury items for the pious consumption of tasteful household goods is emphasized when the narrator compares her to a young housewife whose pride . . . in [her]self becomes a pride in her home. Her home is the new impersonation of herself; it is her throne, her empire. How often do we see the young wife more sensitive to the adornment of her house than the adornment of her person, willing even to retrench and deny in the last, that her home may become more cheerful and attractive! A pretty set of china for her teatable goes farther with her than a gay robe for herself. She will sacrifice ribbons and laces for means to adorn the sacred recesses which have become to her an expansion of her own being. (Stowe [1896] 1967b, 142–43)

That the consumption performed by Eva after her wedding with Harry is pious rather than excessive, and that she hence no longer is the "rich and rather self-indulgent daughter of luxury" (421) as which she appeared for the most part of *My Wife and I*, is on the one hand highlighted by the frequent remarks concerning the economy with which she sets about furnishing her house. "There were chambers," her husband notes in *My Wife and I*, "which seemed to be built out of drapery and muslins, every detail of which, when explained, was a marvel of results at small expense " (Stowe [1896] 1967a, 479). Similarly, the narrator of *We and Our Neighbors* identifies Eva as one of those "domestic artists, who contrive *out of the humblest material* to produce in daily life the sense of the beautiful" (Stowe [1896] 1967b, 45, emphasis added), and remarks that "[t]he little elegances and adornments of her house were those that are furnished by thought and care rather than by money" (421). On the other hand, the piousness of Eva's consumption in the decoration of the house is stressed through repeated comparison of her endeavors to the adorning of an altar. Thus the narrator points out that Eva's efforts in embellishing her house with flowers are not "work in vain" because "[n]o altar is holier than the home altar, and the flowers that adorn it are sacred" (123) and "[m]any an aching back and many a drooping form could testify how the woman spends herself . . . in this sort of altar-dressing for home worship" (167–68).

The host of passages picturing Eva as a "home-artist" (45) have led Douglas to claim that Eva's function in *We and Our Neighbors* remains primarily an ornamental and ornamenting one. In her eyes, Eva is merely concerned with homemaking to create a recreational space for herself and her husband and friends, and thus serves as

the representative of the new impractical heroine increasingly popular in the fiction of mid-nineteenth-century America. Herself self-consciously childlike, not to say childish, Eva is an emblem of play, of leisure, of carefree gaiety, and a symbol of the increasing trust Stowe, in common with her culture, was putting on these qualities as instruments for the new Bushnellian kind of regeneration. ([1977] 1996, 137)

Yet, by its repeated depiction of pious consumption *We and Our Neighbors* makes abundantly clear that Eva's adornments of her house do not merely fulfill an ornamental and recreational function, as Douglas argues, but are meant to promote (human) refinement and civilization, thus serving as an antidote to the "overcivilization" alluded to by Lears (1981, xv). In this perspective, the repeated emphasis the novel puts on Eva's efforts "to keep a quiet, peaceable, restful home" (Stowe [1896] 1967b, 36), where "everybody must be made to have a good time, so that they'll want to come again . . . and get a sort of home feeling about our rooms" (132), takes on a different significance than Douglas claims. Thus Eva's homemaking endeavor, carried out through the pious consumption of "'refined' domestic artifacts" (Merish 2000, 90), is described as her contribution to "the kindly work of humanity" (Stowe [1896] 1967b, 194), or as a "mission work" performed in the home (219). Hence, in the following passage the house's attractiveness is linked to its therapeutic effect on individuals in need of socialization or civilization:

> Even with the most rigorous self-scrutiny, Eva could not find fault with the home philosophy by which their family life had been made attractive and delightful, because she said and felt that her house had been a ministry to others. It had helped to make others stronger, more cheerful, happier. (421)

The two primary examples of this effect are Harry's friend Bolton, who suffers from the consequences of his abuse of "stimulants" as a young man, as well as Maggie, the fallen daughter of Eva and Harry's housekeeper. To both, the Henderson household serves as "a shelter and a strength" (Stowe [1896] 1967b, 441), exerting on them the socializing (in the case of Bolton) and civilizing (in the case of Maggie) effect generally ascribed to pious consumption in the nineteenth century (Merish 2000, 90).

However, more is at stake in Eva's performing "the kindly work of humanity" (Stowe [1896] 1967b, 194) than offering help to people in her immediate vicinity. Throughout *We and Our Neighbors*, Eva pursues the goal of "creating little domesticated replicas of her life" (Douglas [1977] 1996, 252), primarily by means of matchmaking, the logical precursor of homemaking.[21] Accordingly, after she has functioned as the catalyst for two engagements among her sisters and friends, Eva asks her mother-in-law in a letter:

> Mother, doesn't it seem as if our bright, cosy, happy, free-and-easy home was throwing out as many side-shoots as a lilac bush? Just think; in easy vicinity, we shall have Jim and Alice, Angie and St. John, and, as I believe, Bolton and Caroline. We shall be a guild of householders, who hold the same traditions, walk by the same rule, and mind the same things. . . . And it is not merely having good times either; but, mother, the more I think of it, the more I think the making of bright, happy homes is the best way of helping on the world that has been discovered yet. A home is a thing that can't be for one's own self

alone—at least the kind of home we are thinking of; it reaches out on all sides and helps and shelters and comforts others. Even my little experiment of a few months ago shows me that. . . . (441–42)

Although Douglas can conceive of Eva's matchmakings—her production, that is, of further sites of pious consumption—only as "essentially narcissistic" ([1977] 1996, 252), the novel seems to endow this (re-)production of homes in the image of the Henderson household with a different meaning. Not only does the above passage highlight that Eva is no longer a marriage market commodity but has become a female producer, a maker of matches and of homes, but it also pictures her and other homemakers as driving forces in the social change called for by Stowe in *My Wife and I*.

The spirit that the passage just quoted thus expresses is that of Stowe's and Catherine Beecher's manual *The American Woman's Home* (1869), in which "a wealth of scientific information and practical advice are pointed toward a millenarian goal" (Tompkins 1985, 143). Thus, Tompkins argues, Beecher and Stowe's manual clearly reveals that in their eyes (just as in Eva's), "[c]entering on the home . . . is not a way of indulging in narcissistic fantasy, as critics have argued, or a turning away from the world into self-absorption and idle reverie; it is the prerequisite of world conquest— defined as the reformation of the human race through proper care and nurturing of its young" (143). In contrast to Douglas, who is clearly the focus of the criticism of the foregoing passage, Tompkins emphasizes the "imperialistic drive behind the encyclopedism and determined practicality of this household manual," which in her eyes "flatly contradicts the traditional derogations of the American cult of domesticity as a 'mirror-phenomenon,' 'self-immersed' and 'self-congratulatory'" (144), or as an "evasive banality" (Lears 1981, 17). This "imperialistic drive" is particularly obvious in a passage that bears a striking resemblance to Eva's (similarly imperialistic) projection of the spreading of replicas of her household. According to Beecher and Stowe, if "a truly 'Christian family' [were] instituted in any destitute settlement," it would "soon gather a 'Christian neighborhood'" around it; subsequently, they outline, this

> cheering example would . . . spread, and ere long colonies from these prosperous and Christian communities would go forth to shine as "lights of the world" in all the now darkened nations. Thus the "Christian family," and "Christian neighborhood" would become the grand ministry, as they were designed to be, in training our whole race for heaven. (2002, 337)

Commenting on this and similar passages in Beecher and Stowe's manual, Brown evokes the notion of a "manifest destiny" prompting "American women to domesticate and Christianize the world . . . through the work they perform in their homes" (1990, 20). Something similar is also suggested by

Amy Kaplan in her essay "Manifest Domesticity," in which she argues that the domestic work performed by women in nineteenth-century America was perceived as a "cultural work . . . related to the imperial project of civiliz- ing" (1998, 582). This work—which is to considerable extent that of pious consumption—is precisely the work Eva begins to perform in *We and Our Neighbors,* and it is through her home- and matchmaking efforts that, how- ever remotely, "housekeeping [becomes] a political practice and the home a model of political province" (Brown 1990, 20).

By highlighting Eva's performance of pious consumption and its positive effects, *We and Our Neighbors* thus ascribes her an agency that Douglas, who can perceive of Eva and her disestablished companions only as im- potent, passive consumers, was unable to grant her. Thus, although Eva indeed "creates nothing from scratch, as the woman gifted with 'faculty' did," and is therefore "a shopper rather than a worker" (Douglas [1977] 1996, 65–66), forsaking the excessive consumption she practices in *My Wife and I* enables her to turn her home into "a dynamic center of activity, physical and spiritual, economic and moral, whose influence spreads out in ever-widening circles" (Tompkins 1985, 145).[22] Although one should not regard this agency uncritically,[23] it seems wrong to deny its existence alto- gether (as Douglas does for example) because such a denial obscures the extent to which *We and Our Neighbors* exceeds the merely descriptive mode of sociological fiction by promoting a social change capable of remedying the injustices exposed in *My Wife and I.* Certainly, the change envisioned and promoted in *We and Our Neighbors* is not of a radical nature in that it does not put into question that women's primary domain is the domestic sphere. Nonetheless, however, by making this sphere appear as a site whose feminine occupants are endowed with actual agency, the novel attributes these women a power to make an impact on their culture that exceeds the passive and largely impotent "influence" they are granted by Douglas.

## NOTES

1. Among the critics who engage in greater detail with *My Wife and I* are Ann Douglas in *The Feminization of American Culture* (1977); Theodore Hovet in his es- says "Tableaux Vivants: Masculine Vision and Feminine Reflections in Novels by Warner, Alcott, Stowe, and Wharton" (1993, with Grace Ann Hovet), "Rummaging through the Past: The Cultural Work of Nostalgia in Harriet Beecher Stowe's *My Wife and I*" (1996), and "The Power of the Popular: The Subversion of Realism in Harriet Beecher Stowe's *My Wife and I*" (1997); Carolyn L. Karcher in "Stowe and the Literature of Social Change" (2004); and Lisa Watt MacFarlane in "The New England Kitchen Goes Uptown: Domestic Displacements in Harriet Beecher Stowe's New York" (1991). With the exception of Douglas, most of these publications men- tion *We and Our Neighbors* only in passing, if at all.

2. Karcher classifies *Uncle Tom's Cabin* (1852), *A Key to Uncle Tom's Cabin* (1853), *Dred* (1856), and *Lady Byron Vindicated* (1870) as Stowe's "overt protest works," while she counts *The Minister's Wooing* (1859), *The Pearl of Orr's Island* (1862), *Oldtown Folks* (1869), *Poganuc People* (1878), *My Wife and I* (1871), *Pink and White Tyranny* (1871), and *We and Our Neighbors* (1875) among her sociological fiction (204).

3. Although Douglas's study is controversial particularly with regard to the effects she ascribes to feminine disestablishment (see note 6 below) and her negative evaluation of feminine consumption, the concept of "feminine disestablishment" will prove a useful tool in the following analysis in that Stowe's novels *My Wife and I* and *We and Our Neighbors* deal with the phenomenon that Douglas describes. I intend to show, however, that the protagonists of Stowe's two novels find ways of circumventing the restrictions placed upon them by their disestablishment in a manner not considered by Douglas.

4. See Matthaei (1982, 112, 117) for an assessment of the new possibilities for active self-fulfillment becoming available to women in their new role as homemaker.

5. This critical concern implicates, as Hovet observes, the existence of a realist strand in the novel, intended by Stowe as "a realistic portrayal of [women's] situation in a capitalistic and urban environment" in which "she hoped to negotiate social conflict, in this case the conflict between advocates and opponents of women's rights and between radical and moderate feminists" (1997, 3). The feminist characters presented in the novel range from the radical Audacia Dangyereyes, "a lampoon of Victoria Woodhull," over Mrs. Stella Cerulean, modeled on Stowe's younger sister Isabella Beecher Hooker (Karcher 2004, 215), to the more moderate Ida Van Arsdel and Caroline who, as Karcher asserts, "speak for the more conservative and practical fashion of the women's right movement" (2004, 215–16).

6. The foregoing remarks are critical reflections on Douglas's study *The Feminization of American Culture*, which according to Gillian Brown, Jane Tompkins, and other critics is too quick in dismissing sentimental literature as trivial. Thus, according to Lori Merish, "Douglas fails to provide a convincing theoretical account of feminine consumption and women's construction as (sentimental) consumers. . . . Reductively presenting women's consumption (and sentimentalism itself) as a reflex of changes in economic production, Douglas fails to historicize the economic and gender relations she describes, and radically simplifies the complexity of mass culture" (2000, 17).

7. This divide separates rural characters from their urban (sometimes reversed) mirror images. Thus, Ida Van Arsdel is the urban counterpart of Caroline, whereas Harry's mother has a reversed and somewhat grotesque double in Maria Wouverman, the aunt of Eva Van Arsdel.

8. Placed on the rural side of the divide set up in the novel between established and disestablished women, Caroline is accordingly presented as undisestablished in the sense that she is expected to perform the same work as Harry's mother and, perhaps more importantly, in that the role of consumer is not available to her. Nonetheless, other than Mrs. Henderson Caroline is no longer content with her situation and voices her discontent in terms and concepts of the emerging market society. She thus holds an intermediary position in the novel to some extent—also

suggested by the fact that she eventually follows Harry to New York—and in consequence much of the criticism she expresses applies to the situation of women both before and after disestablishment.

9. Pateman quotes from Macpherson's *The Political Theory of Possessive Individualism* (1962).

10. In the case of the Van Arsdel daughters the function of the educator in consumption is primarily fulfilled by their aunt Mary Wouverman.

11. In his projection of Miss Ellery's marriage as an act of selling herself, Harry clearly adheres to the "fiction of separability" according to which an individual's capacities and abilities can be separated from him/her without a loss in self-governance (Pateman 2002, 27). It is obvious that he does so because it enables him to believe in his own autonomy in the light of his prospective future as an employee or wage laborer.

12. See Norma Basch's *In the Eyes of the Law* for a comprehensive discussion of the development of married women's property rights in the United States over the nineteenth century. Although the changes made to the laws beginning in the 1840s made it possible for married women to own property and hence "step into wealth" in the manner outlined by Harry (Stowe [1896] 1967a, 76), Basch cautions that "[t]he revolution that the married women's acts seemed to herald simply did not take place. . . . The changes created by the statutes were either limited or in some areas even illusory" (1982, 30).

13. As Lori Merish points out in *Sentimental Materialism*, the association of women with luxury was already common in the writings of eighteenth-century Scottish thinkers such as David Hume and Adam Smith, whose ideas concerning "commerce in general, and consumption in particular . . . set in place a network of discursive associations . . . that became unexamined conventions of U.S. writings about capitalism throughout the nineteenth century" (2000, 31). In these writings "[t]he view of women as male property objects is insistently figured in the . . . equivalence of women and luxury" (42).

14. Other than Harry, Jim does not yet know of the business failure looming over the Van Arsdels. In the logic of the novel, this failure alone makes the marriage between Harry and Eva possible in that it clarifies that Harry is not what Jim initially suggests—a fortune-hunter.

15. It is remarks such as these—as well as Harry's act of advertising himself, which will be discussed below—which in my opinion necessitate a reconsideration of Hovet's repeated claim that "Harry's belief in romantic love . . . repositions him outside the commodity culture and in opposition to the power structure" (1997, 7, see also 10).

16. Her aunt's opinion of Eva's "usefulness" is revealed in her reply to Eva's complaint that nobody seems to understand "that a woman may be tired of leading a lazy life, and want to use her faculties," and that she would "give all the world to feel that I was of as much real use to anybody as Ida is to papa" (Stowe [1896] 1967a, 266). Although it is clear that the notion of being of "real use" that Eva evokes here refers to an activity in which she is involved as an independently acting subject rather than passive object—what Caroline calls a "life-work worth doing" (111)—all that her aunt can suggest in reply is for Eva to "[m]arry Wat Sydney" if she wants to help her father (267).

17. Veblen defines conspicuous consumption as the "specialised consumption of goods as an evidence of pecuniary strength" ([1925] 1949, 68). Despite the criticism that Veblen's theory of conspicuous consumption has provoked (see Andrew B. Trigg's "Veblen, Bourdieu, and Conspicuous Consumption" for a concise discussion of problematic aspects of Veblen's theory), it is fairly undisputed that "possessions have meanings that help define a sense of personal identity," and that these meanings are "both public and private" (Dittmar [1992] 1997, 98). Thus the wish to own something is often at least partly a wish to indicate "social-material position" (98).

18. The novel's male characters often strengthen this religious argument by giving it a biological turn in order to emphasize that women are essentially (i.e., in the logic of the eighteenth and nineteenth century, god-given) homemakers. Thus, Matthaei outlines, "[a] female was assigned to woman's work on the basis of her distinct biological capacity to bear children; her biology qualified her for the supposedly natural activities of child-rearing and homemaking" (1982, 111). It is under this premise that Harry can ask Caroline when she voices her dissatisfaction with her restriction to the domestic sphere, whether this dissatisfaction were not "with the laws of nature" (Stowe [1896] 1967a, 112), thereby implying that she is revolting against an order set in place by God. A similar remark is made by Uncle Jacob when Harry asks whether Caroline might not be of "that sort of woman who did not wish to marry at all," whereupon the uncle answers: "I doubt the existence of that species" (117).

19. Clearly, in a society in which luxury was commonly associated with "sensual indulgences and misplaced attachment to worldly ephemera distracting individuals from divine truths" (Merish 2000, 34), such materialism had to become a source of conflict. Although Merish refers particularly to "orthodox Protestants" here (34), a similar disapproval of luxury can be found in an "ascetic Protestant work ethic," which is generally said to give way to a more "hedonistic consumption ethic" in the late nineteenth century (Merish 2000, 89). On this issue, see also Weber's *Protestant Ethic*, particularly the chapter on "Asceticism and the Spirit of Capitalism" ([1930] 1985, 155–83).

20. Thus Mary urges Eva "to turn [her] resources all to keeping up the proper air and appearances" with the help of expensive "silks, gloves, shows, etc." (Stowe [1896] 1967b, 463).

21. It deserves to be mentioned that to convince her sisters and female friends to marry the men Eva thinks fit for them, Eva employs, as Douglas remarks, what can be identified as "advertising techniques" ([1977] 1996, 68). In having her do so, *We and Our Neighbors* illustrates the extent to which Eva is formed by her culture. Yet it has to be noted that Eva's intentions differ from those of her parents and aunt in that her efforts are less (or at least less obviously) economically motivated.

22. Tompkins comments here on the home as pictured in Beecher's and Stowe's household manual.

23. The fact that the concept of "manifest destiny" is applicable to this form of social agency makes very clear that it should not be hailed uncritically as an antidote to patriarchal practices. Thus it needs to be considered to what extent this agency implicates women in the perpetuation rather than the subversion of patriarchal power structures (see, especially, Kaplan for a discussion of this situation).

# WORKS CITED

Basch, Norma. 1982. *In the Eyes of the Law: Women, Marriage, and Property in Nine-teenth-Century New York*. Ithaca, NY: Cornell University Press.

Brown, Gillian. 1990. *Domestic Individualism: Imagining Self in Nineteenth-Century America*. Berkeley and Los Angeles: University of California Press.

Dittmar, Helga. [1992] 1997. "Meanings of Material Possessions as Reflections of Identity." In *The Consumer Society*, ed. Neva R. Goodwin, Frank Ackerman, and David Kiron, 97–101. Washington, D.C.: Island Press.

Douglas, Ann. [1977] 1996. *The Feminization of American* Culture. London: Papermac-Macmillan.

Giddens, Anthony. 1985. Introduction to *The Protestant Ethic and the Spirit of Capital-ism*, by Max Weber, vii–xxvi. London: Counterpoint-Unwin Paperbacks.

Hovet, Grace Ann, and Theodore R. Hovet. 1993. "Tableaux Vivants: Masculine Vi-sion and Feminine Reflections in Novels by Warner, Alcott, Stowe, and Wharton." *American Transcendental Quarterly* 7 (4): 335–56.

Hovet, Theodore R. 1996. "Rummaging through the Past: The Cultural Work of Nos-talgia in Harriet Beecher Stowe's *My Wife and I*." *Colby Quarterly* 32 (2): 113–24.

———. 1997. "The Power of the Popular: The Subversion of Realism in Harriet Beecher Stowe's *My Wife and I*." *American Literary Realism* 29 (2): 1–13.

Kaplan, Amy. 1998. "Manifest Domesticity." *American Literature* 70 (3): 518–601.

Karcher, Carolyn L. 2004. "Stowe and the Literature of Social Change." In *The Cambridge Companion to Harriet Beecher Stowe*, ed. Cindy Weinstein, 203–18. Cambridge: Cambridge University Press.

Lears, T. J. Jackson. 1981. *No Place of Grace: Antimodernism and the Transformation of American Culture, 1880–1920*. New York: Pantheon Books.

Locke, John. [1823] 1963. *Two Treatises of Government*. Vol. 5 of *The Works of John Locke*. 10 vols. Aalen: Scientia Verlag.

MacFarlane, Lisa Watt. 1991. "The New England Kitchen Goes Uptown: Domestic Displacements in Harriet Beecher Stowe's New York." *New England Quarterly* 64 (2): 272–91.

Matthaei, Julie A. 1982. *An Economic History of Women in America: Women's Work, the Sexual Division, and the Development of Capitalism*. New York: Schocken.

Merish, Lori. 2000. *Sentimental Materialism: Gender, Commodity Culture, and Nine-teenth-Century American Literature*. Durham, NC: Duke University Press.

Pateman, Carole. 2002. "Self-Ownership and Property in the Person: Democratiza-tion and a Tale of Two Concepts." *Journal of Political Philosophy* 10 (1): 20–53.

Robinson, Lillian S. 1994. "The Traffic in Women: A Cultural Critique of *The House of Mirth*." In *The House of Mirth: Complete, Authoritative Text with Biographical and Historical Contexts, Critical History, and Essays from Five Contemporary Perspectives*, by Edith Wharton, ed. Shari Benstock, 340–58. Boston: Bedford Books.

Rubin, Gayle. 1975. "The Traffic in Women: Notes on the 'Political Economy' of Sex." In *Toward an Anthropology of Women*, ed. Rayna R. Reiter, 157–210. New York: Monthly Review.

Stowe, Harriet Beecher. [1896] 1967a. *My Wife and I; or, Harry Henderson's History*. Vol. 12 of *The Writings of Harriet Beecher Stowe*. 16 vols. New York: AMS Press.

———. [1896] 1967b. *We and Our Neighbors; or, The Records of an Unfashionable Street.* Vol. 13 of *The Writings of Harriet Beecher Stowe.* 16 vols. New York: AMS Press.

Stowe, Harriet Beecher, and Catherine E. Beecher. 2002. *The American Woman's Home.* New Brunswick, NJ: Rutgers University Press.

Tompkins, Jane. 1985. *Sensational Designs: The Cultural Work of American Fiction, 1790–1860.* New York: Oxford University Press.

Trigg, Andrew B. 2001. "Veblen, Bourdieu, and Conspicuous Consumption." *Journal of Economic Issues* 35 (1): 99–115.

Veblen, Thorstein. [1925] 1949. *The Theory of the Leisure Class. An Economic Study of Institutions.* London: Allen and Unwin.

Weber, Max. [1930] 1985. *The Protestant Ethic and the Spirit of Capitalism,* trans. Talcott Parsons. London: Counterpoint-Unwin Paperbacks.

# Index

# About the Editors and Contributors

**Martin T. Buinicki** is the Walter G. Friedrich Professor of American Literature at Valparaiso University. He is the author of *Negotiating Copyright: Authorship and the Discourse of Literary Property Rights in Nineteenth-Century America* (2006), and has published articles in a number of collections and journals, including *A Companion to Mark Twain* (2006), *American Literary History*, *American Literary Realism*, and the *Walt Whitman Quarterly Review*. His book *Walt Whitman's Reconstruction: Poetry and Publishing Between Memory and History* is forthcoming.

**Jennifer Cognard-Black** is associate professor of English at St. Mary's College of Maryland where she teaches nineteenth-century literature and fiction writing, and is the coordinator of the Women, Gender, and Sexuality Program. Her critical work includes articles in *Ms. Magazine*, *College English*, *American Literary Realism*, the *National Women's Studies Association Journal*, and the *Popular Culture Review* as well as four books: a study of cultures of letters among women writers, *Narrative in the Professional Age* (2004), a writing textbook, *Advancing Rhetoric* (2006), an anthology of unpublished letters by women writers, *Kindred Hands* (2006), and an anthology of food writing, *Words Rising* (forthcoming). A Pushcart Prize nominee, her short fiction has appeared under the pseudonym J. Annie MacLeod in journals such as *Another Chicago Magazine*, *The Magazine of Fantasy and Science Fiction*, and, most recently, *So to Speak*.

**Maria I. Diedrich** holds a chair in American studies at the University of Muenster, Germany. Her work focuses on African American studies. She was the founding president of the Collegium for African American Research

(CAAR) from 1992 to 2001; since 1984 she has been a nonresident fellow at the W.E.B. Du Bois Institute at Harvard. Among her publications are *Cornelia James Cannon and the Future American Race* (2011) and *Love Across Color Lines: Ottilie Assing and Frederick Douglass* (1999). She coedited several volumes of criticism, among them *The Black Columbiad* (1994), *Black Imagination and the Middle Passage* (1999), *Mapping African America* (1999), *Monuments of the Black Atlantic* (2004), and *From Black to Schwarz: Cultural Crossovers between African America and Germany* (2009). She is currently reconstructing the communal and individual experience of black Hessians during and after the American Revolution.

**Joseph Helminski** received his Ph.D. in American literature from Wayne State University in 2001. He has taught at Wayne State and the University of Toledo, and is currently a member of the communications/humanities department at Oakland Community College in Waterford, Michigan, where he teaches developmental writing, composition, and American literature.

**Christiane E. Farnan** is chair of the English department, codirector of American studies, and a member of the advisory board for the Center for Revolutionary Studies at Siena College. She teaches courses in early American literature and American cultural studies.

**Faye Halpern** is assistant professor of English at the University of Calgary. Her research interests include sentimental rhetoric, contemporary writing pedagogy, and the relationship between them. She is currently completing her book manuscript, *The Rise and Fall of the Sentimental Oratory: Lessons for a Contemporary Academic Audience.*

**Sylvia Mayer** is chair of American studies at the University of Bayreuth, Germany. Her major fields of research are ecologically oriented literary and cultural studies and African American literature. Her publications include monographs on Toni Morrison's novels and on the environmental ethical dimension of New England regionalist writing. She has edited and coedited several volumes of criticism, among them *Restoring the Connection to the Natural World: Essays on the African American Environmental Imagination* (2003) and *Literature, Culture, Environment: Positioning Ecocriticism* (2005). She is currently the director of the Bayreuth Institute for American Studies (BIFAS).

**Monika Mueller** is senior lecturer in American literature and culture at the University of Stuttgart, Germany. She received her Ph.D. from the University of Alabama and her *habilitation* from the University of Cologne. She has published a monograph on the Hawthorne/Melville relationship, *Gender,*

*Genre and Homoeroticism in Hawthorne's* The Blithedale Romance *and Melville's* Pierre (1996), and another one on George Eliot's transatlantic literary relationships, *George Eliot U.S.: Transatlantic Literary and Cultural Perspectives* (2005). In addition, she has coedited volumes on multiethnic detective fiction and on disgust as a cultural phenomenon.

**William P. Mullaney** currently serves as the dean of arts and sciences at Chandler-Gilbert Community College in Chandler, Arizona, where he also teaches literature. He has recently published articles on John Steinbeck and Zora Neale Hurston.

**Astrid Recker** taught American and English literature at the University of Cologne, Germany, between 2001 and 2008, where she also completed her Ph.D. with a doctoral thesis on Herman Melville's *Moby-Dick* (2008). After receiving her M.LIS from Cologne University of Applied Sciences, she is now head of the library and documentation department of the German Federal Institute for Vocational Training and Education.

**Sarah Ruffing Robbins** is Lorraine Sherley Professor of American Literature at TCU. She is the author of *Managing Literacy, Mothering America* (2004/2006), winner of a Choice book award from the American Library Association, and *The Cambridge Introduction to Harriet Beecher Stowe* (2007). She has also coedited several collections of essays focused on collaborative work in public scholarship: *Writing America* (2004), *Writing Our Communities* (2005), and *Teachers' Writing Groups* (2006). Her most recent book is a critical edition with interpretive essays, *Nellie Arnott's Writings on Angola, 1905–1913* (2011), coedited with historian Ann Pullen. Currently, she is coediting *Bridging Cultures: International Faculty Women Transforming the U.S. Academy*, a collection of narrative essays (memoirs framed by academic analysis), to be published in 2011.